The Search for a Symbol

The Search for a Symbol

"A New Creed" and The United Church of Canada

William R. H. Haughton

WIPF & STOCK · Eugene, Oregon

THE SEARCH FOR A SYMBOL
"A New Creed" and The United Church of Canada

Wipf & Stock
An Imprint of Wipf and Stock Publishers
199 W. 8th Ave., Suite 3
Eugene, OR 97401

www.wipfandstock.com

PAPERBACK ISBN: 978-1-6667-3266-5
HARDCOVER ISBN: 978-1-6667-2661-9
EBOOK ISBN: 978-1-6667-2662-6

03/15/22

All biblical citations are from the author's own translations.

To my father,
the Reverend Lee R. Haughton

A New Creed

We are not alone,
we live in God's world.

We believe in God:
who has created and is creating,
who has come in Jesus,
    the Word made flesh,
    to reconcile and make new,
who works in us and others
    by the Spirit.

We trust in God.

We are called to be the Church:
to celebrate God's presence,
to live with respect in Creation,
to love and serve others,
to seek justice and resist evil,
to proclaim Jesus, crucified and risen,
    our judge and our hope.
In life, in death, in life beyond death,
God is with us.

We are not alone.
Thanks be to God.

(1968; rev. 1980, 1995)

From *Voices United: The Hymn and Worship Book of The United Church of Canada/L'Église Unie du Canada* (Toronto: The United Church Publishing House, 1996) 918–19. Used with permission.

Contents

Preface

HAVING BEEN AN AVID reader of books for most of my life, it has proven a rewarding experience for me to write one now myself. The process has certainly given me a new appreciation for the books of others and a special sense of awe at the thought of those who have been able to produce multiple works of significance. Of course, self-discovery is hardly a sufficient reason for engaging in a major writing project. As Qohelet noted long ago, "The making of many books is without end" (Eccl 12:12). The question is always, why write this book? In this case, the short answer is that it tells a story that was waiting to be told and makes an argument that I felt needed to be made. Fortunately, I found myself in a position to do some research on the topic of "A New Creed" and with sufficient interest to continue pursuing the project through to completion.

The longer answer is a little more complicated. When I studied at the Toronto School of Theology from 2005 to 2007, I did most of my course work in the areas of patristics and theology. When it came time to write my thesis, however, I became captivated by questions about Presbyterian responses to church union and decided to work on that entirely historical topic. Later, around 2009, I began to develop an interest in "A New Creed." I seemed to be noticing it everywhere in United Church life but could find little published on its background and nothing to my mind that would commend its ubiquity. A few initial visits to The United Church Archives in Toronto started to reveal a fascinating picture worthy of further examination. In some ways, the present work represents the fruition of an idiosyncratic course of study that has allowed me to combine my interests in the histories of the early church and of The United Church.

Most of the research and writing for this book was carried out between 2009 and 2012. In that period, while I was serving the congregations of the Port Rowan Pastoral Charge in Erie Presbytery, work and family life allowed me to pursue my church history hobby with some seriousness. From 2012 until 2020, the draft document of what became *The Search for a Symbol* sat untouched on a USB flash drive. Life simply got in the way. During a period of civil restrictions in response to the COVID-19 pandemic in late 2020, I took a week of study leave from my current ministry with the intent of revisiting my manuscript. Deciding that with a bit more research, reorganization, and editing, the task would be worth taking up again, I continued to make use of the ongoing pandemic-related restrictions, as well as a couple more weeks of study leave to chip away at it throughout 2021.

All stories of book writing are unique, and many involve long periods when a manuscript goes untouched for one reason or another. In my case, the unplanned interruption was providential. In the earlier period of my research, I was able to take advantage of one of The United Church's greatest resources, the *Yearbook and Directory*, in a way that would not have been available to me in more recent years. In late 2009, I looked up and essentially cold-called a number of former members of the Committee on Christian Faith. After hearing a brief personal introduction and the reason for my call, each former member I was able to reach was unfailingly generous with his time, insight, and encouragement. To Richard Delorme, Donald Evans, W. O. "Bill" Fennell, Gordon Nodwell, Hugh Rose, and Mac Freeman I owe a debt of gratitude. Mac in particular was even kind enough to review an early draft of what is now my second chapter and provide some feedback.

My initial attempts at writing about "A New Creed" took the form of a couple short papers, one appearing in *Touchstone* and another presented to the Canadian Society of Church History at its 2011 annual meeting in Fredericton, New Brunswick. I recall vividly how my paper at that gathering generated an unusually lively—one might even say heated—discussion. Afterwards, while some of us were on the way to lunch, Marguerite Van Die commented dryly, "Isn't it interesting the conversation generated by a contemporary topic?" A Carlton University sociologist and United Church minister named Tom Sherwood happened to be in attendance at that same meeting. Tom approached me and informed me he had been a member of the Committee on Theology and Faith in the late 1970s when it was working on the inclusive language revision of "A New Creed." That week in Fredericton and later in phone conversation, he was very kind to share his recollections of that process.

Though at that time I didn't envision taking an eight-year hiatus, the pause served me well. During that period, some interesting books on The United Church's history and theology were published. By waiting to resume my own writing, I was able to draw on the pertinent work of Phyllis Airhart, Brian Clarke and Stuart Macdonald, Kevin Flatt, Jeff Seaton, and the various contributors to the helpful anthologies *The United Church of Canada: A History* and *The Theology of The United Church of Canada.* Moreover, I had the chance to mature my own thinking in those years and then come back to look at my manuscript with fresh eyes. In other words, had I finished the project in 2012, I would have missed out on some excellent books in the intervening years. Had I begun only more recently, I would not have been able to speak in 2009 with the then-surviving authors of "A New Creed" who have since gone to be with the Lord.

A number of people were kind enough to offer different kinds of support, encouragement, and feedback during my protracted writing process. In the 2009–2012 phase, some helpful comments and suggestions were returned by the late Geoff Wilkins and Stuart Macdonald. Stuart in particular was able to direct me towards some key literature on secularization and the 1960s, as well as to pose some important questions and challenges to my thinking. In the 2020–2021 period, Claude Cox, Jeff Seaton, and my father Lee Haughton all read the completed manuscript with great care and offered critiques that were incisive and honest. More generally, I have been grateful for treasured friendships with the late Tom Lowry and others who have kindly and consistently encouraged me to pursue my writing. The people of the Port Rowan Pastoral Charge, as well as of the Dalston-Crown Hill and Forest Home United Churches, have helped provide uniquely happy environments in which to do so. I would like to thank also the various staff people at The United Church Archives and at the General Council Office of The United Church who have offered various kinds of assistance at necessary points through the years. In addition, I must thank Matthew Wimer and the team at Wipf and Stock for believing in this project and for their support through the publication process. The many others who have had a shaping influence on my thought and writing are too numerous to name, but I remember them all with thanksgiving. For the more helpful aspects of my work, those named and anonymous others deserve much credit. For those aspects judged less well, I alone deserve the criticism.

My advocacy of the classical creeds in these pages may strike some readers as unexpected, coming from someone in my position. As I myself have wondered about this while working on the book, two particular experiences in my background have come to mind. As a theological student at the Campbell University Divinity School in Buies Creek, North Carolina, from 2002 to 2005, I had many wonderful teachers, including Steven R. Harmon—whose work will be discussed in chapter 6. During the courses I took with Dr. Harmon at Campbell, I greatly enjoyed the experience of reciting the Apostles' and Nicene Creeds in alternating weeks. Dr. Harmon encouraged us to memorize these ancient confessions and to love them.

More recently, I have been reminded of a time longer ago when my dad taught me and my brother to memorize the Apostles' Creed as small children and recited it with us on occasion at bedtime. That wasn't something I recall reflecting on a lot as a child, but now as an adult and as a parent myself, it strikes me as a remarkable gift to have been given. I have not always lived up to my dad's example—in this or in other areas—but there is still time, and I live in hope. In light of this story, some readers may interpret my advocacy of the classical creeds as an attempt to relive a childhood memory. I don't think that is the case here, but any psychoanalytically inclined interpreters are welcome to say it. As a child, I was blessed to have been taught the Apostles' Creed, and the gospel to which it gives voice, by my father. In a small show of gratitude, I am honored to dedicate this book to him.

Abbreviations

Reference Works

BDAG	Bauer, Danker, Arndt, and Gingrich, *A Greek-English Lexicon of the New Testament and other Early Christian Literature*
ODCC	*Oxford Dictionary of the Christian Church*
OED	*Oxford English Dictionary*

Church Organizations

PCUSA	Presbyterian Church in the U.S.A.
SBC	Southern Baptist Convention
UCC	The United Church of Canada
WARC	World Alliance of Reformed Churches

Introduction

The United Church of Canada has attempted, in less than a century of existence, to articulate its theology through the writing and adoption of four major statements of faith—each "in words appropriate to its time."[1] These four documents are the Basis of Union's "Twenty Articles of Doctrine" (1925), "A Statement of Faith" (1940), "A New Creed" (1968), and "A Song of Faith" (2006). One of the more telling aspects of "A Song of Faith," the most recent of these, is the notable deference it shows to one, and only one, of its predecessors: "A New Creed." The authors of "A Song of Faith" wrote reflexively of its status in appendix A, "This statement is not intended to be in any way a replacement of the beloved New Creed" and, of the creed, that "people in the United Church *love* it."[2] In a historical account of the General Council that approved "A Song of Faith," we read, "When the new UCC faith statement, *A Song of Faith*, was presented at the 39th General Council (2006), the chairperson of the Committee on Theology and Faith had to reassure commissioners on several occasions that *Song* was not intended to replace *A New Creed* in the denomination's life. The notion that *Song* might be mandated for use in worship as a substitute for this now-beloved creed was a point of significant anxiety for many."[3]

1. *Song of Faith*, 2.
2. *Song of Faith*, 17 (emphasis in original).
3. Young, "Introduction," 15.

There is no doubt that such love-language accurately describes the sentiment of many in The United Church. "A New Creed" is a salient feature of the denomination's life, particularly in its liturgical expressions but also in its popular mind as well. Mardi Tindal—later the fortieth moderator of the General Council (hereafter, simply "moderator")—once said of "A New Creed," "It's the one thing I've made sure my children know. We say it as a grace at meals because I really want them to know it."[4] Countless sermon series, confirmation classes, and other media have formally and informally helped to develop a living tradition of using, disseminating, and celebrating "A New Creed" among the community of The United Church, from the General Council to its grassroots expressions.[5] In a learned analysis, William S. Kervin draws on the work of George Lindbeck in assigning to "A New Creed" an emergent "cultural-linguistic" role within The United Church. "Its vocabulary and syntax," he writes, "become hallmarks of the UCC's liturgical ethos, theological reflection, and institutional culture—not merely as propositional claims, or even liberal expressions, but as cultural-linguistic touchstones of ecclesial identity."[6]

Now, after more than fifty years, "A New Creed" is not quite so new anymore. Yet, it continues to represent for many something of the innovative and experimental spirit of The United Church. Sandra Beardsall wrote in 2011, "It remains a beloved and well-used liturgical expression."[7] Indeed, over the course of its tenure, "A New Creed" has grown in stature and even emerged as one of the public faces of the denomination. Around the time I first began thinking about this topic, I was sent a package of resources from the General Council Office to help the congregation I was serving to celebrate The United Church's eighty-fifth anniversary, in June 2010. The centerpiece of this package was a DVD that had a feature tellingly entitled *Welcome to the United Church: Celebrating the New Creed.* Also included was a sample promotional bookmark displaying the text of "A New Creed," which we were encouraged to order in bulk at the cost of only shipping and handling. With the advent of the internet age, in which many are looking at computer screens more often than at print-on-paper

4. Best, *Will Our Church Disappear*, 54.

5. See, for example, Lance Wright's *Confirmation That Works.* This privately published resource was widely used over the years in the former Hamilton Conference.

6. Kervin, "Sacraments and Sacramentality," 243–44.

7. Beardsall, "And Whether Pigs Have Wings," 113.

texts, this 1960s era confession has been kept at the forefront of thinking in The United Church through the denomination's official website.[8]

Within the world of The United Church, one phrase is typically enough to remind an audience of "A New Creed" in its entirety and the unique identity of the denomination that produced it. Much as quotations of Scripture (the Law, the Prophets, and the Writings) often function in the Pauline letters, the use of a single phrase from "A New Creed" can serve to recall an entire story, which then gives shape and meaning to its new setting.[9] The latest service book of The United Church—*Celebrate God's Presence*—demonstrates this prominently. With such a title, inspired by and drawn from the text of "A New Creed," worship throughout The United Church is set within the narrative framework of that confession and the unique denominational story it evokes.[10] As Kervin observes, "Its title and chapter headings, drawn from 'A New Creed' [are] thus indicative of that statement's significant presence in United Church worship and theology."[11] Further, the denominational stewardship program has for several years now been labeled "Called to Be the Church." In a more anecdotal way, I remember one pastoral charge I served had a Green Group—a committee that examined the practices of the congregation and their impact on the environment. This group led a Bible study during my time there on environmental stewardship themes called "To Live with Respect in Creation." That same congregation had a fine music director who set "A New Creed" to music and used the piece as a choral anthem with some regularity.[12] This confession has become an important shorthand way of telling our corporate story and of casting our collective vision.

The official service book and website of the denomination as well as the names of congregational study groups are just a few of the many possible illustrations of the way that "A New Creed" has developed a massive presence in and influence on The United Church of Canada. "A New

8. http://www.united-church.ca/. Many congregational websites also advertise "A New Creed" when pointing web surfers to the church's distinctive beliefs.

9. I owe much in this line of thinking to Hays, *Echoes of Scripture*.

10. *Celebrate God's Presence* is itself saturated with the phrasing of "A New Creed." Funeral services, for example, are included under the heading "In Life, in Death, in Life beyond Death."

11. William S. Kervin, "Worship on the Way," in Schweitzer, *United Church of Canada*, 188.

12. DeVries, "Musical Setting." Such an effort is not entirely unique. See Shephard, "Letter to the Editor."

Creed" is seen as a particularly authoritative and important statement of faith for the people of The United Church. One congregation posted a classified advertisement in *The United Church Observer* in 2016 which read, "The New Creed expresses our theology well." This ad was noticed by Sandra Beardsall who then added the comment, "This brief testimony speaks of the depth of regard UCC members hold for their denomination's 1968 attempt to produce a 'modern creedal statement suitable for use in the liturgy.'"[13] By contrast, the Apostles' and Nicene Creeds—the so-called historic or classical creeds—which are of similar length and have also been constitutionally acknowledged within the denomination, tend to elicit very different kinds of responses. Bill Phipps, then thirty-sixth moderator, once made some controversially unorthodox theological remarks in an interview with the *Ottawa Citizen* and later defended himself by saying that his beliefs were "not frozen in the language of early creeds."[14]

In historical perspective, it is not obvious that "A New Creed" should have such a unique place of authority in relation to those confessions that it has implicitly replaced in the faith and practice of The United Church. The founding constitution of The United Church, the Basis of Union, reads, "We, the representatives of the Presbyterian, Methodist and Congregational branches of the Church of Christ in Canada, do hereby set forth the substance of the Christian faith, as commonly held among us. In doing so, we build upon the foundation laid by the apostles and prophets . . . . We acknowledge the teaching of the great creeds of the ancient Church."[15] The United Church itself has produced other doctrinal statements that, like "A New Creed," are distinctly its own and do not bear any undue weight from ecclesiastical tradition or outside influence. The Basis of Union's "Twenty Articles of Doctrine," quoted in part above, set out the theological consensus that was to be a cornerstone of the church union project.[16] In 1940, "A Statement of Faith" was approved by the Seventh General Council. This was a confession intended to update the "Twenty Articles of Doctrine" of the Basis of Union and was of comparable form and content to its predecessor. Its appearance was supplemented by the

13. Beardsall, "Sin and Redemption," 113.

14. Michael McAteer, "What Do United Church People Believe?" in J. Taylor, *Fire and Grace*, 54.

15. Joint Committee, "Twenty Articles of Doctrine."

16. One can find a comprehensive treatment of the doctrine of the Basis of Union in, among other sources, Silcox, *Church Union in Canada*; Chalmers, *See the Christ Stand*; Morrow, *Church Union in Canada*; and Gandier, *Doctrinal Basis of Union*.

publication of a detailed theological commentary by John Dow of Emmanuel College and a catechism that was approved by the Eleventh General Council in 1944 and went on to sell approximately 500,000 copies.[17] "A Song of Faith," the latest doctrinal statement of The United Church, was approved by the Thirty-Ninth General Council in 2006. Taking these other documents into consideration, it is not extravagant to say that "A New Creed" has become a kind of first-among-equals in giving expression to the faith of The United Church—especially in the context of worship, which is the community's central activity.[18] To varying degrees, it could be said that the other confessions with historical pedigree and authority in The United Church do not contain or give practical expression to the faith of the people of the denomination in nearly as meaningful a way.

Edwin Searcy became well known for his successful tenure as minister at University Hill United Church in Vancouver. He wrote in 2009 about his experiences of "A New Creed" and its prevalence in The United Church.

> In 1968 I was fourteen. Our confirmation class studied the "New Creed" that was adopted by the General Council that year. . . . I notice that the church that birthed me has, for the most part, continued along the path that it was on when I was confirmed. The place of the "New Creed" in our church is an important sign that this is so. Since 1968 it has become, in practice, the only creed used in our denomination. Rare is the United Church congregation which says one of the ecumenical creeds. At baptisms and confirmations we recite "our" New Creed. During services of ordination and commissioning at annual Conference meetings we say our New Creed. I suspect there would be an outcry if one of the ecumenical creeds were to replace the New Creed at one of those services . . . we have adopted the New Creed as our sole functioning one.[19]

17. For an excellent summary of the history of United Church doctrinal statements up to the early 1980s, see Clifford, "United Church of Canada."

18. Many today would speak highly of "A Song of Faith" and might make a similar claim for it. In practice, however, its use, status, and emotional appeal do not approach those of "A New Creed."

19. Searcy, "Story of My Conversion," 37. This is a significant statement, because just a few years earlier, Searcy was one of those who spoke in much more glowing terms about "A New Creed" and its place in The United Church: "One of the things about our tradition that seems to be holding firm is our United Church creed . . . . It picked up our ethos and our tradition and tried to restate things that we couldn't say" (Searcy, as quoted in Best, *Will Our Church Disappear*, 54).

More recently, Jeff Seaton confirmed, "This 1968 statement of faith has become virtually the only creed used regularly in United Church liturgies."[20]

There are surely few, if any, who would be able to disagree with these assessments. The classical creeds, which are of comparable length and liturgical intention, have all but disappeared from The United Church in both practice and theory. For some unusually strong evidence of this, one can look to the *Record of Proceedings* of the Thirty-Fifth General Council in 1994, where a seemingly modest petition was brought before the court that the Nicene Creed be used at merely one of its many worship services. Despite its limited scope, this request was denied. As recorded, the minutes show a surprisingly complete rejection.

> Petition No. 100—The Nicene Creed, Submitted by Appleby United Church, Burlington
>
> WHEREAS the Basis of Union (1925) acknowledges "the teaching of the great creeds of the ancient church"; and
>
> WHEREAS the Book of Common Order (1950) and the Service Book for the Use of the People (1969) include the Nicene Creed; and
>
> WHEREAS The United Church of Canada is a member of the World Council of Churches, whose basis is: "The World Council of Churches is a fellowship of churches which confess the Lord Jesus Christ as God and Saviour according to the scriptures and therefore seek to fulfill together their common calling to the glory of the one God, Father, Son and Holy Spirit"; and
>
> WHEREAS the Canberra Assembly (1991) of the World Council of Churches has issued a call to "move towards the recognition of the apostolic faith as expressed through the Nicene-Constantinopolitan Creed in the life and witness of one another";
>
> THEREFORE BE IT RESOLVED that the Church Board of Appleby United Church petition the 35th General Council through Halton Presbytery and Hamilton Conference to include the Nicene Creed in at least one of its worship services.

Having received this petition from a congregation in Burlington, Ontario, the following motion was brought to the floor of the General Council:

20. Seaton, *Who's Minding the Story*, 87.

> WHEREAS The United Church of Canada is a diverse community; and,
>
> WHEREAS the General Council has shown its openness to new and innovative forms of worship; and
>
> WHEREAS the Nicene Creed is a part of our tradition and heritage; and
>
> WHEREAS we value our journey of faith from its beginning to its present;
>
> "THEREFORE BE IT RESOLVED that the 35th General Council ask the Worship Planning Group of this Council to include the Nicene Creed in one of this Council's worship services."
>
> In the discussion there were both positive and negative comments about inclusion of the Creed.
>
> **Defeated**[21]

While realizing that commissioners change from General Council to General Council and that this decision would not likely be binding on subsequent meetings, it seems difficult to imagine that the Nicene Creed would ever again be accepted for use by the court. Evidently, it does not express or even approximate the Christian faith in a way that most United Church people have come to understand it. On the other hand, "A New Creed" has become the creed of, by, and for The United Church. As quoted above, Searcy and Seaton were certainly correct in their observations and intuitions about the relative status of the various credal confessions available within the denomination.

It is not just those creeds that "come from away" that are now widely disregarded by The United Church. At various points in its history, according to the *Song of Faith* booklet, "The United Church has formally expressed its collective faith."[22] Like both the "Twenty Articles of Doctrine" and "A Statement of Faith" before it, as well as the subsequent "A Song of Faith," "A New Creed" is described as the faith of The United Church "stated . . . in words appropriate to its time."[23] Clearly, the popularity of

21. *Record of Proceedings*, Thirty-Fifth General Council, 526, 158.

22. *Song of Faith*, 2.

23. *Song of Faith*, 2. Interestingly, the Forty-First General Council in 2012 approved a remit put to the congregations and presbyteries by the Fortieth General Council in 2009, which declared all four statements of faith—the "Twenty Articles of Doctrine" (1925), "A Statement of Faith" (1940), "A New Creed" (1968), and "A Song of Faith"

"A New Creed" has been more persistent than that of any other doctrinal confession in the story of The United Church. The creed continues to be held as the denomination's statement of faith par excellence. While the influence of other such confessions has been episodic, the authority and impact of "A New Creed" endures. The deep emotional attachment many feel to its words is seen most clearly in the way the writers of "A Song of Faith," the Committee on Theology and Faith of the General Council, felt the need to qualify the implications of their own work. "This statement," as we read earlier, "is not intended to be in any way a replacement of the beloved New Creed. . . . People in the United Church," further, "*love* it." Lest we have any lingering suspicions that "A Song of Faith" is a usurper, despite its being commissioned and approved by the General Council, we read that, "It does not aspire to the same liturgical standing as A New Creed."[24] Michael Bourgeois, one of those on the team that wrote "A Song of Faith," said publicly that many were encountered in the process of its drafting who "thought that 'A New Creed' so perfectly summarized the faith of the church that nothing else was necessary."[25]

Many in The United Church do seem to *love* "A New Creed." This prompts the questions of what it is they love about "A New Creed" and why? The answers are many and varied. Many people who love "A New Creed" seem to have a personal attachment to it because it is what they have been using to express their faith over a period of many years. Through thick and thin, good times and bad, smooth transitions and great upheavals, spiritual stagnation and moments of powerful religious experience, "A New Creed" has been there, giving voice and shape to the faith that is within them. The phrases of "A New Creed" have provided the natural outlet for their spiritual expression. Others recognize and are drawn to the poetic beauty of "A New Creed." Its text has a rhythm and a cadence that make it very easy on the ears. "A New Creed" can legitimately be described as a literary classic of modern religion, and its words are pleasing to those who long for a sense of beauty in their faith.

(2006)—to be "standards subordinate to the primacy of scripture" and included in the doctrine section (in addition to the original "Twenty Articles of Doctrine") of the Basis of Union. In theory, this places all four documents on equal footing, although, by adding the latter three to the "Twenty Articles of Doctrine," the effect is actually a liberalizing of United Church doctrine. See *Record of Proceedings*, Forty-First General Council, 151.

24. *Song of Faith*, 17.

25. Bourgeois, "Awash in Theology."

Yet others appreciate "A New Creed" for what it is not: a statement of things they do not believe or may have come to resent. "A New Creed" is not the Apostles' Creed or the Nicene Creed, and some count this as a tremendous benefit. For those who see the classical creeds as making claims that are unrealistic for modern people and as using antiquated or even offensive language for God, "A New Creed" is refreshingly free of such baggage. As Searcy writes, there are in it "no more embarrassing words about the Father almighty, or the Virgin Mary, or the resurrection of the body, or the ascension into heaven."[26] Both the language of "A New Creed" and the sort of theological approach it represents are also striking in their contrast to those of the Basis of Union's original "Twenty Articles of Doctrine" and "A Statement of Faith." Both of these longer confessions express a relatively more traditional Protestant vision of the Christian faith and in somewhat more propositional terms. "A New Creed" is noteworthy in that its use of language and its thought-forms more obviously bear the imprint of theological modernity. Its words demonstrate sympathy with language that is somewhat more religious than theological and less likely to suggest the attribution of any particular saving significance to Christianity.[27] Notes Hyuk Cho, "A New Creed affirms that God works in a variety of ways, perhaps even through other faiths."[28] This is an appealing belief for many as we grow ever more aware of the human diversity in our world.

One thing however seems especially to set "A New Creed" apart for the people of The United Church: a great many within the denomination see it as providing a distinguishing mark for The United Church of Canada. Whether reciting it wholly or merely alluding to one of its distinctive phrases, it serves to identify them with the unique story and identity of their community. As we will note later, this "We are not alone" confession has had some limited exposure and usage in other denominations and in other countries. Outside The United Church of Canada, it certainly has its admirers. Among such persons, however, who tend to come from culturally similar denominations and whose outlooks have much in common

26. Searcy, "Story of My Conversion," 37.

27. Religion is a word notoriously difficult, even impossible, to define. See Cavanaugh, *Myth of Religious Violence*, 57–85. *Religion* comes from the Latin *religio*, which means "re-binding." Religion, if we can use the term at all, is suited best to what the Romans considered religion. That is to say, religion is properly civil religion—a social construct used to bolster the state and its civic society. Theology, on the other hand, is used here to mean the discernment of God's revelation.

28. Hyuk Cho, "Practising God's Mission beyond Canada," in Schweitzer et al., *Theology of United Church*, 261.

with the people of The United Church, this text is not celebrated to nearly the same degree or considered formally as a creed. What is exceptional among the people of The United Church of Canada is that "A New Creed" has become perhaps the key symbol of the denomination's sense of itself and is therefore a source of pride. Whereas many United Church folk feel that there is not another Canadian church to which they could see themselves belonging, "A New Creed" gives voice and expression to those vital senses of a unique corporate identity and a fragile communal connection. The United Church of Canada is a relatively large and diverse denomination spread across a vast landscape. It can be difficult to maintain understandings and experiences of the shared identity of The United Church. We wonder, what does it mean to belong to The United Church? What is it that holds this community together in fellowship? Presumably, there must be something! "A New Creed" has become a symbol of that *something*.

In the history of Christianity, The United Church is a new kid on the block. It does not have an obvious pedigree that is recognized by many other Christians or an easy way to identify its connection with most other denominations, whether in Canada or abroad. Many well-informed Christians in other countries have no idea what kind of church The United Church of Canada is. I learned this clearly when I studied theology at a university in North Carolina, U.S.A., and would always get quizzical looks when I tried to explain what sort of denomination The United Church is. In places where there is a history of Methodism, Presbyterianism, or Congregationalism, such groups are old enough to be recognized more easily as distinct branches within the family tree of the Protestant Reformation, with their own unique cultures, theologies, and polities. Historically, these traditions have transcended national and linguistic boundaries. Given our unique blend of these three backgrounds, with a polity and a particular history that is unique to our Canadian context, The United Church is welcome at many an ecumenical table but entirely in like company at few. "A New Creed" gives United Church people something to help them make sense of their identity within both the wider church and Canadian culture. As prominent minister John Pentland notes in his book *Fishing Tips*, "our Creed" is one of the relatively few things that hold our denomination together—and it is the only item on his short list of unifying elements that is distinct to The United Church of Canada.[29]

29. Pentland, *Fishing Tips*, 217.

It is my hope that we can engage here in a rich and full examination of "A New Creed" and its significance for The United Church, historically, liturgically, and theologically. In the first chapter, I will offer a brief discussion of the cultural milieu of the 1960s and demonstrate how the spirit of the times of that revolutionary era made possible The United Church's surprising confessional move of producing "A New Creed." Occasioned in a situation of cultural and theological upheaval and inspired by a fortuitous coming together of creative individuals, it will be shown in the second chapter how this document was initially conceived and then written (and rewritten, repeatedly) in order to reorient the confessional posture of The United Church in a fundamental way. In the third chapter, I will show how the text has been used in and become a shaping influence on the liturgical tradition of The United Church. In practice, it has become the only creed used within, advocated for, or even provided to the people of the church. Chapter 4 will offer a discussion of how this confession has been interpreted within nonliturgical literature. Far from operating merely as the originally proposed possible alternative to the Apostles' Creed in services of baptism, "A New Creed" is now The United Church's confession of faith and theological authority par excellence. The fifth chapter will provide a line-by-line reflection and commentary upon the meaning of the "suggestive," "open-ended," and "allusive" words and phrases of "A New Creed."[30] We will see that while much of its language allows room for a traditionally orthodox meaning, each of its phrases seems actually to invite unexpected, nontraditional interpretations as well. Far from being a mere hypothetical, such diverse meanings and interpretations have demonstrably been proposed by United Church leaders. In the sixth and final chapter, I will consider the significance of "A New Creed" for The United Church and suggest some constructive ways for better using both this text and the practice of credal confession in general going forward. Drawing upon the analysis of several scholars who have sought to make sense of the way creeds do, or can, work within the life of the church, I will argue that the act of credal confession is vitally important and helpful for building up Christian faith and community. By virtue of its originally stated purpose and underlying philosophy of language however, "A New Creed" is not able to support the functions proper to credal confession. Rather than helping to form and give voice to an articulate vision of the Christian gospel, "A New Creed"

30. See Robert C. Fennell, "Scripture and Revelation," in Schweitzer et al., *Theology of United Church*, 59.

is seen to be a compromise text, intended to hold together the fragile coalition of The United Church over the last fifty or more years. This, I would speculate, is another reason why it has been so promoted by those in leadership roles and by the institutional structures of the denomination; the products of The United Church Publishing House, for example, have been universally celebratory of "A New Creed."[31] Given these influences, it is not surprising that "A New Creed" has become entrenched at a popular level. Although it is likely to be a deeply contested claim, I will argue that the Apostles' and Nicene Creeds would do a superior job of nurturing informed Christian faith in individuals and also of bringing them together in the bonds of fellowship. The ecumenical witness of the saints over almost two millennia testifies to the strength of this position.

I will demonstrate that "A New Creed" has come to be seen as expressing the faith of The United Church. However much it may be necessary to qualify a description of the church's corporate faith with reference to the personal perspective of a particular individual or to the theological diversity of the church as a whole, the accepted rule is that The United Church holds a faith and that this faith is expressed by the words of "A New Creed." Given that this has involved the setting aside of other possible alternatives, I will proceed on the assumption that the unique status of "A New Creed" in The United Church is a momentous issue calling for our deeper reflection. I will argue that The United Church's use of "A New Creed," especially involving as it does the practical rejection of the classical creeds, is particularly significant because its current usage cuts off the people of The United Church from the church catholic (universal) in a meaningful way. As one recent commentator observes, "Our conversation with the tradition seems to reach back only to 1968" and therefore "we no longer seem able to engage seriously with . . . principle doctrines upheld by most Christians in most places in most eras."[32] I will show that despite its many appealing attributes, the problems with "A New Creed" are not limited to its lack of ecumenical use but that its deficiencies flow inevitably from the fundamental linguistic decisions of its writers and therefore from the reality that its words simply do not and cannot provide an adequate theological summary of the biblical story—its being assumed with the Basis of Union's "Twenty Articles of Doctrine" and reaffirmed by the Forty-First General Council in 2012 that the Bible

31. The evidence of what the denomination's publishing arm publishes is not insignificant. See Seaton, *Who's Minding the Story*, 37

32. Seaton, *Who's Minding the Story*, 87–88.

is the "primary source and ultimate standard of Christian faith and life." Though readers may take issue with some or all of these conclusions, it is hoped that my critique will not be mistaken for criticism in a negative sense. My intention for presenting this study is not to generate any hard feelings but rather to provide for The United Church (and its scholars) an in-depth account of one important aspect of this denomination's story, as well as to offer positive and constructive proposals for its ongoing life. Whether readers find themselves in agreement or disagreement with the various arguments of this book, no doubt all can appreciate the need for such sustained and serious theological reflection on the beliefs and practices of The United Church.

Brief Word about Terms

It is necessary to say something about my use of the terms creed, confession, statement of faith, and so on. Readers will notice that I use these labels somewhat interchangeably. This is done largely for stylistic reasons. The widely held definitions of these terms, which delineate hard and fast distinctions among them, most commonly in regards to length or ecumenical status, are not entirely satisfactory. Because there is value in applying these labels precisely, I will engage in terminology at some more length in chapter 5 in order to determine in what sense "A New Creed" ought to be considered a creed.

1

The 1960s and the Appearance of "A New Creed"

Introduction

RENOWNED UNITED CHURCH HISTORIAN Phyllis D. Airhart once said that "A New Creed" "sounds sort of '60s-ish to me."[1] Her comment was remarkably intuitive, but in what sense? Given that this distinctive confession is so unlike anything that preceded it, in The United Church or elsewhere, questions surrounding the occasion of its appearance are important to consider. As is widely known, the sixties was a period of significant social upheaval that marked a cultural turning point in the twentieth century. This was true not only for mainstream Christian denominations like The United Church of Canada but for Western societies at large. Though North Americans had sought a return to normalcy following the Second World War—certainly a better and more affluent normalcy—any sense of contentment or consensus that had been achieved in the aftermath of V-E Day or V-J Day was fragmented by the 1960s. Worldviews and assumptions having evolved or taken great leaps, some individuals became impatient for society to change as rapidly and as thoroughly as they had done personally. Some of the enduring images of the decade—from the civil rights struggle of the United States and mass protests against the Vietnam War to the sexual

1. Best, *Will Our Church Disappear*, 54.

revolution and the emergence of a rock-and-roll drug culture—represented social developments that would have been unthinkable just a generation earlier. It will be the purpose of the following few pages to demonstrate briefly in what ways this dramatically changing cultural context suggested to many the need for commensurate adaptation on the part of the church. Some in The United Church felt the times specifically necessitated a change in the form and content of their denomination's creed. The confessional transformation embodied by "A New Creed" was precipitated by such feelings and made more viable in the midst of a radically unsettled community.

Defining the Sixties

When we speak of the historical significance of the 1960s, we are not just talking about ten years as counted according to the Gregorian calendar. Rather, the sixties refers to a period of cultural revolution throughout the West. The era not only seemed full of significant events for those who experienced them but has since been acknowledged as such by historians. One of the challenges of assessing this period is the utterly massive body of evidence at hand. Arthur Marwick's influential book *The Sixties: Cultural Revolution in Britain, France, Italy, and the United States* stretches to over fifteen hundred pages. In some ways, it is a very detailed work. In other ways it is, by necessity, highly selective and superficial. The 1960s occurred at a period in human history when burgeoning technologies allowed for unprecedented levels of human communication, as well as the preservation of vast amounts of information across several media, both new and old. In practical terms, there is an overwhelming amount of data that needs to be considered.

Another challenge in assessing the events of the sixties is the task of choosing appropriate start and end dates for this cultural revolution, which did not begin precisely on 1 January 1960 or end on 31 December 1969. The aforementioned Arthur Marwick made his most notable contribution in suggesting the idea of a long sixties from 1958 to 1974. He argues the sixties really began culturally with a new affluence that empowered teenagers economically and drove corporate interests to pursue teens with the development of an adolescent rock-and-roll culture. This accumulation of financial and social currency greatly emboldened the baby boom generation and increased the significance of their responses to events in the world around them. The end of the era came with the winding down of the Vietnam War and the resignation of Richard M. Nixon from the American presidency. While the long sixties concept has been well received, the selection of different dates by other historians symbolizes the challenge of assigning precise beginnings and endings.[2]

Arthur Marwick took his inspiration for the idea of the long sixties from fellow British scholar Eric Hobsbawm and his influential work *The Age of Extremes: The Short Twentieth Century 1914–1991*.[3] I find Hobsbawm's delineation of this era more convincing, from the triggering of the First World War in 1914 to the collapse of the Soviet Union in 1991. There seems to me a thematic continuity within the geopolitics of this short twentieth century and a clear way to distinguish that period from events both before and after. While I agree that there was also an era we can call the sixties, and that the idea of a long sixties is helpful, I am not sure it is quite as easy to demarcate a cultural revolution in that era as it is with the international political turmoil of the short twentieth century. One could conceivably suggest the beginning of a very long 1960s at 1914. This is not to deny the significant impacts of the sixties but to name a particular challenge in assessing them.

Secularization

Of particular interest to the history of The United Church in general and its writing of "A New Creed" in particular is the difficult issue of secularization. It is widely agreed that over the last hundred or more years, the West has secularized. During this period, religious institutions have been disengaged publically and private faith has waned. It is also acknowledged that the cultural developments of the sixties played an important role in this still ongoing story of secularization in Western societies. Precise understandings of the causes, nature, and timing of the long-term secularizing trend, however, remain remarkably mysterious.

Prominent Canadian philosopher Charles Taylor did a helpful job of framing the challenge.[4] While we might sense that religion has waned

2. See Strain, *Long Sixties*.

3. Marwick, *Sixties*, 4.

4. In *Who's Minding the Story*, Seaton offers a very helpful assessment of C. Taylor's *Secular Age*. In it, he cleverly uses Taylor as a lens through which to interpret The United Church's response to the secularization of Canadian society in recent decades.

in both the public and private spheres in the West, he argues, closer examination reveals many exceptions that call into question this general assumption. In Britain, private piety is not prevalent but there remains a prominent role for religious institutions in public life. In the United States, by contrast, there is no state church, but religious belief among individuals remains fairly common. Rather than considering secularization as a linear trend, in isolation, Taylor prefers to suggest that what has been happening in the West is rather a process of pluralization. "The shift to secularity," he writes, is "a move from a society where belief in God is unchallenged and indeed, unproblematic, to one in which it is understood to be one option among others, and frequently not the easiest to embrace."[5]

The emphasis on pluralism within the discussion of secularization is a helpful one. It offers a more rounded consideration of the issue while also allowing for recognition of the way Western societies have become increasingly fragmented along many different lines, not just in regards to questions about the role of religious institutions or about specific personal beliefs. However apt the recognition of this process of pluralization, it is the case that Canadian churches have been experiencing a steady, long-term decline in recent decades. In using Taylor's framework, we would want to place the emphasis on "not the easiest to embrace" rather than on "one option among others." Brian Clarke and Stuart Macdonald show the reality of the church's steady decline convincingly in *Leaving Christianity: Changing Allegiances in Canada Since 1945*, offering a remarkable and detailed statistical analysis of Canadian census data as well as of denominational records. The clear picture, which aligns well with the stated experiences of the participants in these churches, is that churches have been declining in a linear fashion and they do not know what to do about it. But it is not just that these institutions are becoming less popular and retreating from view. It is also that individual Canadians are increasingly moving away from identifying themselves as Christians.[6] While acknowledging both the pros and cons of the institutional decline of Canadian churches, both for society and for the churches themselves, Clarke and Macdonald state plainly, "There is no fix."[7]

5. C. Taylor, *Secular Age*, 2–3.
6. Clarke and Macdonald, *Leaving Christianity*, 21.
7. Clarke and Macdonald, *Leaving Christianity*, 12.

Within the significant corpus of literature on the cultural revolution of the 1960s, there exists a considerable body of writing on the impact of that revolution on religion in Canada in general and even on The United Church in particular. Kevin N. Flatt, in *After Evangelicalism: The Sixties and the United Church of Canada*, argues explicitly for the link between a so-called liberal theological turn and the sudden onset of decline in the nation's largest Protestant denomination. While there has been some legitimate critique of the way Flatt infers causation, he has nonetheless raised an important question about the relationship of Christian theology and of personal belief with visible, institutional manifestations of the Christian church. Seeking to understand these relationships is of particular importance to those coming from a confessional perspective. While I tend to see more correlation than causation, his theological analysis opens up helpful vistas on longer-term currents that do not seem to be captured by more recent statistical trends. Namely, he argues that The United Church's elites had been liberal from their earliest days and that what changed in the 1960s was a sudden, elite-led transformation of the denomination towards a fully liberalized denominational identity.[8] For Flatt, secularism itself appears to fall on the theological spectrum—at the extreme end, opposite conservative Evangelicalism and further left than theological liberalism. This is an understandable view to take from a theological, particularly evangelical, perspective. What is most insightful about his work is the way this theological consideration allows him to frame the historical challenge. "Sometime between 1850 and 2000," he writes, "Canadian mainline Protestantism shifted away from evangelicalism."[9] Keeping in mind that for him a leftward shift away from Evangelicalism seems to be the same thing as secularization, he asks the question when and why did that shift happen? The two broad schools of thought, he shows, indicate either an early shift between 1890 and the First World War or a late shift during the long sixties. Although emphasizing the clear predominance of the latter, Flatt's theological orientation creates openness to the possibility of longer-term historical continuity.

Our assessments of secularization are influenced to a considerable degree by our own theological and institutional perspectives. This is especially so when considering the sixties, which are so recent as to remain in the living memory of many. In noting the importance of personal

8. Flatt, *After Evangelicalism*, 14.

9. Flatt, *After Evangelicalism*, 6.

perspective on assessments of secularization, Clarke and Macdonald remind us that this theory was itself an outgrowth of ideas proposed by Marx and others, that so-called religion was something humanity would simply grow out of.[10] Therefore, secularization is not necessarily an observation. It can be a presupposition based on certain ideological principles. Darwinism and its understandings of evolution provide another set of widely held assumptions that secularization is normative. Inevitably, historical arguments in this area are going to be shaped by the perspectives, presuppositions, and beliefs of the historian.

Taking 1945 as an obviously meaningful starting point for comparison, as Clarke and Macdonald do, it seems likely from the outset that one would conclude that the religious boom of the 1950s rules out a longer-term secularizing trend and indicates a sudden break in the mid-sixties. If the horizons of study are broadened, might the short upward blip of the 1950s be seen as the outlier? This is not so much a critique as a rhetorical question. By choosing a particular viewpoint, we inevitably shape the reality we see. While as a rule I am inclined to look more for continuity than for change, I am compelled by Clarke and Macdonald's assessment of the demographic significance of the baby boomers' sudden and overwhelming rejection of the church publically and of Christianity privately. The baby boomers' affluence led them en masse to become elites and to broaden their horizons beyond those of their upbringing. As a cultural reset built momentum all around them, many boomers decided to leave the religion of their Sunday school behind. Collectively, they might have decided differently and recommitted themselves to Christianity and the church. Many in their cohort did, individually—after all, it was a very large group—but, on the whole, they did not. It appears that the church's decline since the mid-1960s in Canada and elsewhere is largely the demographic outworking of this generational change.[11]

In her brilliant history of The United Church, Airhart comes from a position of sympathy—theologically and institutionally—for the denomination. Drawing on a theoretical model proposed by political scientist Thomas Homer-Dixon, she suggests that the striking shift towards secularism of the 1960s was never a technical problem to be fully grasped or resolved, theologically or structurally. The expansion of state structures in that era pushed the church to the margins of society in areas where it

10. Clarke and Macdonald, *Leaving Christianity*, 12.

11. Clarke and Macdonald, *Leaving Christianity*, 229–30.

had previously been influential, such as in health care and education. The church could neither continue to play the same roles in an increasingly complex technocratic society nor give any pushback to the encroachment of secular institutions. Its newly diminished social status was not something that could be fixed. Rather, The United Church, like its siblings, was facing a colliding and overlapping set of adaptive challenges, understood as panarchy. A concept inspired by the cyclical nature of the ecological realm, panarchy refers to a complex web of interdependence, featuring ongoing tensions between continuity and change as well as between destruction and creativity. Such challenges necessitate considerable adaptation-learning, growth, and letting go on the part of the agent who is as much acted upon as actor. Seen this way, the adaptations of The United Church and of other churches as well were not symbols of apostasy but of creative changes that allowed institutions to preserve the core of their faithfulness for a new generation and life cycle.[12] "The United Church's response to the revolution of the 1960s did not reverse its statistical decline," writes Airhart. "Yet thousands of United Church congregations across Canada still believed themselves 'called to be the Church,' as the New Creed put it, 'to celebrate God's presence.'"[13]

The United Church's Experience of the 1960s

It is beyond the scope of this work to settle the difficult historical questions of secularization. The purpose here is not to determine what exactly secularization is, when it began, or what caused it. Rather, the intention is to show that within The United Church of the sixties, many had an overwhelming sense that things had changed drastically. The argument here is from the recorded experiences that were articulated in The United Church of the era. Like many other churches in North America in the 1960s, The United Church felt waves of change from both within and without. Facing the certain end of their unofficial establishment and the often glaring ineffectiveness of their activities—from preaching to programming to fundraising—many of the mainstream churches[14] ex-

12. Airhart, *Church with Soul*, 258–59.

13. Airhart, *Church with Soul*, 299.

14. I take the helpful point of Clarke and Macdonald that the oft-used term *mainline* is an American one not particularly suited to the Canadian context. See Clarke and Macdonald, *Leaving Christianity*, 7–8.

perienced what John Webster Grant calls "a decade of ferment."[15] Beardsall describes the situation most helpfully in writing, "Growing wealth, suburban expansion, and waves of post-war immigration were remaking the nation. While Canada did not undergo the immense social, political, and racial upheaval experienced by the United States, there was enough social change to deeply affect its churches."[16] That the changes going on around Canadian Christians were or seemed startling is doubtless true. Change is not inherently bad for the church and can often be good. Among Christians of all stripes were those pleased by happenings at the Second Vatican Council from 1962 to 1965. As Beardsall notes, many in The United Church were actually excited by the cultural changes going on in the 1960s.[17] That said, change is often unsettling and difficult for an established institution to accommodate, especially when clear and rigid divisions emerge between those who work eagerly for change and those who strive to preserve what is best from tradition. Such diverging instincts are often basic to the personalities of those involved, making it difficult to bring people together in a meeting of minds.

Evidence of the seismic shifts being felt throughout the Western church is found in the sudden popularity of individuals and ideas that seemed to indicate the inevitability of radical, sweeping change, especially in regard to centuries-old theology. The English bishop John A. T. Robinson, for example, wrote an amazingly popular book, *Honest to God* (1963), which made the case for the widespread adoption of a strikingly modern theology. In it, he attempts to synthesize the thought of Dietrich Bonhoeffer, Paul Tillich, and Rudolf Bultmann. There was nothing especially new in Robinson's argument—though he thought this particular synthesis was original—but its commercial success was remarkable. Printed in an affordable paperback edition, it sold 700,000 copies in its first two years of publication.[18] Like Harvey Cox (*The Secular City*) and others who attained notoriety for furthering the popularization of theological liberalism, Robinson argues that Christendom has ended and with it the meaning of traditional Christian theology. He summarizes this most succinctly in both calling for and confidently predicting the emergence of a "radically new mould and metamorphosis of Christian

15. Grant, *Church in Canadian Era*, 184–204.
16. Beardsall, "And Whether Pigs Have Wings," 99.
17. Beardsall, "And Whether Pigs Have Wings," 99.
18. Berton, *Comfortable Pew*, 122.

belief and practice."[19] That new shape would be conditioned, first, by the idea that "modern man" could no longer believe in a "God above or beyond the world" and, second, that the world needed a Christianity that could be distilled into an "encounter"—an experience capable of effecting psychological and ethical transformation.[20] Though frightening to some, many agreed with Robinson, Cox, and others in suggesting that such a vision—often labeled secular Christianity—offered the hope of a new dawn for both church and society.

Closer to home, the Canadian churches were becoming well aware of such cultural and theological developments and at times even embracing them. The classic expression of this was found in the publication of Pierre Berton's best seller *The Comfortable Pew*. Rather than introducing its usual devotional booklet for Lent in 1965, the Anglican Church of Canada commissioned Berton, a prominent Canadian journalist, to write "an outsider's view of the church." After beginning with an account of his own drifting away from Anglicanism as a young man, and the "white-robed, anthropomorphic God of [his] childhood,"[21] Berton went on to criticize all of the mainstream churches for having become essentially conservative social institutions that uncritically supported the politics of powerful elites and the social ambitions of their middle-class clientele.[22] Perhaps his sharpest critique was aimed at the churches for what they were saying (traditional theology) and how they were saying it (primarily sermons).[23] For Berton, the churches had become self-serving and were therefore unable to address the key social issues that had emerged in that day.

The United Church sought to capitalize on the popular success of *The Comfortable Pew* by producing a short book of its own, *Why the Sea Is Boiling Hot*. In it, Berton and four other journalists wrote essays assessing "the Church from outside."[24] Their critiques mostly echoed those of *The Comfortable Pew*, but the real significance of this volume lies in the responses to each essay written by United Church officials. Though they were quick to defend The United Church, especially over and against its competitors, these denominational leaders were equally quick

19. Robinson, *Honest to God*, 126.

20. Bultmann, "The Idea of God and Modern Man," in *Translating Theology into the Modern Age*, 83–95.

21. Berton, *Comfortable Pew*, 15.

22. Berton, *Comfortable Pew*, 69–89.

23. Berton, *Comfortable Pew*, 101–28.

24. Nicol et al., *Why the Sea*, v.

to join in the chorus of criticism against traditionalism. It is clear they were themselves overwhelmed by the sort of change going on all around them. Then-Moderator Ernest Marshall Howse refers in his response to "the revolutionary setting of our time," and similar notes are struck throughout.[25] Elsewhere, we read, "We live in a new world changing with unprecedented speed," and "We live in an age of unprecedented stress."[26] Clearly, approaches of conservatism or retrenchment did not seem like viable options for these leaders, no matter how articulate the advocates of contrary positions might be.

In *Why the Sea Is Boiling Hot*, The United Church respondents try to show that they understood what kinds of change were occurring and why. In particular, they identify three areas of revolution: technology, education, and economic disparity. It is the first of these that seemed most extensive and threatening to them. "A revolution in technology," we read, "threatens catastrophic changes in the patterns of employment, promises leisure we do not know how to use, concentrates frightening power in the hands of a few machines and decision makers and steadily increases both our affluence and our sense of helplessness."[27]

A perspective similar to that of *Why the Sea Is Boiling Hot* is found in another little book, published also by The United Church's Board of Evangelism and Social Service, *The Big Change*, by Rex Dolan. Then-professor of preaching at United Theological College in Montreal, Dolan offers a more detailed analysis of the social upheaval engulfing the church at the time. He also strongly criticized the inward-looking attitude of the church (he actually calls it "the 'failure' of the church") and advocated the sort of constructive theological renewal proposed by John A. T. Robinson. Dolan's description of the social and cultural changes facing the church of his day is most enlightening. While stressing that the extent of the change going on was truly difficult to grasp, he suggests that it was the technological revolution—"an apparently interminable acceleration in scientific enterprise"—and the public's widespread adoption of "pragmatic scientific attitudes" that were leading to a "critical approach in almost every area of life."[28] In other words, it is not just that people might be threatened by the loss of their livelihoods to machines or that new household appliances

25. Nicol et al., *Why the Sea*, vi.

26. Nicol et al., *Why the Sea*, viii, 49.

27. Nicol et al., *Why the Sea*, vii.

28. Dolan, *Big Change*, 9.

gave them unexpected leisure time, it is that they had adopted a scientific worldview, which made it impossible to accept any sort of religion perceived as primitive. Dolan's book is remarkably insightful in its provision of an articulate, insider's view of a United Church that was trying to identify and wrestle with the massive sociocultural change being felt all around.

Many church leaders and professional theologians were advocating radical changes to Christian faith and practice and were achieving a degree of notoriety for doing so. That there was so much *call* for change however, indicates that change was not always happening as quickly or in quite the way these people wanted it to. John A. T. Robinson, for example, received stark criticism in England from theologians as diverse as C. S. Lewis and Michael Ramsey, then archbishop of Canterbury.[29] In the same era, mass evangelist Billy Graham and theologian Karl Barth both achieved considerable popularity in offering a more conservative message. Despite its commercial success, Pierre Berton's book also caused outrage among many Anglicans, with some even calling for its publication to be forbidden. The United Church, known in part for "its tradition of untraditionalism" was itself a producer of some more cautious attitudes.[30] In 1966, The United Church Renewal Fellowship was formed. For decades, this group continued to protest the spread of theological liberalism in the denomination.[31] Grant portrays well the divergent responses within The United Church when he writes, "Change was greeted in some quarters with enthusiastic approval, in others with hostility and even shock, and in still others with scepticism or an almost complete lack of interest."[32] Among those who tried to resist the modernization of The United Church's doctrinal confession, particularly as that trend was being expressed in the writing and adoption of "A New Creed," were several members of the Committee on Christian Faith, as well as prominent individuals such R. C. Chalmers of Pine Hill Divinity Hall in Halifax, Nova Scotia, and Kenneth Hamilton of the University of Winnipeg.[33]

29. See Ramsey, *Image Old and New*.

30. Grant, *Church in Canadian Era*, 186.

31. Grant, *Church in Canadian Era*, 238.

32. Grant, *Church in Canadian Era*, 200.

33. More on the statements of these individuals will be seen later.

Concluding Reflections on the 1960s and The United Church

In the 1960s, change was a theme foremost in the minds of many Christian leaders in The United Church of Canada and throughout the West. This often overwhelming change was marked by rapid transformations in technology, worldviews, and values—indeed, in almost every area of life. In particular, new technologies were not only changing the way people went about their daily lives but also reshaping their worldviews around the value of progress. The growing sense that newer-is-better began to influence many areas of society, including religious faith and practice. For all the emphases on change and progress that were being articulated at the time, however, we must not be tempted to choose one form of an insider's perspective in seeking to understand what was really going on in that era. We ought not to forget the preserving instincts of the many in that period who reacted with resistance. Although the 1960s were indeed a time of rapid and often unsettling change, the embrace of change by many was not the uniform response of all. Others were guided by an opposite sort of conserving sensibility. Historically, it would perhaps be more correct to conclude that controversy and tumult, rather than simply change, were the social legacies of the era. Theological liberalism, for instance, was neither new nor a change. It had existed in the West for hundreds of years and been present in The United Church since its founding. What nascent theological divisions there may have already been, however, began to mature into serious fractures. It is not likely coincidental that the so-called mainstream churches began their decades-long decline in the early to mid-1960s, a decline that has continued unabated.[34] The bonds that held the church together were seriously loosened. Those who remained were not connected as strongly as they had been, and many became separated altogether. As Robert D. Putnam shows in his now landmark study, it was not just Christian churches that began to experience a breakdown in their received consensus and to decline in both popularity and participation, but congregations of other faiths, labor unions, service clubs, bowling leagues, and virtually every other kind of traditional community grouping as well. The causes Putnam identifies for this decline of social and civic involvement were new pressures of time and money due to the economics of two parents working outside the home, urban sprawl (leading to people living farther from other people and from their place

34. See Clarke and Macdonald, *Leaving Christianity*.

of work), and, above all, the consequences of generational change (baby boomers coming of age), co-mingled with the privatization of entertainment enabled by television.[35]

The cultural developments of the sixties had a great influence on The United Church of Canada. This is shown by the many changes it made throughout its areas of operation. It was not just the form and content of the church's credal confession that were altered but many other of its features as well. Notable was the publication of the New Curriculum series for Sunday school classes and other small group studies—a fascinating story in its own right and one that has been well told.[36] Beardsall argues that, "The United Church's encounters during the 1960s were indeed wide-ranging, running the gamut from new statements on divorce and abortion to fresh church union negotiations, a new formulation of credal faith, and new ways of doing mission at home and globally."[37]

There is a massive body of literature covering every imaginable aspect of the 1960s' cultural revolution—even on its significance for Canadian Christianity in general and for The United Church in particular. Airhart notes that although there is a lack of explanatory consensus on many points, "Scholars agree that the 1960s decisively changed the religious landscape of North America and Western Europe."[38] This chapter has provided a very brief look at the sixties. On the one hand, it has been brief, because most such analyses must inevitably be selective rather than exhaustive. On the other, this is not a broad study of the 1960s but of one of its documents—"A New Creed"—and of that document's ongoing significance for The United Church of Canada. Clearly, however, the unique historical context of the 1960s—in which often overwhelming change and unresolvable community breakdown were being experienced—made more possible the drafting and formal adoption of such a novel statement of faith. When its authors wrote in their report *Creeds* "No one can doubt that we live in an age of rapid change," they signalled both the presence of some contextual influences and their remarkably

35. Putnam, *Bowling Alone*, 277–84.

36. See Flatt, *After Evangelicalism*, 104–43; Airhart, *Church with Soul*, 200–202; and Bradley-St.-Cyr, "Downfall of Ryerson Press," 96–127.

37. Beardsall, "And Whether Pigs Have Wings," 100.

38. Airhart, *Church with Soul*, 258. For helpful summaries of the literature, see also the aforementioned, 196–224; Flatt, *After Evangelicalism*, 3–16; and Clarke and Macdonald, *Leaving Christianity*, 12–23.

keen awareness of them.[39] Subsequent reflection has confirmed the committee's observations. Some years later, Peter Gordon White wrote, "The sixties were a period of disruption and discontinuity for the churches, in a sea of social and political turbulence. It was a time of cultural revolution in North America as elsewhere . . . this Union of Canadian churches in 1925 had not adopted any single creed as foundational but had simply acknowledged 'the teaching of the great creeds of the ancient church.' The work of the committee reflects both the turmoil of the times and the openness of the United Church tradition, brief as that tradition may be."[40] John Webster Grant also argues that The United Church became caught in the turbulence of the age, losing its "sense of running before the wind" in the early 1960s.[41]

A former member of the Committee on Theology and Faith who was involved in that committee's revision of "A New Creed" in the late 1970s told me that, in his view, the original text "was a product of the sixties in all sorts of ways."[42] Any claim about precisely how outside pressures influenced the doctrine of The United Church in the 1960s, however, or changes in its confessional posture needs to be nuanced. The temptation to make connections in a deterministic way, as if it were inevitable that something like "A New Creed" had to appear about the time it did, must be avoided. Many Christian denominations in Canada and elsewhere faced exactly the same societal pressures as The United Church. Some even produced modern confessions of their own—notably the United Church of Christ in the U.S.A. (1959) and the North American arm of the World Alliance of Reformed Churches (1965)—but none produced anything like "A New Creed."[43] The emergence of "A New Creed" was influenced by the interplay of intellectual trends, personal relationships, and institutional dynamics, as well as of creativity—and some might even say of inspiration. In assessing the writing and adoption of "A New Creed" within The United Church of the tumultuous 1960s, we cannot claim to determine causation, but we can certainly identify correlation. The sixties did not cause "A New Creed," but the writing and adoption of this confession fits well within the historical context. The unique features

39. Standing Committee on Christian Faith, *Creeds*, 10.

40. Vischer, *Reformed Witness Today*, 195.

41. Grant, "Only Yesterday."

42. Telephone interview with Tom Sherwood, 30 Nov. 2011.

43. The United Church of Christ and WARC confessions are much more traditional in expression.

of this period allowed the creative impulses behind it to flourish, much as just the right spot in a garden allows a certain plant to thrive as it receives the correct amount of sunlight.

"A New Creed" was written to reflect and adapt to changes being felt within The United Church, changes that themselves found their source in broader social developments. However, The United Church also had its so-called conservatives. Changes were afoot, but specific responses were not embraced by all of its participants. What we see in this history is not so much the emergence of a new theological consensus in The United Church but the rapid and surprising breakdown of an older one. From its founding, a considerable range of theological diversity had existed within The United Church. In the first quarter of the twentieth century, disparate constituencies among Canada's Methodists, Presbyterians, and Congregationalists—Eastern, Central, and Western; urban and rural; rich and poor; liberal and conservative—had coalesced around the vision of a national, broadly-based Anglo-Protestant denomination. During the 1960s, this coalition began to disintegrate. Far from being unaware of this, the Committee on Christian Faith sought and gained permission to craft a radically new form of confession, a key purpose of which was to attempt to hold together the alliance that had existed in The United Church since the time of union. That there were some negative reactions to the committee's new doctrinal confession, coming from both the left and the right, shows that they were not able to achieve this goal completely in their writing of "A New Creed."[44] However, the subsequent story would show that in this aim, they actually achieved some considerable success.

As highlighted at the outset of this chapter, Charles Taylor articulates three distinct ways of understanding secularization: as the diminishing of the role of religion in public life, as the decline of personal belief among individuals, and as the rise of pluralism within society. This last option, he argues, is best able to accommodate the data. It also helps to articulate that something has happened rather than simply that other things—be they the social prominence of religious institutions or private faith—have stopped happening. Secularization, for Taylor, is not a story of subtraction but of creation. "Western modernity," he writes, "including its secularity, is the fruit of new inventions [as well as] newly constructed self-understandings

44. See the contrasting but critical responses of John Burbidge and Berkley Reynolds in "A Creed" (no author). These responses are cited and discussed in Airhart, *Church with Soul*, 274, and Flatt, *After Evangelicalism*, 184–85.

and related practices."[45] Upon reflection, it strikes me that many United Church leaders of the 1960s would have been pleased with Taylor's later framing of secularization. They certainly recognized that their church and others had entered a period of notable decline. They were also aware that the Christian faith was not enjoying the same resonance among their contemporaries that it had once had. They, like the later historian Flatt, tied their assumptions regarding institutional vitality to the personal faith of its individual church members. Yet, whereas Flatt saw a causal connection between liberalism and institutional decline, many of them saw liberalism as the antidote to the decline that they thought would only increase the further one moved to the right of the theological spectrum. United Church leaders were aware that it was not just that Christianity was on the wane but that pluralism was in the ascendency. Despite the oversimplification of their assumptions, their actions can be seen as attempts not just to be appealing within an increasingly pluralistic social context but also to accommodate their church to it. Of this effort, "A New Creed" will be shown to be both exemplary and symbolic.

To grasp the unique significance of the unprecedented writing, adoption, and use of "A New Creed" within The United Church, we must appreciate the revolutionary demands of the 1960s as well as the simultaneous resistance to change that was being summoned. Many expressed an ongoing satisfaction with the received tradition. The tensions that emerged within The United Church reflected the broader social upheaval of the era. Having established that such tumults were being experienced in Canada's most popular Protestant denomination and were significant influences upon both its decision makers and many of its constituents, we will proceed to a detailed examination of the genesis and evolution of the text of "A New Creed."

45. C. Taylor, *Secular Age*, 22.

2

The Text of "A New Creed"

Introduction

"A New Creed" is clearly beloved by many people in The United Church of Canada. Yet, despite its place of authority and prominence in the life and liturgy of Canada's largest Protestant denomination, the origin and evolution of the text of "A New Creed" have been somewhat shrouded in mystery ever since the text's initial presentation to the Twenty-Third General Council in 1968 and its subsequent publication in the *Service Book*. Kenneth Hamilton of the University of Winnipeg—a member of the team that was concurrently negotiating a potential organic union with the Anglican Church of Canada—was quoted at the time as saying that his group had "not the slightest inkling" that such a confession was being drafted. Clearly offended that he and his colleagues, who were involved in a crucial ecumenical dialogue and negotiation, were being left in the dark as some leaders in The United Church sought to redefine its corporate confession, Hamilton went on to call "A New Creed" "tendentious," "extremely superficial," and "slightly ridiculous."[1] Until recently, familiarity with the history of "A New Creed" has been mostly absent. Gretta Vosper was able to refer as recently as 2008 to a "mysterious process" by which the text was composed and then authorized for

1. "Vague New Creed."

liturgical use across The United Church.[2] Victor Shepherd, an expert on the theology of The United Church, once said, "It is difficult to grasp how there came to exist a creed [like 'A New Creed']."[3]

Despite its massive popularity within the denomination, few know enough about where "A New Creed" came from or why it was written. In order to fill a gap in our historical understanding, this chapter will provide a detailed history of the genesis and evolution of "A New Creed." Though a few secondary sources have appeared, with increasing frequency in recent years, most of these are summary in nature. In fact, virtually all that has been published on the subject was stated long ago in *Creeds*—the final report of the Committee on Christian Faith that wrote "A New Creed."[4] By virtue of its aims, *Creeds* itself offers a relatively brief summation of the committee's work.

Though the words of "A New Creed" are now widely perceived as articulating the faith of The United Church, it will be shown that the Committee on Christian Faith, by its own testimony, crafted the phrases of "A New Creed" to be intentionally vague, abstract, and, by implication, unclear. Put another way, "A New Creed" was designed so that individuals could utter the creed with their lips while referring to almost anything they wish, personally and privately. As the committee wrote in its report to the General Council, "The words and statements used are suggestive rather than definitive, making it possible for them to be filled with personal content by those who say the creed."[5] Importantly, this was an implicit acknowledgment on their part that there was no particular theological vision shared widely enough that it could rightly be called the faith of The United Church.

2. Vosper, *With or Without God*, 96.

3. Shepherd, "Testimony of Dr. Victor Shepherd," in Zung, "Bermuda Trial."

4. Notably Clifford, "United Church of Canada"; Kervin, *Language of Baptism*, 183–85; Peter Gordon White, whose account appears in Vischer, *Reformed Witness Today*, 194–95; and Airhart, *Church with Soul*, 273–75. At more length, see Flatt, *After Evangelicalism*, 176–85. A series of helpfully complimentary sketches is also provided in Schweitzer et al., *Theology of United Church*.

5. Standing Committee on Christian Faith, *Creeds*, 18.

The History of the Text

Background

Although the current text of “A New Creed” reflects revisions that were approved by the General Council Executive in 1980 and in 1995, its basic formulation was made in the mid-1960s, in preparation for the Twenty-Third General Council of The United Church in 1968. The impetus for the creation of such a new credal statement within the denomination came as early as 1965, according to the Committee on Christian Faith, when that group was studying a draft baptismal liturgy that had been proposed by the Committee on Church Worship and Ritual for inclusion in the upcoming *Service Book*. Finding some broad discomfort with the suggested rubric “The Apostles’ Creed shall be said by all,” committee members sought and gained permission from the Sub-Executive of the General Council to write a “profession of faith, suitable for liturgical use, as a possible alternative to the Apostles’ Creed.” Following the Twenty-Second General Council in 1966, in time for which such a task had not been possible, the Committee on Christian Faith asked for and then received an enlarged, threefold mandate from the Sub-Executive of the General Council:

1. To examine the status and authority of the classical creeds in The United Church of Canada today.
2. To collect and examine representative modern statements of faith.
3. To attempt to formulate a modern credal statement suitable for use in the liturgy, with special reference to the new order for the administration of the sacrament of baptism.[6]

The result of the committee’s work over the next two years was a brief confession of faith entitled “A New Creed” and a booklet, *Creeds: A Report of the Committee on Christian Faith*, in which the group summarized its activity and advocated for the confession of faith it had written. Upon the approval of the General Council Executive, “A New Creed” appeared in the 1969 *Service Book* alongside, and controversially before, the Apostles’ and Nicene Creeds, as well as “A Statement of Faith of The United Church of Christ in the U.S.A.” (1959).[7]

6. Standing Committee on Christian Faith, *Creeds*, 5.

7. *Service Book for Use of People*, 310–14. In the ministers’ edition, the creeds

The historical account given in *Creeds* contains a helpful summary of the writing of "A New Creed." Unfortunately, it provides the virtual extent of the information known by many about the origins of "A New Creed," and, while interesting, it seems to raise more questions than it answers. Most pointedly, how could a small committee decide to set in motion a process of radically redefining the confession of the faith of The United Church so quickly and so quietly, simply because some of its members were uncomfortable with a particular liturgical rubric of introduction for the Apostles' Creed? To shed some much needed light on this story and suggest answers to this and other possible questions, we must turn to the archival records of the Committee on Christian Faith and examine what it was doing in the mid- to late 1960s.

The Work of the Committee on Christian Faith

As mentioned, the origins of "A New Creed" came as early as 1965. At the beginning of that year, the Committee on Christian Faith had designated, somewhat informally, a group of individuals to approach and possibly meet with a similar committee of the Presbyterian Church in Canada with a view to producing a joint statement of faith.[8] Clearly, there was an appetite among committee members to prepare a doctrinal confession of some kind. It is worth remembering that by this point the wider theological unrest of the age had already reached deeply into The United Church. As of 1965, there were at least two former moderators who were publically opposed to reciting the Apostles' Creed.[9] In February of that year, *The United Church Observer* printed an editorial entitled "Don't Make Us Recite the Apostles' Creed," which argued, among other things, that a minister should not even have the right to include it, by choice, in a baptismal service. While a joint effort with the Presbyterians never got off the ground, a better and more important opportunity availed itself to the committee shortly. In May 1965, the Committee on Christian Faith found itself examining a baptismal liturgy that had been proposed for the forthcoming *Service Book* by the group entrusted with its production,

---

were on the inside covers, both front and back. As we will see in the next chapter, the different confessions and creeds were labeled differently with the value-laden terms "Historic" and "Contemporary."

8. Standing Committee on Christian Faith, "Meeting Minutes" (11 Jan. 1965, box 5).

9. See, for example, Howse, *Roses in December*, 194.

the Committee on Church Worship and Ritual. Concerned for its part, like the *Observer*, by the suggested formula "The Apostles' Creed shall be said by all," the Committee on Christian Faith voted to "request [to the Committee on Church Worship and Ritual] that the Apostles' Creed be *permissive* rather than obligatory as suggested in the service [emphasis in original]." The committee went on to agree, moreover, "that we request permission from the Executive or Sub-executive of the General Council to attempt to draft a brief profession of faith suitable for liturgical use as a possible alternative to the Apostles' Creed." They went on to qualify their planned request by saying that "this . . . does not alter the United Church's acceptance of the historic creeds as indicated in the Basis of Union."[10] In response to this request, the Sub-Executive of the General Council passed the following motion: "At the request of the Committee on Christian Faith, it is agreed that permission be given to the Committee to attempt to draft a brief profession of faith, suitable for liturgical use as a possible alternative to the Apostles' Creed, especially in the New Order for the administration of the Sacrament of Holy Baptism."[11] For some time, no further action was taken on the issue, as the committee was occupied with other matters that needed to be addressed more urgently in preparation for the Twenty-Second General Council in 1966. By the fall of 1966, however, the process of actively developing a brief doctrinal confession was put in motion. At the committee's October meeting, members were charged to consider bringing a credal statement for presentation at the next meeting.[12]

When the Committee on Christian Faith next gathered in November 1966, a handful of well-known creeds was distributed among the members for perusal and discussion, notably those of the United Church of Christ in the U.S.A. (1959) and the North American Area Council of the World Alliance of Reformed Churches.[13] For the next meeting, members were asked to secure yet more such credal statements for examination, whether they be collected from churches, groups, or individuals, or perhaps even texts composed by committee members themselves. Certain of

10. Standing Committee on Christian Faith, "Meeting Minutes" (10 May 1965, box 5).

11. Standing Committee on Christian Faith, "Meeting Minutes" (3 Oct. 1966, box 6).

12. Standing Committee on Christian Faith, "Meeting Minutes" (3 Oct. 1966, box 6).

13. See Standing Committee on Christian Faith, *Creeds*, 18–19.

them were also commissioned to prepare papers for presentation at upcoming meetings on such pertinent topics as "The History of the Classical Creeds," "The Place of the Classical Creeds in the Credal Documents of The United Church of Canada," and "The Essential Function and Content of a Creed Today." The committee had clearly begun to envision a broader task, which would need to be carried out in a comprehensive and systematic manner. As a result, they would need an enlarged mandate. It was then decided, at the suggestion of committee members Donald Mathers of Queen's Theological College and Ernest Long of Church House, to "request the Sub-executive of the General Council to enlarge the terms of reference from that of simply writing a brief doctrinal confession to taking on a detailed analysis of creeds and credalism both within and beyond the boundaries of the United Church."[14] The threefold mandate received from the Sub-Executive, noted above, was the direct result of this request. As is now clear, this broader vision came to be extremely important in shaping the course and the result of the committee's work over the next two years.

In subsequent meetings of the Committee on Christian Faith, taking place over a period of several months, there was a great deal of discussion and debate on the subject of creeds in general and the best method of trying to write a new one in particular. However, little progress was made on the task of writing a creed that would be suitable for use in the liturgy of The United Church. The job of writing a confession that would be both appropriate and, given the existence and ready availability of the traditional alternatives, sufficiently compelling certainly seemed a difficult one. It was a goal made more difficult by the fact that committee members often disagreed intensely among themselves over almost every relevant issue that came up in discussion. Years later, former committee members vividly recalled the level of disagreement and dispute that surrounded their deliberations.[15] At its meeting of 12 December 1966, for example, the presentation of some historical papers was followed by a dispute over the fundamental nature of the committee's mandate. Carl

14. Standing Committee on Christian Faith, "Meeting Minutes" (14 Nov. 1966, box 6); and Standing Committee on Christian Faith, *Creeds*, 5.

15. Mac Freeman referred to "a real division" and "a deep divide" on the committee (telephone interview with Freeman, 7 Dec. 2009). When asked if he had any particular memories of the process, Richard DeLorme responded with a chuckle, "We fought a lot" (telephone interview with DeLorme, 7 Dec. 2009). To be fair, all members of the committee with whom I spoke continued to think highly of one another and, to a person, seemed to enjoy their time on the committee very much.

Moore argued that a short credal statement was not needed at all, although perhaps a newer and more detailed (longer) confession might be useful, such as that recently produced by the United Presbyterian Church in the U.S.A. This was countered by, among others, Donald Mathers who argued that the classical creeds were already too detailed, causing consternation among many. He claimed that a newer creed was needed, which featured, were it to be useful at that time, "an out" or "conscience clause" of some kind. Moir Waters of Robinson Memorial United Church in London, Ontario, countered further that the committee would not produce a creed to replace all others but simply add one to the list of possible options. Discussion naturally turned later in that day to the Apostles' Creed and the complex issues its use evoked. Two main positions emerged among committee members on the use and interpretation of the Apostles' Creed. On the one hand, there were those who argued that the theological vision it expressed needed to be demythologized through the drafting and use of an alternative statement. On the other were those who believed that the difficulties presented by the use of the Apostles' Creed should be overcome by teaching the laity what it meant. Among the latter was W. O. "Bill" Fennell of Emmanuel College, who charged his fellow committee members to think long and hard about whether they indeed wished to discard the theological truth of the Apostles' Creed. In response to this debate, Richard McLean, another traditionalist, who was the minister at Chalmers United Church in Kingston, Ontario, offered to provide the text of an amplified or paraphrased version of the Apostles' Creed for the next meeting.[16]

On 9 January 1967, the Committee on Christian Faith reconvened and essentially carried on its unfinished discussion from the previous meeting. Richard Delorme from Valleyfield, Quebec, presented a paper entitled "A History of the Classical Creeds," in which he proposed the thesis that creeds represented simply the "meeting of history and dogma." Wolfgang Roth, a minister in Chesley, Ontario, responded firmly from a traditional perspective that "the Apostles' Creed is a sign of the church's continuing apostolicity."[17]

On 13 February, another meeting produced yet further debate about the Apostles' Creed and the fundamental desirability of writing an

16. Standing Committee on Christian Faith, "Meeting Minutes" (12 Dec. 1966, box 6).

17. Standing Committee on Christian Faith, "Meeting Minutes" (9 Jan. 1967, box 6).

alternative creed. Richard H. Davidson cited the results of a survey that indicated that half of all ministers in The United Church did not want to say the Apostles' Creed, even at the sacrament of baptism. R. Gordon Nodwell of Mount Dennis United Church, Toronto, again offered a response grounded in the older tradition: the Apostles' Creed should be retained in baptism. He noted that the use of the ancient creed did not signify full comprehension but simply a desire to align with a particular community and its faith. Discussion continued to focus on the broad questions of a creed's role and usefulness. One cannot help but notice in the committee's meeting minutes a waning of enthusiasm for their task, as disagreements had led to an impasse. Some members even asked to be relieved of their responsibility for preparatory assignments. Professor Mathers, an able administrator, kept the committee moving forward by reminding them of their need to bring a report to the next General Council in 1968 and proposed an outline for one on which he had already begun work.[18]

On 10 April, the committee gathered once again to address some of the nagging questions that had continued to hinder real progress. Hugh A. A. Rose from Eastminster United Church, Toronto, then chair of the committee, presented a paper entitled "Classical Creeds in United Church Documents." One of those who had argued strongly for the need and desirability of writing a modern creed, he offered the provocative argument that "the United Church has carefully avoided use of the ancient creeds." He offered as evidence, among other things, that the 1944 catechism did not mention either the Apostles' or Nicene creeds. For his part, Nodwell suggested that a discussion would be needed on the relationship between ordination and any credal statement that the committee would draft. "Those who teach and lead in the church," he argued, "must be expected to affirm a more fully orthodox understanding of the faith than those who are private members." The remainder of this meeting was spent in planning for the committee's final report to the General Council.[19]

It seems that the Committee on Christian Faith had found itself in an ever-deepening rut. It was going over the same issues again and again while making little progress toward the actual writing of a creed that would be suitable for use in The United Church. The personal perspectives

18. Standing Committee on Christian Faith, "Meeting Minutes" (13 Feb. 1967, box 6).

19. Standing Committee on Christian Faith, "Meeting Minutes" (10 Apr. 1967, box 6).

of the committee members, by now well known to one another, had only become entrenched.[20] That their final report was already being prepared does not signify that there was very much from their deliberation worth reporting. In May, the committee met once again, though no new ground was broken.[21]

Until this point, the Committee on Christian Faith had been meeting in a conference room at the General Council Office, 85 St. Clair Avenue East, Toronto—commonly known as Church House. In June, then Chairman Mathers called the committee to Queen's Theological College in Kingston, Ontario, for two days of retreat and deliberation. Fennell opened the discussion with a paper on "The Uses and Authority of Creeds." In it, he proposed a distinction be held between creeds and confessions, the former being primarily liturgical and the latter being primarily constitutional. In light of this, creeds should be doxological and guides to the interpretation of Scripture as well as instruments of mission and ecumenism. The Apostles' Creed, he argued, has performed these tasks extremely well and "should be given a place of great importance in the church." From this, there followed what seems to have been a surprisingly rich and, at times, heated discussion. Though many of the various comments recorded are too nuanced to be lifted out of context, it is clear that a great diversity of perspectives was represented—from those who valued the classical creeds to those wanted to have the use of a more modern one with "as universal a language as possible" and even others who thought a suitable creed was neither likely nor desirable. Professor R. M. "Mac" Freeman of Victoria College and Nodwell later circulated a sheet of paper to their colleagues with a series of eight recommendations that argued, among other points, that the Apostles' Creed should be used and taught in the church, though qualified with an appropriate introduction by worship leaders. All kinds of other creeds should also be made available to the church—including any new ones to be drafted by the committee.

Another significant discussion of the committee during its time in Kingston revolved around the appropriate formula of introduction for the Apostles' Creed, were it to be used in worship. Following debate, it

20. In *The Language of Baptism*, Kervin noted among the committee members "a range of attitudes toward the historic creeds—a mixture of patristic witness, Puritan rejection, liberal suspicion, and ecumenical appreciation" (185).

21. Standing Committee on Christian Faith, "Meeting Minutes" (8 May 1967, box 6).

was voted that the following rubric be recommended for the *Service Book*: "Let us confess the Christian faith as it has been confessed by the historic Christian church in the Apostles' Creed." Though approved, this deeply divided the committee. Its records indicate that a "sizeable minority" was against any *confession* of the Apostles' Creed, even if it were qualified as "historic." Freeman, who articulated this principle most often and most firmly, insisted that he would accept only a formula of introduction that included, "Let us hear . . ." Another member, or members, protested that authority had been sought and given to the committee to compose a new creed precisely "because we had questioned the use of the Apostles' Creed in the new baptismal service." Counter to this it was argued that "our encouragement of the use of the Apostles' Creed in a worship service does not deter us from preparing a new creed, or creeds, of our own."

Toward the conclusion of its two-day retreat, the committee examined an assortment of modern creeds and statements of faith that had been distributed among them. After someone commented that the recent Methodist hymnal in the United States had included a collection of such doctrinal confessions, it was generally agreed that in addition to the Apostles', Nicene, and new United Church creeds, some of these should be included in the *Service Book* as well. "Such a collection," it was noted, "would have tremendous ecumenical significance." The various items now before the committee were discussed, and general criteria for evaluating them were suggested. Any suitable statement of faith, it was agreed, should make mention of 1) God the Father, 2) God the Son, 3) God the Holy Spirit, 4) the church, and 5) the kingdom. Upon adjournment, a commissioning was given "that members of the Committee are invited to write a brief statement (approximately 150 words), doxological in emphasis and to include the 5 main ingredients . . ." for presentation at the next meeting.[22]

For months, the Committee on Christian Faith seems to have toiled in vain. It had found disagreement over almost every issue, including the value of the fundamental task it had been assigned, namely the writing of a doctrinal confession for use in the baptismal liturgy of The United Church. Though it did not leave Kingston with the first words of a new faith statement or even a breakthrough in consensus, for that matter, it did seem to discover a renewed sense of energy. Whether from a newness of setting or an inspired piece of leadership by Mathers or both, committee

22. Standing Committee on Christian Faith, "Meeting Minutes" (12–13 June 1967, box 6).

members seemed hopeful of making headway at last. It is from this point that the history of "A New Creed" becomes especially interesting.

In September, the committee reconvened at Church House in Toronto. John Fullerton of Keene, Ontario, presented a paper on "The Desirability of A New Creed," a topic that continued to be a lightning rod for discussion. Donald Evans, a professor of philosophy at the University of Toronto, offered a lengthy rebuttal to Fullerton in which he reiterated the desirability of a new creed. Evans was opposed, in general terms by Fennell and more pointedly by former moderator Angus J. MacQueen who argued: "1) It is a fallacy to say recitation of a creed unites Christians; 2) Repetition of a creed does not aid a church doctrinally and; 3) Creeds do not lend joy or praise to worship." Since no member of the committee had yet brought a creed for consideration, each was asked again to attempt to write one and bring it to the next meeting.[23]

At the beginning of the next monthly meeting in October, Richard Davidson, a Toronto-based minister who served also as the chair of the Committee on Church Worship and Ritual, presented a new translation of the Apostles' Creed—which had come from a study group within the Roman Catholic Church—and this version was "received favourably" by the committee. It was clear that the committee had to do something constructive with the Apostles' Creed, even though a few would no doubt have been happy to relegate it to the archives. Both Davidson and Freeman were asked to prepare a translation of the Apostles' Creed for the next meeting, taking into consideration the benefits of this Roman Catholic edition and others.[24]

Though Freeman was given involvement in this ongoing project, it is another of his contributions that has to be seen, in retrospect, as one of massive historical significance. In October 1967, he submitted to the committee the following text of a creed he had written:

23. Standing Committee on Christian Faith, "Meeting Minutes" (12 Sept. 1967, box 6).

24. Standing Committee on Christian Faith, "Meeting Minutes" (16 Oct. 1967, box 6).

I believe that
Man is not alone.

- God has created and is creating us.
- God has worked in history and is working to liberate us for true humanity in community.
- God has come among us in the true man Jesus and comes among us today in the Spirit of our risen Lord to deliver us from alienation from God, our fellows and ourselves.
- God has called and is calling us into the company of Jesus with whom we are chosen to be servants, by whom others are also set free.

Man is not alone.
- In life, in death, in life beyond death we are in the presence of God.

Believing that we are offered life and liberation from beyond our human resources, I trust God and commit my existence to his purpose.

It is apparent that Freeman's submission is the seed from which "A New Creed" grew. Later, he recalled getting the idea for a creed that begins with "Man is not alone" after reading the phrase in an article by John C. Bennett of Union Theological Seminary in New York.[25] Though the confession recited today is significantly altered, several of his distinctive phrases remain in revised form. We note in particular "man is not alone" at or near the beginning of the text; God . . . "has created and is creating"; "is working [in] us"; "has come . . . in the true man Jesus"; "has called and is calling us" to, among other things, service; "man is not alone" repeated towards the end of the creed; "in life, in death, in life beyond death," we are in a proximate relationship with God; and a reference to "trust" in God.

25. Years later, Mac Freeman recalled having seen the article either in *The Christian Century* or perhaps in a smaller journal such as *Christianity and Crisis* (telephone interview with Freeman, 7 Dec. 2009). Conversely, Donald Evans believed "Man is not alone" came from the renowned 1951 book of that title by Abraham Joshua Heschel. These reminiscences are not necessarily contradictory. Bennett and Heschel were well known to each other and were even colleagues. Bennett could have borrowed the phrase from Heschel. I have not found an instance of Bennett's using "Man is not alone." However, he did write the phrase "This is God's world" in Bennett, "Some Objections to Coexistence." If this were what Freeman recalled to me some forty years after having served on the Committee on Christian Faith, it goes to show what a remarkably sharp memory he had.

In general, the committee was pleased with Freeman's submission. Though it was really the first attempt by a committee member to draft a creed for consideration, it is clear that several of its phrases and emphases found favor in that they remained in the version of "A New Creed" submitted to the General Council for approval. Some members expressed a need to have reference at the beginning of the text to "the hiddenness" and "the mystery" of God. Others thought that themes like "new creation" and the "kingdom of God" were important omissions. Still, a strong feature for many was this text's ability both to invite confession from the whole community and to encourage life-commitment on an individual basis in baptismal or confirmation contexts. Although there was some further discussion of the final report to be prepared by the committee—and even of Fennell's paper from the Kingston meeting—the bit was in the mouth. Richard Delorme was commissioned to comment on and rewrite Freeman's creed for the next meeting.[26]

In November, the committee reconvened at Church House. By this time, real progress was being made towards the goal of drafting a creed for presentation to the next General Council in 1968. While time constraint was likely a spur for the group's increased productivity, there must have been something about Freeman's creed that stimulated the once stagnating deliberations of the group.[27] Early in the November meeting, James MacKenzie presented a creed that was essentially a paraphrase of the Apostles' Creed.[28] It was not widely liked. Freeman then presented a slightly revised version of his creed and, following some discussion, was commissioned to revise it further based on suggestions that were made. The most significant of these was to change "I believe" in the first line to "We believe."

After this, the committee turned to the revision of Freeman's original creed by DeLorme. Both his submission and the further suggestions it engendered are extremely significant because they mark further progress

26. Standing Committee on Christian Faith, "Meeting Minutes" (16 Oct. 1967, box 6).

27. Telephone interview with Mac Freeman, 7 Dec. 2009. Freeman later remembered that prior to his submission of a creed, things "looked hopeless." The idea of speaking to the loneliness of the modern person with "Man is not alone" sparked, he said, "a creative explosion in the group." In this, he confirmed what seems clear from committee records.

28. Standing Committee on Christian Faith, *Creeds*, 34–35.

toward the text of the creed that was eventually presented to the General Council. DeLorme submitted the following:

> We believe that:
> Man is not alone; he lives in God's world.
> We believe in the God of this world and other worlds.
> – In God Who has created and is creating us.
> – In God Who has come among us in the True Man, Jesus.
> – In God Who, in Jesus, reconciles us to himself and others.
> – In God Who, by His Spirit, liberates us to serve.
> We believe in this God.
> Therefore:
> Man is not alone; he lives in God's world.
> – In life, in death, in life beyond death, we are in his presence.
> We believe in the God of this world and other worlds.
> We commit our existence to Him.[29]

The similarities of this text to the committee's final draft—which was the original version of "A New Creed"—are apparent. The underlined phrase (emphases in original), "Man is not alone; he lives in God's world," which has become the trademark of "A New Creed," finds its distinctive arrangement here—keeping in mind that Freeman originally wrote simply, "Man is not alone." Its repetition at the end of the creed represents an emphasis shared by this creed and the final version. From Freeman were borrowed other phrases, which had been modified to a more final form: "We believe . . . In God Who has created and is creating us" and "Who has come among us in the True Man, Jesus." DeLorme's version also seemed to strike a middle ground between Freeman's and the final draft in referring to the Spirit in the second stanza of the creed. As a separate line following the second stanza, his "We believe in this God" is a line whose echoes are still heard today in "A New Creed," which reads, "We trust in God." Also, he closely followed Freeman with "In life, in death, in life beyond death, we are in his presence." Perhaps even more significant features of DeLorme's revision are its brevity and its rhythm. While Freeman coined a number of unique phrases that have remained in "A New Creed," his prototype was much longer and more descriptive, featuring more complex sentences. DeLorme authored fewer original phrases but seems to be the one who provided the basic literary structure of the creed. He wrote a shorter statement with more concise phrases. He also introduced the sense of poetic expression to the committee's creed.

29. DeLorme, "Revised Creed."

DeLorme's work was very well received by the committee. Considering how much of his work remains in "A New Creed," this is hardly surprising. His creed was "commended for," among other things, "its sense of humility in a vast universe." Almost as interesting as DeLorme's revisions of Freeman are some of the other suggestions made to him. We note especially that he was asked to omit, in the third line, "the God of this world and other worlds." If we remove this phrase, and also the opening line "We believe that," we get a creed that starts like this:

> Man is not alone; he lives in God's world.
>
> We believe in God . . .
>
> > Who has created and is creating us,
> > Who has come among us in the True Man, Jesus . . .

Clearly, the committee was getting closer to "A New Creed" as it appeared in the *Service Book*. We ought to take notice of a suggestion that was made to alter "Man is not alone; he lives in God's world" to "We are not alone; we live in God's world." Though this exact change was made many years later by a reconfigured committee, it was not made by DeLorme or by the Committee on Christian Faith at this point. DeLorme's use of "reconcile" was dropped by the committee at the time but later made its way back into the approved text of the creed.

In retrospect, this meeting of 13 November 1967 was a seminal event. However, the committee's task was by no means complete, and a report had to be made to the General Council in just a few months' time. A decision about the place and authority of other creeds in The United Church—especially the Apostles' Creed—was still to be reached. Since little progress had been made on this front, and since neither Davidson nor Freeman had been able to produce a satisfactory version of the ancient baptismal confession, both Fennell and E. C. Blackman were commissioned to do so.[30]

By the time of the December 1967 meeting, the Committee on Christian Faith was on the way to completing the work it had been assigned. Blackman presented a paraphrase of the Apostles' Creed, based on what he presumed to be its earliest Latin text. Though his translation was commended, he was asked to prepare another—this time of the so-called *textus receptus* of the Apostles' Creed, "along the lines of the New

30. Standing Committee on Christian Faith, "Meeting Minutes" (13 Nov. 1967, box 6).

English Bible."[31] Meanwhile, Mathers presented a draft of the final report, and committee members were satisfied with the form that it was taking. In it, he had prepared a list of "7 Points of Agreement" that described the modest portions of common ground that had been reached by the committee and is essentially the material presented under the heading "Our Consensus" in *Creeds*.[32] The points of agreement and disagreement within the group had become entrenched by this point.

The focus of attention then returned to the creed of the committee, which was continuing to take shape. DeLorme presented another revision of his own and Freeman's work, but members preferred his previous submission. Freeman brought forward another version:

> We believe—
>
> We are not alone; beyond man, hidden but not unknown, is God.
> - God has created and is creating us.
> - God has worked in history and is working to liberate us for true life in community.
> - God has come among us in the true man Jesus and comes among us today in the Spirit of our risen Lord to deliver us from alienation from God, ourselves and our neighbours.
> - God calls us into the company of Jesus as servants to set others free.
> - God gives us hope that in the end there is no bondage to evil and death.
>
> Man is not alone; in life, in death, in life beyond death, we are in the presence of God.
>
> Believing that we are offered liberation and true life from beyond our human resources, I trust God and commit my existence to his purpose.

This edition of Freeman's creed had not moved closer to the text of "A New Creed," but it is telling to realize what elements of the creed were by then firmly established: "We are not alone"; "We believe . . . God has created and is creating us"; "God has come among us in the true man, Jesus"; the repetition of "Man is not alone"; and "In life, in death, in life beyond death . . ." had each been carried forward in several versions as the core elements around which the committee would shape its final creed. In

31. For Blackman's fascinating translated and annotated version of the Apostles' Creed, see Standing Committee on Christian Faith, *Creeds*, 23.

32. Standing Committee on Christian Faith, *Creeds*, 6.

this revision, however, Freeman did make a couple of changes that subtly influenced the final draft. First, he brought a further emphasis on the Spirit's activity in our midst, an emphasis that is important in "A New Creed." Second, he coined a phrase "God calls us into the company of Jesus . . ." that made it into "A New Creed" as "He calls us into his church" and remains today as "We are called to be the church."

A third version of the creed was also put forward for discussion by Donald Evans:

> We believe that we are not alone.
> We believe in the one God, hidden yet not unknown.
> He has created and is creating us;
> He has come among us in the true man, Jesus;
> He reconciles himself to us in the risen Christ;
> He liberates us to love and serve our neighbour in the power of his Spirit;
> He rules over human history to bring true community for all mankind;
> He loves us in life, in death, in life beyond death.
> We trust him, we worship him, we seek to do his will.

Evans had written it during the previous meeting in November and passed it around at that time, virtually as soon as he finished it. Though it was only now being discussed one month later, we can see how, in the context of the previous meeting, he was trying to revise DeLorme's creed in light of the group's discussion. Some of the ideas suggested to DeLorme were taken up by Evans. Several aspects of Evans's creed are likely to have had a bearing on the committee's final product. Like that of DeLorme, his draft was brief and employed concise phrases. We know that the committee wanted to use this sort of structure and style, not least for purposes of encouraging people to memorize the creed. Two particular phrases seem to have been first proposed by Evans. "To love and serve" is still found in "A New Creed" to this day. "We trust him" also is a phrase that, though placed differently, made it into "A New Creed" as printed in the *Service Book* and remains today in a slightly revised form. We can see that the general content and style of "A New Creed" was taking shape. The committee members sensed this, and former Moderator MacQueen was commissioned to "write a creed, keeping in mind those of Rev. R. M. Freeman, Professor Donald Evans and Rev. R. H. DeLorme's two versions."[33]

33. Standing Committee on Christian Faith, "Meeting Minutes" (11 Dec 1967, box 6).

When it reconvened again in the new year, the Committee on Christian Faith continued further down its path. Nodwell, who had begun chairing the committee to free up some extra time for Mathers's other work, presented the most up-to-date list of modern confessions, and it was agreed that that of the United Church of Christ in the U.S.A. should be recommended, in the final report, for inclusion in the *Service Book*. Following this, MacQueen made a presentation. Surprisingly, he brought forward a set of five different creeds, four of which were original to him—and one of which appeared in *Creeds* under his authorship.[34] Though his writing efforts were received favorably, only one was thought worthy of serious discussion, his revision of the so-called "Freeman-DeLorme Creed." This name for the creed under consideration is telling. By this point, there was a prototype of "A New Creed" with which the committee was working, and its primary authors were considered to be Freeman and DeLorme. MacQueen's version read:

> We believe that
>
> We are not alone; we live in God's world; He created us spiritual beings for loving community with Himself. He has come among us in the true man, Jesus Christ, and reconciles us to Himself and our fellowmen. He dwells with us by His spirit of truth, freedom and love, and calls us to serve His kingdom in the world. He gives us hope through the cross and resurrection of Jesus Christ that we are not doomed to sin and death.
>
> In this God is our faith and peace and joy. To him we commit our lives forever.[35]

We can see in this revision a number of features common to Freeman's prototype and its various revisions—the phrase "We are not alone" in particular. The reference to God's coming in Jesus, the "true man," and other themes were carried forward. In other ways, MacQueen deviated from the pattern. He went slightly longer again and with more description. Also telling are the distinctive suggestions he made, which appear to have been ignored. His reference to the hope God gives "through the cross and resurrection of Jesus Christ" was an interesting omission, to say the least, from the text of "A New Creed" that the committee later presented to the General Council. Nonetheless, other members of the committee, including Nodwell, Alex Farquhar, and Mrs. H. C. Wyman were

34. Standing Committee on Christian Faith, *Creeds*, 35.

35. MacQueen, "Revision of Freeman-DeLorme Creed."

asked to take MacQueen's creed, along with those of Freeman, DeLorme, and Evans, and present another version at the next meeting.[36]

In February, the committee again gathered for its monthly meeting in Toronto. Mathers announced that he had finished sections 3–5 of the final report to be made to the General Council. Discussion quickly turned to the completion of a creed. On behalf of the group that had been assigned to writing it, Nodwell submitted the text:

> Man is not alone; he lives in God's world.
> We believe in God:
> Who has created and is creating,
> Who has come in the True Man, Jesus,
> Who works within us and among us by his Spirit.
>
> We believe in Him.
>
> He calls us into his Church, to love and serve our fellow men, and to share in his kingdom.
> In life, in death, in life beyond death, he is with us.
> We are not alone; we believe in God.[37]

It is clear that this revision had moved remarkably close to the final creed of the committee. The use of "Man is not alone" instead of "I believe" or "We believe" to begin the text found its genesis here, as did a number of other features dictated by a quest for sheer brevity. God is now the one "Who has created and is creating," in general and not with particular reference to "us." The phrases referring to Jesus and to the Spirit had approached their final form. Following MacQueen, but in opposition to previous revisions, the Spirit was not predicated upon Jesus, thus leaving open the ancient debate over the *filioque*—the procession of the Holy Spirit from the Father *and from the Son*. "He calls us into his church" was quite like the "He calls us to be the church" of the text that was eventually approved.

Precisely as this version was being pared down to a minimum and was approaching its distinct and recognizable form, a breakdown in the committee's consensus reemerged forcefully. Freeman argued against the repetition of "We believe in" and also suggested redefining the call of God as "out of the world" rather than "into his church." Fullerton "objected to the failure [of this creed] to relate the three persons of the Godhead into one." However, no action was taken on his criticism. Most interesting was

36. Standing Committee on Christian Faith, "Meeting Minutes" (8 Jan. 1968, box 6).

37. Nodwell, "Some Modern Creeds Discussed."

the critique of Farquhar, one of the three people who had been charged with drafting the current revision. As opposed to Nodwell and Wyman, he stated a desire to include the phrase "God . . . who loves us in this life and beyond." He considered the phrase, "In life, in death, in life beyond death . . ." to be redundant. A possible revision of the creed, based on group discussion, is included in the committee's meeting minutes this way:

> Man is not alone; he lives in God's world.
> We believe in God:
> Who has created and is creating,
> Who has come to us in the true man, Jesus,
> Who works within us and among us by his Spirit.
> We believe in him.
> He calls us into his church:
> To celebrate his presence,
> To love our fellow men,
> To uphold his kingdom.[38]

To a certain extent, the consensual model had begun to fall apart. Several phrases and the shape of the creed were generally agreed upon by committee members, but a number of its aspects were still quite objectionable to certain individuals. However, time was running out.

When the group gathered again in March, Mathers announced that they had only until 15 April, barely one month away, to complete their work and finalize their report for the General Council. Since the report he had been working on was almost finished, he asked some other members of the committee to have a close look at it. After a discussion of the brief recommendations to be made to the General Council and of some final responsibilities, Mathers made plans to finish the report with Freeman's help. There was also, at this meeting, "a final discussion" of the text of the creed. Each member of the committee was invited to comment. (MacQueen was absent and had written a letter, which was read aloud at the meeting.) It was decided, at this late hour, that the creed still needed some mention of the "historic work of Jesus." The chair, Nodwell, was to go away and prepare a final draft, taking note of suggestions and incorporating them into the text where necessary.[39]

38. Standing Committee on Christian Faith, "Meeting Minutes" (12 Feb. 1968, box 6).

39. Standing Committee on Christian Faith, "Meeting Minutes" (11 Mar. 1968, box 6).

At the committee's March meeting, Dorothy Wyman of St. Catharines, Ontario, presented several possible phrases of introduction for the Apostles' Creed, and one was chosen. Afterward, Secretary Rose wrote to the Church Worship and Ritual Committee, which was working on the *Service Book*, concerning a proposed introductory formula for the Apostles' Creed. Rose stated that his committee were requesting of their counterparts "that the following introductory formula be recommended for use with the Apostles' Creed: 'Let us repeat the historic expression of the Christian faith known as the Apostles' Creed.'"[40] The Committee on Church Worship and Ritual responded that its members were not at all happy with this phrase, proposing "say together" rather than "repeat." Thus the matter was sent back to the Committee on Christian Faith, where it sparked a renewed debate at the meeting of 8 April. "At least one . . . member of the committee wanted a stronger statement than is implied with 'say together' and indicated we should seek an unambiguous statement." Evans and Mathers were content with "Let us say together . . ." and moved its adoption. Wyman, however, pleaded for "repeat," arguing that "say together" was synonymous with "confess" and that this was not acceptable with reference to the Apostles' Creed. She argued, "'Let us say together the historic expression . . . ' is ugly and awkward sounding." Freeman agreed with her, adding that "say together" would lead to "dishonesty in public worship." After this, the group voted and "say together" was carried 6 to 5. At this point, Mathers left the room and went to visit the Committee on Church Worship and Ritual, which was also meeting at Church House that day. He told his colleagues there that one member was satisfied with "repeat" but totally opposed to "say together." While there was no strong opposition to "Let us repeat . . .," "Let us say together . . ." left his group "badly split." After it was suggested by the Committee on Church Worship and Ritual to use "Let us repeat together . . .," Mathers returned this idea to the Committee on Christian Faith who concurred. A similar formula of introduction for "A New Creed," "Let us repeat together a contemporary expression of Christian faith . . ." was adopted as well.

Before concluding its work, the committee spent some time on the crucially important task of putting the final polish on the creed it would present to the General Council. Nodwell brought before the members something like this version of the creed:

40. Rose, "Letter to Richard H. N. Davidson."

Man is not alone; he lives in God's world.

We believe in God:
Who has created and is creating,
Who has come in the True Man, Jesus,
Who works within us and among us by his Spirit.

We trust him.

He calls us to be his Church:
To celebrate his presence,
To love and serve others,
To resist evil and proclaim his kingdom.

In life, in death, in life beyond death, he is with us.
We are not alone; we believe in God.[41]

To this text were made only a few minor revisions. In light of discussion within the group and some informal feedback that had been received from outside, especially in a letter from R. C. Chalmers, a professor at Pine Hill Divinity Hall, the committee accepted a revision and expansion of the reference to the work of Christ. To the line "Who has come in the true Man, Jesus" was added "to reconcile and renew." Further expansion was also made to a later line in the creed. What once read "He calls us . . . to resist evil and proclaim his kingdom" became "To seek justice and resist evil. / We proclaim his kingdom." There was also a discussion of whether or not to use capital letters in one or both of the words in the phrase "true man." We find that though "the committee noted it is better theologically to use lower case for both words . . . the theologically uneducated might accuse the committee of an unorthodox emphasis on the humanity of Jesus if lower case were used, and therefore it was decided to use lower case for 'true' and upper case for 'Man.'" With these revisions, the final text of the creed for submission was:

Man is not alone; he lives in God's world.

We believe in God:
Who has created and is creating,
Who has come in the true Man, Jesus, to reconcile and renew,
Who works within us and among us by his Spirit.

We trust him.

41. No piece of paper seems to exist with this penultimate draft, either in the committee's meeting minutes or elsewhere, although it can be guessed at with some confidence.

He calls us to be his Church:
To celebrate his presence,
To love and serve others,
To seek justice and resist evil.

We proclaim his kingdom.

In life, in death, in life beyond death, He is with us.
We are not alone; we believe in God.

At the conclusion of this revision, it was decided to recommend the creed to the General Council.[42]

Just one week later, on the day of the deadline for its report, the Committee on Christian Faith met again briefly to make sure it had all its ducks in a row. There was a further brief discussion of the use of upper and lower cases in "true Man." A motion to use lower case for both words was defeated. To conclude business, Freeman was charged with doing a final edit of the report.[43]

At the General Council

The text of "A New Creed" was first presented to the whole church at the Twenty-Third General Council, which met in Kingston, Ontario, at the end of August and beginning of September 1968. It was on the morning of Thursday, 29 August, in Sydenham Street United Church that the time came for the Committee on Christian Faith to make its report, which was presented initially by Mathers. Following Mathers's presentation, Rose spoke to the report in more detail.[44] Despite the massive effort of the committee, its creed was in for a bit of a rough ride and was ultimately not accepted by the General Council. Rose recalled, "I remember being suitably intimidated standing before council and even more so when Ernie Howse, former moderator and minister of Bloor Street, and George Johnston, prof of New Testament at Emmanuel, neither of whom had the reputation of being conservatives, poured scorn on a creed that didn't begin with I believe and then went on to dare to pretend to keep company

42. Standing Committee on Christian Faith, "Meeting Minutes" (8 Apr. 1968, box 6).

43. Standing Committee on Christian Faith, "Meeting Minutes" (15 Apr. 1968, box 6).

44. *Record of Proceedings*, Twenty-Third General Council, 56.

with the 'Historic Statements of the Church Catholic.'"[45] For some time, the proposed creed was discussed on the floor of the Council. No doubt, many positive aspects were highlighted along with the negative.[46] Possible revisions to the text of the creed were also bandied about in open discussion.[47] Though further details of the events in question probably remain outside the possibilities of historical inquiry, it is clear enough what happened: the creed was sent back to the committee for further revision. Here again appeared the figure of R. C. Chalmers, a corresponding member of the Committee on Christian Faith from Maritime Conference, who had never been happy with the creed to begin with. He had said as much to a visiting journalist. In an interview, Chalmers called the new creed "theologically thin" before going on to say that, "It will have no authority in the church, so we're not getting very excited about it. I wouldn't use it."[48] It was Chalmers who "moved that the new Creed be referred back to the Committee on Christian Faith with the request that it be redrafted in a manner that will give more adequate expression of the Christian Gospel for our time, and that the Committee report to the Executive of General Council which shall have power to issue."[49] This motion was carried, and the creed was sent back to the Committee on Christian Faith for further revision.

Back to the Drawing Board

The Committee on Christian Faith reconvened within weeks of the General Council and made its reconsideration of the creed an "immediate priority." If a confession were to be ready for the *Service Book*, any

45. Email to author from Hugh A. A. Rose, 12 Dec. 2009.

46. Many thought at this time that this initial version of the creed was the best that could be hoped for and were disappointed that it was eventually to be revised. Moir Waters, a member of the Committee on Christian Faith, preached a sermon on "A New Creed" from his Robinson Memorial United Church pulpit, London, Ontario, on the Sunday immediately following the General Council. He expressed his sheer amazement that such a confession could have been referred back to the committee: "This is the creed that was rejected!" He commended the creed to his congregation for liturgical use and encouraged his parishioners to memorize it. See Waters, "Sermon." John Burbidge later slammed the General Council Executive for capitulating to "the orthodox" in approving later revisions to "A New Creed" in, "A Creed" (no author), 18.

47. *Record of Proceedings*, Twenty-Third General Council, 56.

48. "Vague New Creed."

49. *Record of Proceedings*, Twenty-Third General Council, 56.

revisions would have to be made quickly. Rose reported to his colleagues the experience of the General Council. He recounted the criticisms of George Johnston and R. C. Chalmers. He also said, "There appeared to be no opposition to the effort to write creeds, but considerable concern as to the form and content of the Creed." A couple of letters to the committee from concerned individuals were read, highlighting the view that the creed featured "inadequate Christology" and that it "lacked depth." George Johnston sent in a suggested revision of the creed, which is at least interesting enough to print in full:

> As disciples of Jesus the risen Lord,
> And as men who live in the Father's world,
> We affirm our faith together.
> We believe in one God,
> Who has created the world and is creating still;
> Who spoke by the prophets;
> Who revealed himself uniquely in Jesus
> And reconciles us by the spirit of Jesus.
> God has called us to be his church,
> Celebrating his presence with joy,
> Loving and serving our fellow men,
> Seeking justice for all and fighting against evil everywhere,
> Joining with artists and scientists and all men of good will to make peace on earth.
> We now commit ourselves to this God,
> We give the glory to his holy Name.[50]

Although Johnston's creed is not important in and of itself and did not provide the basis for the committee's own revisions, it is interesting to note the key phrases his revision maintained, along with the expansion of certain other features he found lacking in the text that had been presented to the General Council.

A more substantial piece of correspondence was received from R. C. Chalmers, with a detailed list of ten criticisms of the committee's creed. In general, he called it "theologically 'thin'—a sort of mini-theology," and he claimed that it had several "serious omissions." His criticisms, since they had a notable impact on the deliberations of the committee, are worth quoting at length:

> 1. It begins with a statement about man, not about God.

50. Johnston, "A Proposed New Creed."

2. It begins—and ends—on a negative note—NOT. A creed should be entirely affirmative.
3. The word God may mean many things. The word Father, or Our Father, should designate God's character. The Creed nowhere refers to God's love and thus it would seem all the more necessary to refer to God as Father.
4. The New Creed is very weak in Christology. Jesus is only "true Man." Could not a Hindu say this of Gandhi, or a Buddhist of Buddha? We are Christians and this would appear to make it necessary to use the title Christ. Further, since the earliest confession was about Jesus being LORD, and the Church's reference to Him as Saviour, should not these terms or titles also be used? Since Christology is the very heart of any Christian Creed it would seem that we require at least a second line in it to sum up Christ's Incarnation, His ministry and teachings, death and resurrection, ascension and parousia. All of these, very briefly and yet meaningfully, are referred to in the Statement of Faith of The United Church of Christ.
5. Spirit should read Holy Spirit. There should be a few words to designate who He is and what He does. The present form of the New Creed might be interpreted as identifying the Spirit with the Spirit of Jesus and this raises some Trinitarian questions.
6. The New Creed says "He calls us TO BE His Church." The Statement of Faith of The United Church of Christ says "He calls us INTO His Church." The Church is Christ's Body, not ours. Should not a descriptive word like fellowship be used to designate what is meant by the Church?
7. "To celebrate His presence"—If this has reference to the Lord's Supper I would strongly urge that some mention should also be made concerning Baptism.
8. The next two lines of the New Creed are "social service" alone. What about evangelism? Something should be said, as in the Statement of Faith of The United Church of Christ, about the witness of the Church throughout the world to the proclamation of the Gospel.
9. The last line is partly redundant and therefore should be omitted. As stated previously, it is also negative. It would be much better to end

with "God is with us"—a sentence which might also be used at the beginning of the Creed.

10. In preparing a New Creed for our Church which would speak of the essentials of the Christian faith the doctrine of our Church as set forth in the Basis of Union, as well as in our own Statement of Faith and Catechism, which are teaching instruments, should be clearly kept in mind.[51]

Committee members spent a good deal of time discussing Chalmers's criticisms. While some were considered more valid than others, most were dismissed by consensus. The committee did acknowledge that the implied double negative of "not alone" "could fail to address adequately the human condition" to which they wanted to speak. The "lack of any reference to historic events of crucifixion and resurrection" was also recognized. Yet, on other points, Chalmers failed to convince. "God who comes to reconcile and renew," they agreed regarding his point 3, "seems to us to express both the traditional concept of the fatherhood of God and the active love of God." "The Creed's statement that God Himself has come in Jesus expressed a high Christology," they thought in response to point 4, "identifying both Jesus being the Living Lord, yet 'the' (rather than 'a') true Man." "TO BE," further to point 6, "is deliberately put in place to indicate an activist sense of church membership, rather than a passive relationship to an institutional entity." Regarding Chalmers's seventh point, "Celebrate his presence" was not intended as a reference to the Lord's Supper but to "all types of worship." Lastly, the phrase "proclaim his kingdom" they decided was "intended to express evangelism." After a lengthy day of discussion, the committee members went away with a lot to think about. Rose, who was now chair, charged the members to send him any of their ideas about revising the creed for distribution at their next meeting.[52]

On 21 October 1968, the Committee on Christian Faith reconvened and decided immediately that they would have to complete any revision of "A New Creed" that day in order to have it approved by the General Council Executive in November in time for it to be published in the *Service Book*. But how would they be able to do in one day what they had not been able to accomplish in months of work? Hugh Rose had taken

51. Chalmers, "New Creed."

52. Standing Committee on Christian Faith, "Meeting Minutes" (23 Sept. 1968, box 6).

the proactive step, in the weeks leading up to the meeting, of seeking some outside help. Father Gregory Baum, then of Saint Michael's College, Toronto, was a very well-known and influential Canadian theologian. He had been a *peritus*, or theological advisor, at the Second Vatican Council and had played a role in liaising with ecumenical observers at the council. Baum was also acquainted with some of the theological professors who sat on the Committee on Christian Faith—people like Mathers, Evans, and Freeman. Earlier in the year, and before the committee had completed the final draft of their creed for the General Council, Evans, a faculty member in the department of philosophy at the University of Toronto, had shown it to Baum.[53] Baum then went on to write a review of the creed in *The Ecumenist*, a journal that he edited.[54] In his review, entitled "A New Creed," Baum showed himself in favor of the attempt to write new creeds in general and of the draft of "A New Creed" that was being prepared in The United Church. Baum liked the method of starting the creed with human reference and also the verbal, action-oriented descriptions of God. His main criticism of the creed was that it did not refer to a divine eschatological judgment and therefore seemed to allow Canadian Christians go on living "a comfortable life, possibly in a nice suburb."[55] Hugh Rose, on this occasion, announced that he had written Baum and asked him "if he would care to make specific suggestions regarding revision in the proposed creed." Baum had replied, however, that he could not do so, "as he felt it would be inappropriate in his position."[56]

The committee members were left to hammer out any revisions quickly and without any help. Fortunately, Evans, who had initially sought Baum's review, had come to the table with a paper he had written based on the discussion at the committee's September meeting as well as the feedback received via Baum's article.[57] Most of the day was spent in a line-by-line discussion of the creed, largely on the basis of Evans's proposed revisions. The text of the creed he presented was this:

53. Telephone interview with Donald Evans, 7 Dec. 2009.

54. A copy of Baum, Review of "New Creed," can be found in the archival records of the Standing Committee on Christian Faith, The United Church of Canada Archives, 82.204c, box 3, file 41.

55. Baum, Review of "New Creed."

56. Standing Committee on Christian Faith, "Meeting Minutes" (21 Oct. 1968, box 6).

57. Evans, "Possible Revision of Creed."

Man is not alone, he lives in God's world.
We believe in God:
    who has created and is creating,
    who has come in the true Man, Jesus, to reconcile and renew,
    who works within men and among men by his Spirit.

We trust him.

He calls us to be his Church:
    to celebrate his presence,
    to love and serve others,
    to seek justice and resist evil,
    to proclaim the risen Jesus, our judge and our hope.

In life, in death, in life beyond death, God is with us.
We are not alone.

In his paper, Evans made a number of comments that are revealing of the committee's outlook and therefore the final content of the creed. Significantly, the first line remained unchanged. "There was again general agreement within the committee," wrote Evans, "that the creed should start with man; the agreement was supported by Gregory Baum's article." The committee felt the need to address an "existential conviction," and "Man is not alone" seemed by far and away the best manner of doing so. The first change suggested by Evans came in the fifth line where "who works within us and among us by his Spirit" became "who works within men and among men." This change was in response to the criticism of many and was intended to signal the work of God's Spirit outside the church. Evans suggested in his paper that "who works in us and others" was a possible alternative.

The most significant revision proposed in Evans's draft was to expand the phrase "We proclaim his kingdom" and to move it onto the bottom of the previous stanza as a qualifier of "He calls us to be his Church." The new line reads, "to proclaim the risen Jesus, our judge and our hope." These changes, he argued, accomplished a number of things. First, in response to the criticism of R. C. Chalmers, "to proclaim" was used to emphasize evangelism, as "We proclaim" might indicate that proclamation is nothing more than a summary of the other things the church does, such as "celebrate his presence" and "love and serve others." Reference to "the risen Jesus," further, "is more explicit in expressing the conviction that Jesus is alive." "Our judge and our hope," finally, introduced the elements of divine judgment on a fallen world and also of an eschatological hope into the creed. While adding further detail to the creed in order to satisfy critics, Evans's proposals about explaining Jesus's life and significance were cagey. He wrote, "My proposal leaves open the possibility of various interpretations of the resurrection" and, further, "is open to various interpretations as to the way in which the risen Jesus is our hope."

Two other more minor revisions were proposed by Evans. First, he concluded the second to last line, "In life, in death, in life beyond death," with "God is with us" instead of "he is with us." Taking into account the revisions of the previous line, from "We proclaim his kingdom" to a fuller account of Jesus's significance, Evans thought it necessary to mention God explicitly, not just Jesus, as the one who is with us always. Finally, Evans removed the last phrase of the creed, "we believe in God," leaving the final line to read simply, "We are not alone." He thought that the "we believe in God" was redundant and also saw a value to finishing, as starting, "with a statement about man, that is, about man in relation to God."

On the basis of Evans's proposed revisions, the committee was able to make its changes to the creed in a timely and satisfactory manner. They left most of the creed in the form in which it had been presented to the General Council, making only a few alterations. The text they produced and sent to the Executive of the General Council is printed here.[58]

> Man is not alone, he lives in God's world.*
>
> We believe in God:
> who has created and is creating,
> who has come in the true Man, Jesus, to reconcile and make new,
> who works in us and others by his Spirit.
> We trust him.
>
> He calls us to be his church:
> to celebrate his presence,
> to love and serve others,
> to seek justice and resist evil,
> to proclaim Jesus, crucified and risen, our judge and our hope.
>
> In life, in death, in life beyond death, God is with us.
> We are not alone.
>
> Thanks be to God.**
>
> *This line may be used as a versicle, with the rest as a response.
> **This line is still under consideration as a possible addition.

58. Standing Committee on Christian Faith, "Report on Creeds."

Since much of the discussion of the changes to the creed was covered by Evans's paper, we can move fairly briefly through the committee's final revisions and the rationale for them. Most of the creed remained unchanged, including especially the distinct opening line "Man is not alone, he lives in God's world." The committee reified its desire to begin the creed by addressing the existential condition of human loneliness, which they felt was the major issue in their modern world.

Among the changes to the creed were, in the fourth line, "who has come in the true Man, Jesus, to reconcile and make new" instead of "reconcile and renew." "Make new" was thought to be more biblical. In the fifth line, "who works in us and others by his Spirit" replaced "who works within us and among us." This change was made to "be more specific about the work of God outside the church."

The most major change to the creed came to the original phrase "We proclaim his kingdom." The committee followed Evans's wording almost completely, except that it added further a note about Jesus's crucifixion. Rather than his proposed "to proclaim the risen Jesus, our judge and our hope," the committee came up with the words "to proclaim Jesus, crucified and risen, our judge and our hope." This new line nicely tied together the crucifixion and the resurrection of Jesus, linking them with God's divine judgment and the eschatological hope of Christians.

The concluding lines, beginning "In life, in death" and ending "We are not alone," followed Evans's text exactly. A final addition, new to this particular draft of the creed, was the closing line "Thanks be to God." Though not universally liked, "This additional line appealed to several members of the committee as making the creed more useful liturgically and in expressing joy in the Gospel." Though here the line was marked with a double asterisk as being "still under consideration," it has survived in "A New Creed" as we find it today. With these changes, the creed was sent by the committee to the General Council Executive for approval. There was some discussion surrounding the creation of a version *en français*, but the committee felt that this was beyond its terms of reference and should be left to the National Committee on French Work.[59]

The fate of "A New Creed" was then in the hands of the General Council Executive. On 5 November 1968, Rose went before the Executive. He distributed two handouts: the report of the committee's revisions to the creed and Evans's paper, on which the former was largely based.

59. Standing Committee on Christian Faith, "Meeting Minutes" (21 Oct. 1968, box 6).

Rose presented the revised text of the creed and explained the changes that had been made. Those in the room appear to have been pleased with the creed now before them and they gave it their blessing. The minutes of the General Council Executive record its reaction: "After discussion, it was moved and agreed that general approval be given to the revised Creed for use in congregations and that it be included in the *Service Book*."[60] Thus it was that "A New Creed" was entered into the official doctrine of The United Church of Canada.

One week later, Rose reported back to his colleagues on the Committee on Christian Faith. He described his presentation, the discussion of the Executive, and, most importantly, the approval that had been given to the creed. Rose, along with Freeman, then took on the task of preparing a booklet for publication, which appeared under the title *Creeds*. With that, committee members immediately moved on to other business.[61]

Later Revisions to the Text of "A New Creed"

Following the approval of the General Council Executive, "A New Creed" was published in the 1969 *Service Book* as the first of the four creeds or confessions included.[62] As is obvious to anyone familiar with the creed today, however, the text of "A New Creed" currently in use is not precisely that which was first published. Barely a decade after it was approved, there was a desire to have it altered to reflect principles of inclusive language.[63] The impetus for taking this step seems to have come, at least in some measure, from the disbanding and reconstitution of the Committee on Christian Faith. In March 1977, it was reported to the General Council Executive that the Committee on Christian Faith had become too unwieldy—it was too large, met too infrequently, and was paralyzed by diversity. Therefore it was not effective, visible, or credible to the wider church. In its place

60. United Church of Canada General Council, "Executive Meeting Minutes" (5 Nov. 1968, box 32).

61. Standing Committee on Christian Faith, "Meeting Minutes" (12 Nov. 1968, box 6).

62. *Service Book for Use of People*, 310.

63. Clifford expressed his surprise that "A New Creed" was not gender-inclusive from the beginning, given the rise of feminism in the church during the 1960s and the presence of two women, Dorothy Wyman and Katharine Hockin, on the Committee on Christian Faith, which drafted the original. See Clifford, "United Church of Canada," 18.

was created a new group called the Committee on Theology and Faith, which would consist of no more than twelve people and meet regularly in Toronto, under the leadership of then Chair Peter Gordon White. The General Council Executive approved this change, and it was affirmed by the Twenty-Seventh General Council meeting in Calgary later that year.[64]

One of the early tasks of the new Committee on Theology and Faith was to take a fresh look at "A New Creed." In late 1979, the committee took a motion to the General Council Executive with regards to a suggested revision of the creed. We read in the meeting minutes of the latter: "Following a review of the New Creed, the Committee recommended to the Executive that the first versicle of the New Creed be revised to read, 'We are not alone, we live in God's world.'" It was a natural suggestion as, by this time, many across the church were already making this change privately in congregational recitation.[65] The Executive supported the change but asked the Committee on Theology and Faith to go even further, passing a motion "that the [entire] Creed be revised to make it inclusive in its language."[66]

Two major questions emerged in the course of the committee's work. First, should "A New Creed" (or any such text) be revised and updated or simply left alone as a historical document? The majority of the committee believed "A New Creed" could be revised in good faith—a position felt to be indicated by the popularity of this confession within the denomination. Second, should Scripture be quoted in a creed? This question arose specifically in regards to the revision to the fourth line proposed by Tom Sherwood, that "the true Man, Jesus" become "Jesus, the Word made flesh." Some in principle opposed the use of such directly biblical language but offered only "polite dissent."[67]

The work of revision was completed in one year. Peter Gordon White went again before the Executive and presented, with reference to the motion of November 1979, an inclusive language revision of "A New Creed":

64. *Record of Proceedings*, Twenty-Seventh General Council, 187–89.

65. Telephone interview with Tom Sherwood, 30 Nov. 2011.

66. United Church of Canada General Council, "Executive Meeting Minutes" (21 Nov. 1979, box 34). As an aside, it was mentioned to the Executive on this occasion that the Committee on Theology and Faith would be recommending to the Twenty-Eighth General Council that a commission be established "to develop a more 'up-to-date' Statement of Faith for use in The United Church of Canada."

67. Telephone interview with Tom Sherwood, 30 Nov. 2011.

We are not alone, we live in God's world.

We believe in God:
who has created and is creating,
who has come in Jesus, the Word made flesh,
to reconcile and make new,
who works in us and others
by the Spirit.

We trust in God.

We are called to be the church:
to celebrate God's presence,
to love and serve others,
to seek justice and resist evil,
to proclaim Jesus, crucified and risen,
our judge and our hope.

In life, in death, in life beyond death,
God is with us.

We are not alone.

Thanks be to God.

Here, we have moved almost completely to the version of "A New Creed" used today. This text is considered gender-inclusive, at least insofar as it has eliminated any masculine reference or masculine pronouns for God, Jesus, or humanity.[68] "Man" is now "we" or "us." "His" is now "God's." Perhaps the most theologically significant change is from "the true Man, Jesus" to "Jesus, the Word made flesh." Don Schweitzer has argued, "The Christology of *A New Creed* changed" in this grammatical revision, replacing "the emphasis on Jesus revealing what it means to be fully human with an affirmation of the divinity of Jesus, of Jesus as the incarnation of the second person of the Trinity."[69] With these changes, the Executive was happy to approve the revised creed. Their meeting minutes record "that the Executive of the General Council approve the revised version of this New Creed, authorizing whatever steps are necessary to have this

68. Kervin has argued recently that, according to the typology proposed by Marjorie Proctor-Smith, the current language of "A New Creed" would be better understood as nonsexist rather than inclusive. See Kervin, "Sacraments and Sacramentality," 236–39.

69. Schweitzer, "Christology of United Church," 137.

New Creed made known and used in The United Church of Canada."[70] It is worth noting the implicit ideology of this motion. Though "A New Creed" was initially proposed, and then drafted, to provide an option for the people of The United Church, especially for those who did not want to use the Apostles' Creed in services of baptism, it was now the case that the denomination would take "whatever steps necessary," including the bearing of financial implications, "to make this New Creed . . . used in The United Church of Canada." "A New Creed" was hardly just an option anymore. Rather, it had become, in relatively short order, *the* confession of the denomination.[71]

This "We are not alone" version of "A New Creed" had more staying power than its "Man is not alone" predecessor. Yet it has itself had one more stage of revision to date. In 1994, a petition from Toronto Conference called "Renewing the Creed" was brought to the Thirty-Fifth General Council meeting in Fergus, Ontario. Although this was a lengthy petition, it can be summarized as expressing a desire that "A New Creed" reflect a growing awareness in church and society of environmental issues and that "there is a need for our confessional language to reflect this awareness." The significant portion of the petition reads:

> Therefore be it resolved that the 69th annual meeting of Toronto Conference petition the 35th General Council of The United Church of Canada to amend the United Church Creed to explicitly acknowledge our responsibility for the integrity of creation and our place in it, by including between the lines "to seek justice and resist evil" and "to proclaim Jesus, crucified and risen, our judge and our hope" a phrase such as one of the following—to care for creation, to live in harmony with creation, to pursue the integrity of creation, to walk softly on the earth, to heal the earth—the final wording and placing would be determined by the Theology and Faith Committee.[72]

Following the success of this petition at the General Council, the Committee on Theology and Faith later settled on the phrase "to live with

70. United Church of Canada General Council, "Executive Meeting Minutes" (19 Nov. 1980, box 34).

71. Since it had not been done initially in 1968, one wonders why at this point the decision was not taken for the General Council as a whole to reconsider the status of "A New Creed" and possibly to issue a remit, so that congregations and presbyteries would have a voice in such a significant alteration to the doctrinal confession of the church.

72. *Record of Proceedings*, Thirty-Fifth General Council, 526–27.

respect in Creation," including it immediately following "We are called to be the Church: to celebrate God's presence." Other suggestions such as "to care for the earth," for example, were "felt to be too anthropocentric, failing to acknowledge the interrelationality of humankind and the earth."[73] "A New Creed," as revised and approved by the General Council Executive in 1995, reads:

> We are not alone,
>   we live in God's world.
>
> We believe in God:
>   who has created and is creating,
>   who has come in Jesus,
>   the Word made flesh,
>   to reconcile and make new,
>   who works in us and others
>   by the Spirit.
>
> We trust in God.
>
> We are called to be the Church:
>   to celebrate God's presence,
>   to live with respect in Creation,
>   to love and serve others,
>   to seek justice and resist evil,
>   to proclaim Jesus, crucified and risen,
>   our judge and our hope.
>
> In life, in death, in life beyond death,
>   God is with us.
> We are not alone.
>
> Thanks be to God.[74]

Harold Wells has argued that the adopted revision of "A New Creed," with its call "to live with respect in creation," marked a key step in The United Church's move toward "ecotheology."[75]

Thus we find "A New Creed" as it is used today in The United Church of Canada. This may not be the text as it exists forever. "A New Creed" may be revised again; only time will tell. There may yet be need for more historical analysis in the future.

73. H. Wells, "Good Creation," 91. See also 100n70.

74. *Voices United*, 918. Used with permission.

75. H. Wells, "Good Creation," 90.

Implications

In this chapter, we have uncovered a detailed and interesting history of the text of "A New Creed," which has not been widely known. *Creeds*, the report of the Committee on Christian Faith, provides a brief summary of this story. Other, similarly brief historical sketches exist in secondary sources. What is it we can learn from this more detailed history? Three things come to mind. First, there is an intrinsic value to having a historical consciousness, to knowing something about the past. For the many people of The United Church who recite "A New Creed" from time to time, it will be of value to understand the reason this confession exists and why it takes the form it does. The story of "A New Creed" is an interesting one, and it is edifying for the people of The United Church to learn about important events and figures in the history of their denomination. Such knowledge can deepen our spiritual life as individuals and also strengthen the bonds of fellowship among us.

The second important lesson to be learned from the story of "A New Creed" is the implicitly negative reason and purpose for its creation. "A New Creed" was drafted because there were some—possibly many—in The United Church at the time, not least on the Committee on Christian Faith, who had a strong aversion to the use of the Apostles' Creed in worship. In fact, it was the potential inclusion of the Apostles' Creed in the baptismal order of service in the forthcoming *Service Book* that generated a reaction among committee members and led them to seek permission to write an alternative confession.[76] The unwillingness to confess the same faith, with the same words, on the same occasions as had been done in The United Church to that point, according to its constitution and custom, underlies the recitation of "A New Creed" from its genesis to the present. The Committee on Christian Faith acknowledged this in stating that "a dissatisfaction" with the received consensus was its primary motivation in creating a new confessional text.[77] Contrary to the widely held assumption in The United Church today, "A New Creed" was not written to express the faith of the denomination. Its writers, and many of their

76. For a comment on the use of the Apostles' and Nicene Creeds in The United Church during its first forty years, see Young, "Introduction," 14. Note also the inclusion of these texts in *The Hymnary of The United Church of Canada*, 771, and *The Book of Common Order of The United Church of Canada*, 121, 122, 139, 147, 148, 157, 158, 304, 305.

77. Standing Committee on Christian Faith, *Creeds*, 10.

contemporaries in the 1960s, did not think there was one. Rather, this text was created as a means of allowing people to sidestep the confession of what had previously been assumed to be that faith.

Third, there is the related matter of what the words of "A New Creed" were intended to do positively: to help The United Church manage a breakdown in its received consensus. We have seen that "A New Creed" was not written to express the faith of The United Church because, as acknowledged at the time, there was no such thing. Of course, many loved "A New Creed" from the beginning, including several members of the Committee on Christian Faith. Even among that small group, however, there was little commonality of opinion. Some, like R. K. N. MacLean, did not think The United Church should be replacing the classical creeds but doing a better job of teaching them to the people.[78] Fennell did not think "A New Creed" would have any kind of legs in the church.[79] *Creeds* tells us that among the arguments heard repeatedly in committee meetings were "This is not an age for writing creeds," "Nothing can take the place of the classical creeds," and "If we can continue to use the Bible, we can continue to use the classical creeds."[80] The records of the Committee on Christian Faith, whose members found themselves "often . . . in vigorous argument," show that the purpose and value of "A New Creed" were seen from the beginning as pragmatic.[81] Its conciliatory phrases were the product of debate and negotiation. Through an emphasis on the existentialist ideology of encounter, its primary aim was to equivocate on matters of theology in order to accommodate the individual consciences of those holding significantly different beliefs. While some committee members valued the classical creeds and their place in the ongoing life of The United Church, many more were opposed to their use as statements of faith, especially in liturgical contexts. In the conclusion of *Creeds*, the committee shows how it tried to bridge that gap with its new text in writing, "The words and statements used are suggestive rather than definitive, making it possible for them to be filled with personal content by those who say the creed."[82] The classical creeds clearly did not offer, according

78. Telephone interview with Mac Freeman, 7 Dec. 2009.

79. Telephone interview with Gordon Nodwell, 15 Dec. 2009.

80. Standing Committee on Christian Faith, *Creeds*, 9–16.

81. My own conversations years later with surviving committee members confirmed this. When asked if they had any memories of their time working on "A New Creed," fierce disagreement was invariably the first thing mentioned.

82. Standing Committee on Christian Faith, *Creeds*, 18.

to its majority, such a benefit. When discussion moved naturally then to the precise relationship between the words uttered by an individual in worship and that person's actual beliefs, they wrote that "the Bible admittedly requires interpretation . . . . A creed, however, should be a statement that can be used to express convictions with little or no reservation and not much interpretation."[83] The committee's lack of consensus is shown clearly in that, despite its best efforts, the creed it wrote could not meet its own standard. "A New Creed" expressly requires much interpretation by all who in saying it must mentally fill its words and phrases with their own personal understanding. It is telling of the politically oriented compromise reached that while this text may eliminate the need for much personal reservation, it actually amplifies the necessity of interpretation.

Simply put, in the 1960s, the classical creeds were not held to express the religious beliefs of many members of the Committee on Christian Faith, and no interpretive lens appeared likely to redeem those ancient confessions in their eyes. Against that backdrop, "A New Creed" was written to allow diverse personal expressions of faith. Its authors stated, "If creeds are meant to express a consensus of belief . . . then this is the worst possible age for writing them. The impulse that has driven us to discuss new creeds is not so much that we have a new consensus to express as a dissatisfaction with the consensus we have inherited."[84] "A New Creed" is now widely assumed to express the faith of The United Church. It is the only confession used with regularity or widespread acceptance in the life and worship of the denomination. These are developments that were likely unanticipated when the creed was first conceived of, written, and authorized for inclusion in the *Service Book*.

83. Standing Committee on Christian Faith, *Creeds*, 15.

84. Standing Committee on Christian Faith, *Creeds*, 10.

3

"A New Creed" in the Liturgy of The United Church

Introduction

In the previous chapter, we saw how "A New Creed" was drafted in a time of social upheaval as a kind of conciliatory or diplomatic text, intended to manage the breakdown of theological consensus being experienced in The United Church of Canada in the 1960s and to buttress its fragile, institutional coalition. Initially proposed as an alternative to the Apostles' Creed in a service of baptism, "A New Creed" was later formalized as a concession to the irreducible diversity of beliefs and perspectives within the denomination. In this chapter, we will move on to examine the evidence of The United Church's official liturgies—in the service of which "A New Creed" was created. Specifically, we will consider in what formal liturgies "A New Creed" has been included, where in these orders of service it has been placed, and with what language it is introduced. This study will help us to see what, if any, viewpoints have been taken and advocated regarding "A New Creed," implicitly or explicitly. It is the argument of this chapter that "A New Creed" has come to be portrayed liturgically as uniquely important and authoritative for The United Church. While allowance has generally been made for the use of other confessions, such as the classical creeds, alternatives have seldom been used in practice. Perhaps most surprisingly, given the stated purpose of its creation, "A New Creed" has come to be seen as The United Church's confessional statement par excellence. Rather than serving as a mere alternative, it has come to be the overwhelming norm.

Our word liturgy comes from the Greek *leitourgía*, meaning the work of the people. The worship of a Christian community is so central to its very reason for being that liturgical language and structures are foundational. Worship, to put it more bluntly, is where the rubber meets the road. As Mary John Mananzan describes it, "the liturgical aspect" is fundamental to the Christian life. Liturgy is essential, she argues, because it represents "the dialogical exchange between God's self-revelation and man's faith response." Rather than allowing this conversation to be told solely through or even collapsed into preaching, "liturgical celebration" becomes a "re-enactment . . . of the Christian community" of the divine-human drama of salvation.[1]

In contrast to other media, the form and content of corporate worship tend to bear the weight and imprint of ecclesiastical authority—regardless of the polity within which a given community worships. Though often locally revised and edited in the case of The United Church, liturgies are published and distributed by the courts of the church.[2] Having been prepared by experts and authorized with a stamp of institutional approval, liturgies become almost sacred texts in their own right, bearing much of the responsibility for the theological instruction of the faithful. Even amidst the messiness and diversity of worship practices in a denomination like The United Church, liturgical language carries authority. In a congregational context, it may be a minister who has decided whether the congregation will recite a creed and, if so, what creed it will be. If it is not the minister, then likely it would be a council, session, worship committee, or other arm of governance that would make that decision. In all likelihood, worship leaders will introduce a chosen creed with language that will provide the interpretive lens through which it will or ought to be seen by the congregation. In light of these considerations, the liturgical

1. Mananzan, *"Language Game" of Confessing*, 137–38.

2. Thomas and Bruce Harding described this local-national tension as being expressed through "ordered liberty" within The United Church tradition. "The overarching theme of this history of worship in The United Church of Canada has been the tension between *order* and *liberty* (cf. the Preface to the *Book of Common Order*). Each congregation is free to follow worship patterns of its own choosing, but these patterns are to be informed by the official orders of the church" (Harding and Harding, *Patterns of Worship*, 271).

contexts in which "A New Creed" appears in The United Church are significant for the religious life of its people.

The Liturgical Resources of The United Church and Their Histories

The United Church of Canada has always had a liturgical tradition in print, as did its antecedent denominations at the time of union. As early as 1 December 1925, barely six months after the birth of the new denomination, a booklet was prepared that gathered into one volume several orders for special services—such as those for baptism, communion, weddings, and funerals—from the existing resources of the Congregationalist, Methodist, and Presbyterian churches. This booklet, *Forms of Service*, was approved by the Second General Council in 1926 and distributed to congregations for use in a variety of worship settings. The Second General Council did not content itself with this achievement. It also established a standing committee—the Committee on Church Worship and Ritual—which quickly began the task of preparing a hymn book and a service book in order to seed a distinctively United Church liturgical tradition.[3] *The Hymnary* (1930) and *The Book of Common Order* (1932) then appeared in relatively short order. *The Book of Common Order* was a comprehensive service book that featured orders for regular and special services, as well as an extensive collection of prayers, a table of weekly Scripture readings, and creeds. *The Hymnary* provided primarily for the musical needs of United Church congregations at worship, but it also offered a limited collection of written prayers and the text of the Apostles' Creed.

In the early to mid-1960s, worship in The United Church was still being shaped by the use of *The Hymnary* and *The Book of Common Order*—the latter's having been revised and expanded as recently as 1950. Though both the Apostles' and Nicene Creeds were printed in *The Book of Common Order* and made permissible in its orders of service for baptism and communion, the actual use of the classical creeds in The United Church was inconsistent in its early decades. As John H. Young notes, their use consisted mostly of the Apostles' Creed at services of baptism and the Lord's Supper.[4] It is worth keeping in mind that copies of *The Book of Common Order* were

3. Harding and Harding, *Patterns of Worship*, 16–27.

4. Young, "Introduction," 14.

not usually put in the pews. Worshippers typically had in hand only the Apostles' Creed, as it was printed in *The Hymnary*.

The primary sources of study for the liturgy of The United Church as it bears upon the more recent history of "A New Creed" are those service materials that have been published since the approval of "A New Creed" by the General Council Executive in November 1968. In chronological order, the liturgical resources of particular significance are the two editions of the *Service Book* (1969), *A Sunday Liturgy* (1984), *Baptism and Renewal of Baptismal Faith* (1986), the *Service Book for Use in Church Courts* (1993), *Voices United* (1996), and, the most recent major liturgical resource of the denomination, *Celebrate God's Presence* (2000). Also worthy of consideration will be *The Hymn Book* (1971), the experimental *Voices United: Services for Trial Use 1996–1997*, and select versions of "Celebration of a New Ministry"—a template based on the order of the same name in the *Service Book for Use in Church Courts*—which now are generally distributed electronically and used widely across Canada for what have often been known as covenanting services.

There are some excellent scholarly studies of The United Church's liturgical tradition, two of which bear special mention. One is *Patterns of Worship in The United Church of Canada: 1925–1987*, by Thomas and Bruce Harding. Based on the graduate-level research of this father and son, *Patterns of Worship* describes in rich detail the worship practices of The United Church from its inception until the 1980s. Brilliantly, the book provides the fascinating histories of each liturgical resource produced and published by the denomination during the period in question. The primary thesis of the Hardings is that the worship patterns of The United Church tradition have reflected a dialectical tension between "order and liberty." A second work of note is William S. Kervin's *The Language of Baptism: A Study of the Authorized Baptismal Liturgies of The United Church of Canada, 1925–1995*. In a different type of study from that of the Hardings, Kervin took a very close look at The United Church's baptismal services in particular. While primarily a historical and liturgical study, it is also a theological and even exegetical one. Kervin's thesis is that the baptismal liturgies of The United Church in each successive generation "show an evolution toward the classic (patristic) liturgical forms of Christian initiation gleaned from the liturgical scholarship of the day."[5] He also shows how the move to more traditional

5. Kervin, *Language of Baptism*, xviii.

forms of baptismal liturgy was balanced by the adoption of progressively more modern or liberal theological content. Though the present study of "A New Creed" in its liturgical contexts within The United Church does not seek to build directly on the arguments of these other works, it does take into account their excellent and fascinating research. We will see here that since the appearance of "A New Creed" in 1968, the more classical expressions of the Christian faith have been largely jettisoned in favor of this newer confession. This text has been consistently presented in worship as expressing the unique faith of The United Church.

The Service Book (1969)

Thomas and Bruce Harding introduced their account of the genesis and production of the 1969 *Service Book*: "Throughout the 1950s there was considerable impetus within The United Church of Canada for a revision of its two primary worship resources: the 1930 *Hymnary* and the 1932 *Book of Common Order*. The major concern was the lack of congregational participation in United Church worship."[6] After a buildup of popular sentiment across the denomination, the Eighteenth General Council meeting in Kingston, Ontario, in 1958 commissioned the Committee on Church Worship and Ritual to revise *The Book of Common Order*.[7] Intended to have been completed perhaps as early as 1965, the *Service Book* appeared after some hurried, last-minute revisions by the Committee on Church Worship and Ritual only in the spring of 1969. The ministers' edition was published first, followed shortly afterward by a version to be kept in the pews so that congregations could follow along and participate more frequently and fully in worship.

The *Service Book* is important for the study of "A New Creed" in a number of ways, not least of which is that "A New Creed" was written on the occasion of its preparation.[8] The method used by the Committee on Church Worship and Ritual in creating the volume was to prepare draft services and send them to the wider church for comment.[9] In one poten-

6. Harding and Harding, *Patterns of Worship*, 125.

7. *Record of Proceedings*, Eighteenth General Council, 90, 119. Noted in Harding and Harding, *Patterns of Worship*, 126n290.

8. Although, ironically, as Kervin notes, "A New Creed, having originated as a result of revisions to the services of baptism in the *Service Book*, ended up virtually absent from its baptismal liturgies" (Kervin, "Sacraments and Sacramentality," 234).

9. The use of such a method is partly why it took so long to finish the service

tial order of service for baptism, the Committee on Church Worship and Ritual had included the recitation of the Apostles' Creed with the rubric "The Apostles' Creed shall be said by all." This inclusion drew the ire of many in the denomination, including some members of the Committee on Christian Faith.[10] It was this that led the Committee on Christian Faith to seek the permission of the Sub-Executive of the General Council to write a modern creed that could be used instead of the Apostles' Creed.

The *Service Book* is also significant because, on a more practical level, it was the first place "A New Creed" was published with authorization for liturgical use in The United Church. In the ministers' edition of the *Service Book*, "A New Creed" is printed on the inside front cover, whereas in the people's edition, it appears on page 310. In both cases, it is placed with "A Statement of Faith" of the United Church of Christ in the U.S.A. as well as the Apostles' Creed and the Nicene Creed. In both editions, "A New Creed" is first in order. It is likely that "A New Creed" became a formal title by virtue of its appearance in the *Service Book*. Previously, the Committee on Christian Faith had not given it a definite title. Both inside and outside that committee, the text was known by a number of names: "a new creed," "A Creed," "the new creed," "The United Church Creed," and others—each of them provisional.

The recitation of a creed or confession was never mandated in the *Service Book*. In the earlier history of The United Church, the use of creeds had never been required or consistent. In large measure, this was due to the influence of congregationalism—a tradition that has always resisted the suggestion that any religious authority might usurp the Bible or an individual's conscience. To mandate the recitation of a creed, all of a sudden, would have been a radical departure for persons from that tradition and now as well for those from the newer United Church tradition that had drawn heavily from it. Also, the spirit of the times worked against the imposition of traditional expressions of classical Christianity. That said, the Committee on Church Worship and Ritual clearly wanted to make available to the denomination some more classical elements of Christian liturgy, including recitation of the ancient creeds. This is evident in the various orders of service provided in the *Service Book*. The first order for "The Celebration of the Lord's Supper" outlines a service in three movements: "The Approach," "The Word of God Proclaimed and

---

books. The other important reason, understandably, was that the cultural unrest that had influenced the church made it difficult to produce a consensus about anything.

10. Standing Committee on Christian Faith, *Creeds*, 5.

Acknowledged," and, finally, "The Word of God Enacted," which would include an offering, the Lord's Supper, and a closing.[11]

Within this order of service, a creed was included as an option in the second movement, "The Word of God Proclaimed and Acknowledged." This implies that a key function of a creed, at least in this context, would be to summarize the message of the Bible in response to the reading of Scripture and the sermon. The *Service Book* goes on to state, in the annotated portion of the outline, "Then the minister and people may make profession of the faith of the church by singing or saying the Nicene Creed or the Apostles' Creed or We praise thee, O God."[12] In the second, "contemporary" order based on the foregoing outline, which used more modern language—especially "you" and "your" instead of "thee" and "thou" for addressing God—we find simply that "A creed may be said."[13] In both examples, the recitation of a creed was entirely optional. Essentially, the introduction to the *Service Book* stressed the right of the minister to do whatever he or she wanted. We read:

> In the United Church of Canada there are no prescribed forms of worship, except part of the ordination service. Worship in the United Church of Canada is guided by directories. This means that liberty is given to each minister to use his own words in any prayer. In a directory rubrics refer to structure and content, not language. It is in this context that the use of "shall" and "may" in the rubrics is to be understood. "Shall" indicates not prescription but preference, a recommendation that an act should be done or a type of prayer said. "May" suggests some particular act or prayer but without the preference involved in "shall."[14]

Whatever compromise in language was reached, among committee members themselves, as well as between the Committee on Church Worship and Ritual and the General Council, the preferred option seems to have been that a communion service with traditional language would include the classical creeds (or the *Te Deum*), while the version with more colloquial language would most likely be accompanied, if by any confession at all, by "A New Creed."

11. *Service Book for Use of Ministers*, 2.

12. *Service Book for Use of Ministers*, 5.

13. *Service Book for Use of Ministers*, 16. See also the "Introduction" for the service book's definition of "contemporary."

14. "Introduction," in *Service Book for Use of Ministers*, n.p.

Another of the *Service Book*'s orders is a second outline for "The Celebration of the Lord's Supper." It follows a slightly different three-part order: "The Introduction," "The Ministry of the Word," and "The Holy Communion."[15] Though couched in so-called traditional language—God's being addressed with Elizabethan pronouns—this service offers an interesting variant on the rubric of introduction for a creed. Following the sermon, we find, "A creed may be said or sung, or the hymn Te Deum may be sung."[16]

Ironically, given the original impetus for the writing of "A New Creed," creeds are featured even less prominently in the "Services of Initiation" referred to in the *Service Book* as outlines for "The Baptism of Children" and "Adult Baptism and Confirmation." Each of these "Services of Initiation" takes place in four movements: "The Approach," "The Word," "The Action," and "The Response."[17] Whereas in the communion services the recitation of a creed was tied liturgically to the public reading of Scripture and preaching, in these services it was included under the "Profession of Faith" and tied more closely to the sacrament itself. Symbolically, this would give the creed the function, not of summarizing Scripture or responding to "The Word" but of representing the faith of the global community into which the candidate was being initiated.[18] In the first order for "The Baptism of Children," "The Action" begins with the minister's reading of two passages of Scripture—Matthew 28:18–20 (the Great Commission) and Mark 10:13–16 ("And Jesus said, 'Let the children come to me'")—followed by some teaching about baptism. After this comes the promise of the congregation, followed by the phrase "Then may the Apostles' Creed be said by all." Then come the promises of the

15. *Service Book for Use of Ministers*, 22.

16. *Service Book for Use of Ministers*, 24.

17. *Service Book for Use of Ministers*, 38–74. The service book states that "sermon and supper belong together as the full diet of public worship" but also provides outlines for services that would not include either of the sacraments. The second of these orders takes a relatively simplified form. The first, interestingly, features three movements (like those for the Lord's Supper) but (like those for rites of initiation) uses the language of approach, word, and response (76–83).

18. See Harding and Harding, *Patterns of Worship*, 163n403. Committee on Church Worship and Ritual Member Hugh Matheson is quoted as saying, "The Apostles' Creed is the symbol of faith that is historically identified with baptism [in the Western church]; we have used it here as the means whereby the church expresses the faith with which the child is surrounded."

parent(s) and the act of baptism.[19] The place of the Apostles' Creed in this order is tenuous; it's being introduced by the without-preference "may." By the second order for the baptism of children, surprisingly, couched in more contemporary language, the creed has disappeared entirely.[20]

The two orders for "Adult Baptism and Confirmation" are almost identical to those for the baptism of children. Only minor variations appear in the final two movements of worship: "The Action" and "The Response."[21] Again, the place for a creed is not with "The Word" but with the rites of baptism and/or confirmation, under the heading "Profession of Faith." In the first order, following the reading of scriptural imperatives and some theological explanation for the acts of baptism or confirmation, we find "The people may stand and say the Apostles' Creed."[22] Questions would then then be put to the congregation and to the candidate(s). In the second order, the one written in up-to-date language, we find simply "A Creed (optional)."[23]

The last features of the *Service Book* bearing significance for "A New Creed" are the placing of the text and its suggested formula of introduction. "A New Creed" (and also "A Statement of Faith" of the United Church of Christ in the U.S.A.) is included with the suggested phrase of introduction "Let us repeat together a contemporary expression of Christian faith." Conversely, the Apostles' and Nicene Creeds might be introduced with the words "Let us repeat together the historic expression of Christian faith known as the Apostles'/Nicene Creed."[24] As we saw, the suggested formulae of introduction caused great debate within the Committee on Christian Faith, as well as between it and the Committee on Church Worship and Ritual. While some wanted an introduction involving something like "Let us confess" or "Let us say together," others insisted on something like "Let us repeat." In the *Service Book*, the compromise became "Let us repeat together."

The precise text of "A New Creed" appears slightly differently in the *Service Book* than it does in any of the reports of the Committee on

19. *Service Book for Use of Ministers*, 42–45.

20. *Service Book for Use of Ministers*, 53. In place of a creed, we find simply these instructions: "Let us pray in silence for the gifts of God's Spirit."

21. *Service Book for Use of Ministers*, 56.

22. *Service Book for Use of Ministers*, 61.

23. *Service Book for Use of Ministers*, 71.

24. The creeds appear on the inside covers of the ministers' service book and on 310–14 in the people's edition.

Christian Faith. In their final presentation to the General Council Executive in November 1968, and even in the second edition of *Creeds* (1975), there is a footnote to "A New Creed," which says that the opening phrase "may be used as a versicle, with the rest as a response."[25] In the *Service Book*, the opening phrase of the creed is used as a versicle only.[26] This looks a bit bizarre on paper, especially since the minister is already instructing the congregation with a phrase of introduction, "Let us repeat together." Why would he or she then introduce the creed further by saying, "Man is not alone, he lives in God's world"? It seems most likely that the Committee on Church Worship and Ritual, comprised mostly of self-styled traditionalists, simply could not see itself clear to printing a creed that did not begin with "I believe" or "We believe."[27]

Conclusions about the Service Book *and "A New Creed"*

"A New Creed" was written on the occasion of the preparation of a new book of services for The United Church and in response to those liturgical writers who wanted to introduce the more regular use of the Apostles' Creed at baptism. That the writing of "A New Creed" was necessary indicates the discord that existed between the Committee on Church Worship and Ritual and the Committee on Christian Faith. While the latter group was somewhat more liberal in outlook, the former tended to see itself as more conservative and traditional. This difference between the two seems evident in a number of ways. The Committee on Church Worship and Ritual displayed an interesting treatment of the text of "A New Creed" in making its distinctive opening phrase a versicle only, meaning that the congregation would make a more properly credal statement beginning with the words "We believe." The traditionalism of the Committee on Church Worship and Ritual was also evident in their unwillingness to introduce the Apostles' Creed with simply "Let us repeat," feeling that this "emasculated" doctrinal confession.[28] They also subverted the aims of the Committee on Christian Faith by specifically suggesting the

25. Standing Committee on Christian Faith, *Creeds*, 22.

26. *The Concise Oxford Dictionary* (9th ed.) defines versicle as "each of the short sentences in a liturgy said or sung by a priest . . . and alternating with responses."

27. Harding and Harding, *Patterns of Worship*, 164n405.

28. Kervin, *Language of Baptism*, 185.

classical creeds in some sacramental orders of service, especially the first order for communion, while only leaving the matter open in others.

All of that said, the Committee on Church Worship and Ritual found itself swept up, either intentionally or unintentionally, in the prevailing spirit of liberalism within The United Church. The use of a creed as a confession or profession of faith is only ever optional in each of the orders of the *Service Book*. In some services, notably the second order for baptism, it is entirely absent. In other services, creeds "may" be said. "May," as the *Service Book*'s introduction suggests, is weaker than "shall" and is not intended to carry a preference. Further, the classical creeds are used only in the services that are uniquely marked by their use of more traditional language, meaning the old-fashioned practice of addressing God with archaic pronouns. Though it is notable that the Committee on Church Worship and Ritual provides alternate orders of service in relatively more traditional and more contemporary language, the suggestion of using classical creeds particularly in the former implies that these ancient confessions are more sentimentally important. They are a matter of taste. The liberalizing pressures felt by the editors of the *Service Book* are evident also in the formulae of introduction agreed upon for the creeds. While the two committees wrestled over "confess" and "repeat," the more telling words in the final rubrics are "contemporary" and "historic." The classical creeds are to be introduced as "the historic expression of the Christian faith," while "A New Creed" would be known as "a contemporary expression of Christian faith." While historic describes something that *was* significant in the past, contemporary is a word for something that is with the times or current.[29]

The *Service Book*, like "A New Creed," was born not of a new consensus but amidst turbulent times and a general breakdown of religious consensus within church and society. At this stage, "A New Creed" was not the faith of The United Church. Due to the upheaval of the era, The United Church of Canada did not have a theological consensus to express. We can see how the language of the *Service Book* intended to accommodate a diverging spectrum of belief within the denomination and began to suggest a trend in this direction. Creeds, whether ancient or modern, in its various services, were never more than mildly suggested, implying that the classical creeds did not carry a lot of weight with many people in The United Church. The interesting role of creeds in the liturgies of the

29. See the definitions of *The Concise Oxford Dictionary* (9th ed.), 288, 643.

Service Book made manifest the institutional tug-of-war that was going on behind the scenes. The move to a historic-contemporary dichotomy between the classical creeds and "A New Creed" indicated the likely direction in which The United Church would move.[30] As we go on to examine later liturgical developments in the denomination, we will see that this is precisely what has happened.

The Hymn Book (1971)

A personal memory of The United Churches of my childhood in the 1980s was the sight of the green service books and red hymn books sitting side by side in the pew racks. These two volumes represented the second-generation United Church worship books, having replaced *The Book of Common Order* and *The Hymnary* respectively. Though it came from the same era as its sibling the *Service Book*, *The Hymn Book*'s creation resulted from a very different creative process. While the liturgies of the *Service Book* were written with a view to the emerging spirit of ecumenical convergence in the 1960s, *The Hymn Book* was produced as a concrete expression of a then-hoped-for, but ultimately unsuccessful, organic union between The United Church and Canada's Anglicans. As early as 1943, the Church of England in Canada began to give signals that it was interested in pursuing the visible unity of Christendom in Canada with willing partner churches.[31] Twenty years later, both The United Church and the by-then-renamed Anglican Church of Canada had appointed parallel committees of "Tens" to consider the possibility of a merger. In a somewhat concurrent development, there had been in The United Church, since the middle of the 1950s, growing calls for a new hymnal to replace *The Hymnary*. In 1962, after years of agitation from the grassroots, the Twentieth General Council commissioned the production of such a replacement volume.[32] In 1964, The United Church proposed, through its Ten, that a new hymnal be created jointly with the

30. Kervin notices another important first step in the openness around creeds in the *Service Book*: "the first intentional permission for the use of other baptismal symbols" (Kervin, *Language of Baptism*, 157).

31. Grant, "Leading Horse to Water," 165.

32. Harding and Harding, *Patterns of Worship*, 168–69.

Anglicans. After the Anglican General Synod gave its agreement in 1965, work on the project was begun.[33]

Finally published after almost six years of labor, *The Hymn Book* was a controversial volume from its beginnings. In part, it seems to have suffered as a legacy to the failed project of union. United Church folk often thought it "too Anglican," note Thomas and Bruce Harding, while their Anglican counterparts similarly considered it "too United Church."[34] Ironically, the issue of worship books was itself sometimes given as a reason for the undesirability of union. "One would . . . have supposed, from contrasting denominational reactions," notes John Webster Grant with a hint of sarcasm, "that by the Sunday after union all the prayer books would have vanished from Anglican churches and reappeared in United pew racks."[35]

The Hymn Book is of some interest for our consideration of creeds. Unsurprisingly, "A New Creed" was not included. This makes sense, given that the *Service Book* had just been published and also that this new hymnal was a joint project with the Anglican Church of Canada. In the "Liturgical Appendix," however, near the back of the book, the Nicene and Apostles' Creeds were included alongside liturgical settings for sung portions of Holy Communion and some Psalms. The Nicene Creed was included set to music at 507d, and the Apostles' Creed for recitation at 510b. Thomas and Bruce Harding note that this "Liturgical Appendix" was an Anglican preference.[36]

Of particular interest is another personal memory. In 1996, the United Church congregation of my youth bought a set of new *Voices United* hymnals. At that time, our copies of *The Hymn Book* were given away to congregants (rather than boxed up and put in storage, as happened in many other places). I have my copy still and have long-noticed that it displays the text of "A New Creed," printed on a half-sheet of 8"x11" paper and glued carefully to the inside front cover. This was a telling practice and not an uncommon one.

33. "Preface," in *Hymn Book*, n.p.

34. Harding and Harding, *Patterns of Worship*, 195–201.

35. Grant, "Leading Horse to Water," 173.

36. Harding and Harding, *Patterns of Worship*, 187.

A Sunday Liturgy (1984)

As we saw, the creation of the *Service Book* was motivated largely by an increasing desire that there be greater oral participation in worship by United Church congregations. As was also the case in some other Protestant denominations, there occurred a parallel movement in the Roman Catholic Church, reaching its climax in the Second Vatican Council (1962–1965), to increase participation and accessibility for the laity. Among the liturgical reforms to come from that council was a mass in which the priest was to face the congregation and also to speak in the vernacular rather than in Latin. Stemming from the retrieval of worship practices through the scholarly study of early Christian history, these concurrent transformations across different traditions came to be known as the ecumenical convergence. The *Service Book* represented an early step along this path for The United Church, though it was by no means the only or final such step. As part of a broader structural realignment within The United Church in the 1970s, the Committee on Church Worship and Ritual was merged into a new Committee on Liturgy, under the Division of Mission in Canada, effective in 1980. In 1983, that committee was renamed the Working Unit on Worship and Liturgy. An early priority of this group was the production of new orders of service, built upon those of the *Service Book*, which would further incorporate liturgical, theological, and cultural developments of the previous decade and a half, especially in light of the ongoing ecumenical convergence.[37] The first of these orders to appear was *A Sunday Liturgy for Optional Use in The United Church of Canada*, in 1984.

Like the *Service Book*, *A Sunday Liturgy* reflected a desire to encourage a word-and-table shape to worship in The United Church. Thus, the Lord's Supper continued to be normative and those services without communion were intentionally set as variations from the standard. The outline in *A Sunday Liturgy* featured an order of service in four movements: "Gathering," "Service of the Word," "Service of the Table," and "Sending Forth."[38] On an initial examination of this outline, it is not immediately evident where a creed or confession might be placed. In this sense, such a recitation was even more inconspicuous than it might have been in a liturgy based on some of the outlines in the *Service Book*. In the annotated portion of *A Sunday Liturgy*, we find that creeds were given

37. Harding and Harding, *Patterns of Worship*, 243–55.

38. Working Unit on Worship, *Sunday Liturgy*, 4.

as an option under "Responses to the Word" within the "Service of the Word." As in the *Service Book*'s first order for the Lord's Supper, creeds would therefore be tied to the reading of Scripture and preaching, both to summarize the biblical story and to give the congregation an opportunity to respond to the preaching. The use of creeds, however, was by no means emphasized. We read, "There may be silence and/or individual reflections on the Word, a creed, a hymn, an invitation to Christian discipleship, baptism, reaffirmations of faith, testimonies, announcements of congregational life and work, individual concerns gathered for the Prayers of the People."[39] It is difficult to know quite what to make of this description. The "Introduction" to *A Sunday Liturgy* declares, "Liturgy tells the story of the Christian faith in this and in all times and places." Further, the service it contains was meant to reflect "the ecumenical convergence that is now under way among many denominations."[40] The idea of corporate, doctrinal confession using the classical creeds might seem a good fit within such sentiments. Despite this, there is no pride of place given to such confession in *A Sunday Liturgy*. "A creed" may be said, but it does not stipulate which creed. It is easy to get the impression that creeds are not important at all, their being on par with the "announcements" and even "silence and/or individual reflections." *A Sunday Liturgy* also notes, "There is no need for a creed when the Great Thanksgiving comes later"—its being a common feature of the Lord's Supper, of which the authors encourage more regular celebration, in any case. What is more, "One of the historic creeds (Apostles' or Nicene)," we read, "may be said on occasion as a means of affirming the unity of the church throughout the ages."[41]

What reflective writing we find in *A Sunday Liturgy* (the "Introduction" and "Guidelines" sections) on the subject of creeds refers broadly to the classical creeds. Far from being embraced, however, these creeds were somewhat marginalized when singled out as appropriate for only occasional use. Even when used sparingly, they were not held to express the faith of The United Church. Notably, "A New Creed" was not explicitly described as containing the faith of The United Church either.

39. Working Unit on Worship, *Sunday Liturgy*, 9.

40. Working Unit on Worship, *Sunday Liturgy*, 6.

41. Working Unit on Worship, *Sunday Liturgy*, 42.

Baptism and Renewal of Baptismal Faith (1986)

A later volume in the Services for Optional Use series was entitled *Baptism and Renewal of Baptismal Faith*. Unlike *A Sunday Liturgy* and other "for optional use" booklets, which borrowed language heavily from other sources, this was written entirely from scratch by the members of the Task Group on Christian Initiation of the Working Unit on Worship and Liturgy. Two particular members of that task group, Jim Taylor and Jim Dowden, wrote the various drafts that were then worked on by the group as a whole.[42]

The broad outline for the order of service used in *Baptism and Renewal of Baptismal Faith* was that taken from *A Sunday Liturgy*, with the baptismal portion's being inserted essentially between the sermon and communion. The outline of this baptismal portion reads:

> Introduction
> Presentation of Candidates for Baptism / Those Renewing their Baptismal Faith
> Renunciation and Declaration and Congregational Profession of Faith
>   Questions and Responses
>   Corporate Profession of Faith
> Prayer of Thanksgiving and Pouring of Water
> Action of Baptism / Action of Renewal of Baptismal Faith
> Blessing[43]

What is especially significant about this baptismal service in relation to "A New Creed" is the "Corporate Profession of Faith." The placing of the profession suggests that the writers, like those of the services of initiation in the *Service Book*, wished it to symbolize the faith with which one was going to be surrounded at baptism. For the "Corporate Profession of Faith," two options were provided: the Apostles' Creed and "A New Creed." A separate formula of introduction was given for each. The Apostles' Creed was to be introduced with the words "Let us with the whole church confess our faith." "A New Creed" was to be introduced with "Let us join in a statement of our communal faith."[44] This was explained in the booklet: "In response, the congregation stands . . . and then joins with them to confess the faith of the church in a creed. There are two options in this service—the ecumenical Apostles' Creed (historically, the baptismal

42. Harding and Harding, *Patterns of Worship*, 256–62.

43. Task Group on Christian Initiation, *Baptism and Renewal*, 4.

44. Task Group on Christian Initiation, *Baptism and Renewal*, 10–11.

profession) and the contemporary credal statement of The United Church of Canada. Notice that each has its appropriate introduction."[45] As compared to the *Service Book*, the rhetoric of theological debate seems to have cooled. While there was not necessarily a theological consensus among the members of the Task Group on Christian Initiation, they did not spend long trying to find common theological ground and therefore did not seem to think it worth fighting over.[46] There was no longer a forced then-now dichotomy between official doctrinal positions and the creeds or confessions that express them. The Apostles' Creed was not relegated to the dustbin of the past as a "historic expression of the Christian faith" but referred to as the faith of "the whole church."

Baptism and Renewal of Baptismal Faith takes a theological and liturgical position that is stunning in its subtlety. While the classical creeds and the Christianity they express are not quite degraded as before—as this baptismal service was intentionally set within the ecumenical convergence—"A New Creed" is significantly elevated in status. While "A New Creed" was made permissible in the *Service Book*, it was done so somewhat sheepishly, as the Committee on Church Worship and Ritual simply did not share the same theological tendencies as the Committee on Christian Faith. In *Baptism and Renewal of Baptismal Faith*, "A New Creed" is explicitly declared to be the parallel of the Apostles' Creed. Unlike those that appear in the *Service Book*, this service names and affirms "A New Creed" as a fully appropriate baptismal confession. It does so in describing "A New Creed" as "our communal faith." It seems difficult to overstate the significance of this. "A New Creed" was described explicitly, in a quasi-official liturgical document of The United Church, as the faith held in common by the denomination. In this document, it became fully acceptable to see this United Church faith as that into which an individual was baptized. Kervin notes that the liturgy of *Baptism and Renewal of Baptismal Faith* "points to the fact that the contemporary 'United Church Creed' is gaining the status of a baptismal symbol (even overtaking the Apostles' Creed in popular appeal)."[47]

45. Task Group on Christian Initiation, *Baptism and Renewal*, 17.

46. Harding and Harding, *Patterns of Worship*, 261n663. Harding and Harding record, from the meeting minutes of the Task Group on Christian Initiation for 17 Jan. 1986, "The chair expressed the view that theological consensus is not likely to be reached by this group but that we need to work at the task(s) in the knowledge of each other's biases."

47. Kervin, *Language of Baptism*, 258.

Conclusions about Baptism and Renewal of Baptismal Faith *and "A New Creed"*

Baptism and Renewal of Baptismal Faith made two key assumptions that have had theological and spiritual significance for The United Church of Canada. First, it formalized a particular interpretation of the linguistic function of "A New Creed" by describing it as "our communal faith." This is important because, as we saw, "A New Creed" was written not to express a collectively held theological vision but, ironically, to facilitate the relatively private profession of personally held beliefs. Clearly, the kinds of language needed for these two distinct purposes are different. That once suggestive words were now declared as definitive, in a sense, means that the theology of The United Church was thought to have become crystallized in a particular way.

Second, the explicit elevation of "A New Creed" to the status of a baptismal symbol signified that a baptism conducted in The United Church was not necessarily a baptism of initiation into the holy catholic church, because "A New Creed" is the confession of no other branch of the Christian church. Of course, many coming from even a more traditionalist perspective would make the key point that any baptism with water, "in the name of the Father, and of the Son, and of the Holy Spirit," is widely considered a catholic one in the ecumenical realm. But the purpose here is not to quibble over whether any individuals have received a legitimate baptism. It is simply to identity that, in this document, The United Church appeared to open the door to a rite of initiation that intentionally sidestepped the faith of the universal church.[48] Or, put another way, it might be The United Church of Canada into which one is welcomed at baptism rather than the one, unitary church spoken of in the New Testament. While some might also respond that *Baptism and Renewal of Baptismal Faith* was always "for optional use" and never authorized by the General Council, this document was nonetheless published by The United Church. Additionally, it has been treated widely as an authorized liturgy within the denomination.[49]

48. For the argument of one person who wanted The United Church to abandon baptism in the name of the Triune God, regardless of the spiritual and practical consequences, see Cawley, "United Church of Canada," 74–75: "The United Church is likely to make a permissive decision . . . if a strong consensus develops that the Trinitarian formula does indeed represent a sexist understanding of God, then the United Church is likely to declare that it cannot be required, even if the ecumenical cost is painful."

49. Kervin treats *Baptism and Renewal of Baptismal Faith* in his *Language of*

Service Book for Use in Church Courts (1993)

Given its particular polity and national scope, The United Church has always had a need for liturgical resources that provide directories and other materials for special services beyond the weekly and pastoral needs of local congregations and communities. Services of ordination or induction would be familiar examples, but there have long existed other liturgical occasions and requirements at meetings of presbyteries and conferences (now regions) as well as the General Council. In the earlier history of The United Church, many such resource materials were contained in *The Book of Common Order* alongside such pastoral directories as those for Public (Sunday) Worship, The Solemnization of Matrimony, The Burial of the Dead, and so on.[50]

In 1958, in anticipation of the production and publication of the next generation of liturgical resources to replace *The Book of Common Order*, the General Council directed that separate editions for ministers, congregations, and church courts be prepared. Eleven years after the ministers' and people's versions appeared, in 1969, came the *Service Book for Use in Church Courts* (1980). An edition revised and updated by the Working Unit on Worship and Liturgy in connection with the services "for optional use" was published in 1993.[51] A brief perusal of the *Service Book for Use in Church Courts* reveals its consistency with the other publications of that series, particularly *A Sunday Liturgy* and *Baptism and Renewal of Baptismal Faith.*

The *Service Book for Use in Church Courts* contains services for induction ("Celebration of a New Ministry"), the reception of candidates for the ministry or minsters from other denominations—although, interestingly, not for ordination in The United Church—as well as local church-building dedications and the installation to office of presbytery chairs, conference presidents, or General Council moderators. The volume's final pages feature a "Service of the Table" that could be inserted into any of its directories as desired or appropriate.[52]

Baptism. The writers of later liturgies have also given it significant weight. See Hymn and Worship Resources Committee, *Voices United: Services for Trial Use*, 6, and the denomination's latest liturgical resource, *Celebrate God's Presence*, 6.

50. *Book of Common Order*, 217–43.

51. *Service Book for Use in Church Courts*, 4.

52. *Service Book for Use in Church Courts*, 92–95.

The use of credal confession is highlighted somewhat prominently in the *Service Book for Use in Church Courts*, its being included in the "Celebration of a New Ministry," "Reception of a Candidate," "Union of Congregations," and "Constituting a Congregation," as well as the services of installation to offices in the various courts of the church. The rubrics follow closely those of *Baptism and Renewal of Baptismal Faith*. In each of the directories in which a creed is included, it is under the heading "Renewal of Baptismal Faith." Both the Apostles' Creed and "A New Creed" are given as options. The formula of introduction for the former is "Let us stand and with the whole church confess our faith." "A New Creed" is to be introduced with "Let us stand and join in a statement of our communal faith."[53] In the volume's introduction, its authors describe their thinking:

> In appropriate places, both the traditional Apostles' Creed and the United Church Creed have been provided. Within the reformed tradition, it is to be understood that provision of service materials constitutes a directory for worship, placing a responsibility on planners to be sensitive to local, national, ecumenical, and historical needs witnessed in the assembly of the people of God.[54]

Indeed, the *Service Book for Use in Church Courts* reflects this Reformed tradition of common order rather than the Anglican or Roman Catholic traditions of common prayer. There is liberty for worship planners to make use of variations according to certain local preferences. As with *Baptism and Renewal of Baptismal Faith*, however, the *Service Book for Use in Church Courts* is striking in its declaration that "A New Creed" is properly an expression of Christians' baptismal faith. Given the continued labeling of "A New Creed" as "our communal faith" and the overwhelming preponderance of its actual selection in such services, there remains little doubt about which creed has been thought to express the faith of The United Church.

Voices United (1996)

The Thirty-Third General Council of The United Church, meeting in 1990, instructed the denomination's Hymn and Worship Resource Committee to produce a new volume to guide the liturgy of the church,

53. *Service Book for Use in Church Courts*, 8.

54. *Service Book for Use in Church Courts*, 4.

which would replace the *Service Book* (1969) and *The Hymn Book* (1971). In 1994, the Thirty-Fifth General Council determined that The United Church still needed two separate, likely substantial worship resources, one being primarily a hymn book and the other being primarily a book of services.[55] In 1996, after approximately five years of work by the large Hymn and Worship Resource Committee, *Voices United* was published. It remains the primary hymn book of The United Church today. Yet, *Voices United* is more than simply a hymnal. The reason for this can be traced back to the original mandate of the committee that prepared it. As its subtitle suggests, *Voices United* is (or at least was initially intended to be) *The Hymn and Worship Book of The United Church of Canada*. In addition to approximately seven hundred hymns, *Voices United* contains a three-year lectionary, a number of prayers, creeds, an extensive psalter, musical settings for communion, and even orders of service for daily prayer, which can be expanded into full services of Sunday worship if necessary.[56] Precisely because *Voices United* has functioned as a source of liturgical material within The United Church and because it contains creeds, it needs to be considered among those liturgical resources significant for the study of "A New Creed."

The section containing creeds in *Voices United* begins at page 918. On that page, the Apostles' Creed appears first, followed by "A New Creed." On the page opposite, we find the same order, but with texts *en français*.[57] It is worth noting that the French *credo* does not function in quite the same way as "creed" does in English. While the range of meanings is much the same—and indeed *le Credo* can be a casual way of referring to one of the ancient Christian creeds—it is not formally a title. The Apostles' Creed is known by the ancient term "symbol"—*Le Symbole des Apôtres* among Francophones.[58] In its French translation, "A New Creed" is not referred to as a symbol but as a confession, the "*Confession de foi*

55. *Voices United: Hymn and Worship Book*, viii, and Hymn and Worship Resources Committee, *Voices United: Services for Trial Use*, 5.

56. Managing Editor John Ambrose writes, "These services can be made as simple or elaborate as an occasion requires" (Ambrose, "Introduction," in *Voices United: Hymn and Worship Book*, xi).

57. Some printings include the French text of the Apostles' Creed at p. 919, while others include only the French version of "A New Creed."

58. The Nicene Creed is similarly known in French as the *Symbole de Nicée-Constantinople*, although the French version of this confession is not provided in any of the liturgical resources of The United Church.

de L'Église Unie du Canada." Prepared by the Consistoire Laurentien, the translation reads:

> Nous ne sommes pas seuls,
>   nous vivons dans le monde que Dieu a créé.
>
> Nous croyons en Dieu
>   qui a créé et qui continue à créer,
>   qui est venu en Jésus, Parole faite chair,
>   pour réconcilier et renouveler,
>   qui travaille en nous et parmi nous par son Esprit.
>
> Nous avons confiance en lui.
>
> Nous sommes appelés à constituer l'Église:
>   pour célébrer la présence de Dieu,
>   pour vivre avec respect dans la création,
>   pour aimer et servir les autres,
>   pour rechercher la justice et résister au mal,
>   pour proclamer Jésus, crucifié et ressuscité,
>   notre juge et notre espérance.
>
> Dans la vie, dans la mort,
>   et dans la vie au-delà de la mort,
>   Dieu est avec nous.
> Nous ne sommes pas seuls.
>
> Grâces soient rendues à Dieu.[59]

This *Confession* is a good and literal translation of "A New Creed" into French. Apart from a few idiomatic differences, it preserves the form and content of the English original remarkably well. One difference of significance is the phrase "Nous croyons en Dieu . . . qui travaille en nous et parmi nous par son Esprit." Literally, this means "We believe in God . . . who works in us and among us by his Spirit." That latter part of this sentence, both in its use of "his Spirit" and "who works in us and among us," is very reminiscent of early drafts of "A New Creed." It paints a quite different picture than does the description of God "who works in us and others," a phrase that was modified between the rejection of "A New Creed" by the General Council in the late summer of 1968 and its acceptance by the General Council Executive that November in order specifically to mention the work of God *outside* the Christian church. Lest we think this merely an idiomatic difference in translation, we can

59. *Voices United: Hymn and Worship Book*, 919. Used with permission.

see later on in the "*Confession de foi de L'Église Unie du Canada*" that the phrase "to love and serve others" is rendered "*pour aimer et server les autres.*" Neither the French language nor the translators of "A New Creed" were without the ability to render "others" very closely. All that said, this *Confession* is an excellent translation of "A New Creed."

Turning the page over once more, we find the Nicene Creed—in English only. Then, from pages 922 to 927, we find several consecutive leaves with both the Lord's Prayer and "A New Creed" printed in several different languages: Cree, Japanese, Korean, Taiwanese, Chinese, and Filipino. Each of these translations of "A New Creed" was prepared by the Ethnic Ministry Council of The United Church for congregations whose services are conducted in these languages. While this is surely to be commended, one might rightly ask, why have not translations of the classical creeds been provided as well?

Conclusions about Voices United *and "A New Creed"*

On the one hand, *Voices United* remains an almost omnipresent influence in the life and worship of The United Church, and its significance for the study of "A New Creed" cannot be denied. On the other, we must be careful not to assign it too much significance. A variety of creeds, including "A New Creed," is included in this well-worn volume, but the creeds' use or placement is prescribed for no kind of service in The United Church. Further, there are no formulae of introduction suggested for the corporate recitation of these creeds. However, the matter of translation and translations is raised, such as we had not encountered in the previous liturgical resources of the denomination. From the fact that "A New Creed" is provided in translation for many different language groups within The United Church while the classical creeds are not, we can deduce that "A New Creed" is thought to be the primary liturgical confession of The United Church of Canada. Conversely, the Apostles' and Nicene Creeds appear to be presented somewhat as tokens. Through its French translations, *Voices United* offers the idea of making a helpful distinction between the symbol of the apostles and a confession of faith of The United Church of Canada.

Celebrate God's Presence (2000)

Following the Thirty-Fifth General Council in 1994, the work of preparing a new service book for the denomination was separated from the production of a new hymnal. Consequently, several members of the Hymn and Worship Resource Committee endeavored, as the Liturgical Resources Subcommittee, to create a new volume that could meet the broad, ongoing liturgical needs of The United Church. The initial draft of their work appeared as *Voices United: Services for Trial Use 1996–1997*. This booklet was sent out across the church, prior to the Thirty-Sixth General Council in 1997, with a comment form that could be filled out by individuals or groups and returned to the subcommittee.[60] Though it was not a particularly brief resource, "evaluation of that document . . . highlighted the need for a more comprehensive collection."[61] Following the sentiment of the Thirty-Sixth General Council in 1996, that the preparation of a new service book was on the right track, a Book of Services Committee was formed to focus on completing the project. It began its work in 1998. Though freed to focus on this one project, the committee found itself "challenged (and, at times, overwhelmed) by the magnitude of the task."[62] The end result of its labors was *Celebrate God's Presence*, which appeared in 2000 and is destined to remain the latest service book of The United Church for some time to come. It is a large volume, bound in a four-inch three-ring binder. Though practically speaking it would be too big and too expensive to be put in the pews—and was not designed with this intention—*Celebrate God's Presence* encourages much of its contents to be "freely copied" into many other formats, such as Sunday bulletins or PowerPoint projections, "for use in public worship in The United Church of Canada."[63] A central strategy of the project appears to have been to provide as much material of as many different types and from as many different sources as possible.

Celebrate God's Presence is a remarkably important volume for the study of "A New Creed." Continuing the trajectory of the denomination's liturgical resources since 1969, it operates under the assumption that "A New Creed" uniquely contains and expresses the faith of The United

60. Hymn and Worship Resources Committee, *Voices United: Services for Trial Use*, 5.

61. *Celebrate God's Presence*, xiii.

62. *Celebrate God's Presence*, xiii.

63. *Celebrate God's Presence*, 8.

Church. Yet, it goes far beyond its predecessors in this regard. The first clue to this is seen clearly in the title, *Celebrate God's Presence*—a phrase taken intentionally from "A New Creed." Beyond its title, this resource is replete with the language and thought-forms of "A New Creed," so much so that an exhaustive study along these lines would be both copious and unwieldy. For example, note how the Book of Services Committee described its theological foundation.

> Theologically, the Committee sought liturgical resources which would help the church:
>
> - Celebrate the presence of God, who is revealed in the biblical story and uniquely in Jesus, the Word made Flesh, and who by the Spirit is at work in the church and in the world;
> - Express and nurture our relationship with God, challenging and sustaining us in Christian living with one another and with all of creation;
> - Invoke the power of the Holy Spirit to reconcile, heal, and make new.[64]

Phrases like "celebrating the presence of God," "Jesus, the Word made Flesh," and "to reconcile . . . and make new," as well as key theological ideas like the nature of God's work outside the church all suggest the influence of "A New Creed."

Numerous other elements of *Celebrate God's Presence* are drawn explicitly from "A New Creed" as well. Orders of service for funerals and memorials are included under the heading "Celebrate God's Presence 'In Life, in Death, in Life beyond Death.'" This is explained in the introduction to the section: "In a Christian funeral the promise of hope is to be proclaimed: 'In life, in death, in life beyond death, God is with us. We are not alone.'"[65] There is also a section of services that can be organized around ecological themes, such as "Blessing of Seeds and Soil" and "Blessing of the Fisheries," headed "To Live with Respect in Creation."[66] There are orders for special services entitled "To Reconcile and Make New" and "To Resist Evil." The latter section is introduced with the words, "Most Sundays, we pray, as Jesus taught, 'deliver us from evil.' Each time we recite A New Creed, we say, 'We are called to be the Church, to seek justice

64. *Celebrate God's Presence*, xiii–xiv.

65. *Celebrate God's Presence*, 442.

66. *Celebrate God's Presence*, 613–36.

and resist evil.' The United Church of Canada has a strong tradition of confronting social injustice and evil."[67]

In other ways also, *Celebrate God's Presence* makes it clear that "A New Creed" has become the doctrinal confession of and for The United Church par excellence. Significantly, "A New Creed" is listed along with the Apostles' and Nicene Creeds under the heading, "Historic Creeds and the Lord's Prayer." One cannot help but notice the subtlety with which this move has been made. There is no explanation as to the relationship of "A New Creed" with the classical creeds. We find simply the assumption made on historical grounds that it is on equal footing with them. As in *Voices United*, however, we find that, in practice, "A New Creed" is really superior to the Apostles' and Nicene Creeds, because it alone is offered in translation to linguistic minority groups—French, Cree, Chinese, Japanese, Korean, Filipino, and Taiwanese—within the denomination. By contrast, the Apostles' Creed is not offered in even one other language.[68] In this sense, *Celebrate God's Presence* has gone beyond even *Voices United*, which at least in some printings offered to French speakers *Le Symbole des Apôtres*. Given the inclusion of "A New Creed" under the heading "Historic Creeds," there is now no distinction evident between what is properly the Christian faith confessed throughout history and that confessed by some in The United Church in recent decades. The only distinction evident is between two creeds that were not commended for use across the cultural diversity of the church and one—"A New Creed"—that was.

Celebrate God's Presence suggests a word-and-table shape of worship, which its editors drew from the ongoing ecumenical convergence and based more intentionally upon the orders of service from *Voices United: Services for Trial Use 1996–1997* and *A Sunday Liturgy for Optional Use in The United Church of Canada*.[69] Yet unlike these previous volumes, *Celebrate God's Presence* does not suggest an outline or order of service as such, but "A Pattern for a Sunday Service" to consist of four movements: "Gathering," "Word," "Thanksgiving," and "Sending Forth." This pattern is broad and permissive. As articulated in its annotated portions, virtually any element of the service can be put in more than one place or left out altogether if one takes its words literally.[70]

67. *Celebrate God's Presence*, 680.

68. *Celebrate God's Presence*, 218–24.

69. *Celebrate God's Presence*, 6.

70. *Celebrate God's Presence*, 7. Even the reading of scripture and preaching could be omitted from a service of the word. We read, "The Bible is opened to the people

While "a creed or affirmation of faith" can be included in any service of worship, primarily as "a response to God's Word," this element is not particularly suggested for services of communion. However, corporate credal confession is emphasized in services of baptism and labeled therein as an "Affirmation of Faith."[71] It is noteworthy in the "Celebration of Baptism" service that *any* creed may be used to symbolize the faith into which the individual is welcomed at baptism and also that the language and thought-forms of "A New Creed" have thoroughly influenced the service as a whole. Candidates for baptism (or their parents) can be asked, "Do you believe in one God: Father, Son, and Holy Spirit?" or "Do you believe in God, who has created and is creating, who has come in Jesus, the Word made flesh, to reconcile and make new, and who works in us and others by the Spirit?" After this profession of faith, all are then asked for a "Commitment to Seek Justice and Resist Evil." As an alternative to a question of accepting Jesus as Savior and Lord, candidates or their parents (or sponsors) can be asked, "Will you proclaim Jesus, crucified and risen, in your words and actions?" Another later question is, "Will you join with your brothers and sisters in this community of faith to celebrate God's presence, live with respect in creation, and love and serve others?" If there are godparents participating, they can be asked, "Will you grow in faith with this child, trusting that, 'you are not alone, you live in God's world'?"[72] These are all examples of the language of "A New Creed" having greatly influenced the baptismal liturgy of The United Church. Considering that the corresponding order in *Voices United: Services for Trial Use 1996–1997* suggested "A New Creed" as *the* corporate baptismal confession but did not borrow so heavily from its phrasing in the questions put to participants, we can assume that the editors of *Celebrate God's Presence* were essentially asked to do so by the church.[73] That *Celebrate God's Presence* seems as far as possible to *permit* practices that were in use in The United Church, we can assume further the words and phrases of "A New Creed" were already being employed in these sorts of ways.

---

through the reading of portions of scripture, through preaching, music, *or* other arts and media" (emphasis added). No doubt, such elements of worship as Scripture reading(s) and preaching are still considered normative practices in the denomination, but this goes to show how flexible "A Pattern for a Sunday Service" is.

71. *Celebrate God's Presence*, 325.

72. *Celebrate God's Presence*, 332–38.

73. See Hymn and Worship Resources Committee, *Voices United: Services for Trial Use*, 60–68.

Conclusions about Celebrate God's Presence *and "A New Creed"*

Celebrate God's Presence is the most recent service book of The United Church and the one most indicative of the church's current liturgical practices. From the volume's title to its organization to the very contents of its wording, *Celebrate God's Presence* is saturated with the language of "A New Creed." To the extent that it goes beyond previous service books of The United Church in this regard, it is evident that there has been a progression in which the role and influence of "A New Creed" have increased, while those of the classical creeds have decreased.[74] This is all the more clear in that while "A New Creed" is considered equally historic with the classical creeds, it alone is provided to those worshipping in languages other than English and so commended to the church. *Celebrate God's Presence* is a concrete and clear example of what Kervin argues about the influence of "A New Creed" on The United Church of Canada when he writes, "Its vocabulary and syntax become hallmarks of the UCC's liturgical ethos, theological reflection, and institutional culture—not merely as propositional claims, or even liberal expressions, but as cultural-linguistic touchstones of ecclesial identity."[75]

"Celebration of a New Ministry"

As a last example of the prominence of "A New Creed" in the liturgy of The United Church, we will look briefly at the order of service for the "Celebration of a New Ministry: An Act of Covenanting for Ordained and Commissioned Ministers [now known as diaconal]." This service—and its less common equivalent for use in instances where lay people are serving in ministry—is used throughout The United Church to mark the beginning of a minister's tenure in a particular ministry setting. Appearing first in the *Service Book for Use in Church Courts*, this directory is now widely distributed electronically in various editions by the regions (formerly presbyteries and conferences) that oversee pastoral relationships and conduct so-called covenanting services.[76] In some ways, the forms this order of service has taken in these electronic distributions are less

74. William S. Kervin, "Worship on the Way," in Schweitzer, *United Church of Canada*, 188.

75. Kervin, "Sacraments and Sacramentality," 244.

76. See "Celebration of a New Ministry" in *Service Book for Use in Church Courts*, 5–14, and "Covenanting Service."

significant for us than the evidence which has been found in the service books of The United Church. It may be a bit of an anti-climax to look at it here. Because the available revisions are so new, however, and because we have the ready opportunity to compare this order in its original form with its concrete expressions in actual services of covenanting, we will find a revealing glimpse of how "A New Creed" is typically used in The United Church today.

The various outlines of "Celebration of a New Ministry" in common use are similar to the communion order in *Celebrate God's Presence*, an order that similarly is derived from that in *A Sunday Liturgy*. Generally, its five movements are "Gathering," "Presentation," "Service of the Word," "Covenanting Action," and "Response to the Covenant"—the last of which can include prayers, an offering, communion, and any concluding portions of the service.[77] In its original form, two options are provided for the "Renewal of Baptismal Faith" within the "Covenanting Action": the Apostles' Creed and "A New Creed." As in the *Service Book for Use in Church Courts*, an introductory formula is given for each: "Let us stand and with the whole church confess our faith," for the Apostles' Creed, and "Let us stand and join in a statement of our communal faith," for "A New Creed."

Interestingly, there are numerous locally approved revisions to this directory that have changed, among other things, the credal portion of the order. From my time as a candidate for ministry from Waterloo Presbytery in the late 2000s, I have a document entitled "The Approved Guideline of Covenanting Service for Use in Waterloo Presbytery." In it, "A New Creed" is *the* prescribed confession. Middlesex Presbytery in the former London Conference, where I was an intern in 2007–2008, used a similar order called "A Service of Covenanting," which also included "A New Creed" not as an option but as the approved creed. My current region, Shining Waters, has its approved covenanting service document available online, and it also features "A New Creed" as the "Affirmation of Faith" at the beginning of the "Covenanting Action" portion of the service.[78]

We need also to keep in mind that such orders of service are often modified even further before they ever see the light of day in an actual worship bulletin. Such printed orders of service are easy to find

77. This exact naming of the five movements does not match any one of the common variations of "Celebration of a New Ministry" that I have seen, as they all have slight differences from one another, but it does represent a consensus of them.

78. "Pastoral Relations Liasons."

and provide revealing insights into the liturgy of The United Church as it is actually practiced. I have found that, if anything, "A New Creed" is even further elevated in status by these occasional edits. I have made a point of collecting such orders of service from my own presbyteries and region over the years, as well as from others. In almost every case I examined, save one, the Apostles' Creed was omitted as an option and "A New Creed" was included. In those examples, the formula of introduction was often borrowed from the denominational template and worshippers were invited to "stand and join in a statement of our communal faith." However, in practice, this language of introduction has itself often been modified. Among the many bulletins I have collected by attending covenanting services or by acquiring from colleagues, I have found one example where "A New Creed" is described with the rubric "Renewal of Our Baptismal Faith" and another where it is introduced with the words "Let us stand and with the whole church confess our faith." The Apostles' Creed is sometimes, on *very* rare occasions, substituted in these kinds of services, but this always stems from the initiative of the minister being covenanted and his or her willingness to go against the grain.[79] Though mine has been an entirely unscientific sampling, I would certainly welcome anyone to present evidence of contrary practices.

Conclusions about the "Celebration of a New Ministry" and "A New Creed"

In practice, the "Celebration of a New Ministry" service has not carried the same weight as have other liturgies published in the various service books of The United Church. Still, it remains a telling example of how "A New Creed" is understood and used within The United Church's worship. Especially when comparing this order in its template form with those modifications in real use, we see that "A New Creed" is even more esteemed than the formal document would suggest.

79. In the one and only covenanting service where I have ever seen the Apostles' Creed in the order of service, I witnessed the "presbytery rep" conducting the service go off script and verbally criticize its inclusion at length before finally introducing it for recitation by the gathered congregation.

Conclusions

Since "A New Creed" was first approved by the General Council Executive in 1968, there has been a steady stream of liturgies produced by and for The United Church. Beginning with the *Service Book* and moving through *Celebrate God's Presence*, each generation of liturgical resources has made space for the use of creeds in corporate worship—particularly in services of baptism and communion—and each has especially commended "A New Creed" to the people of The United Church. While the classical creeds are generally permitted, one gets the clear sense that their use is to be limited and irregular, while "A New Creed" is presented as a doctrinal statement to be used freely and regularly, because it most certainly gives expression to the faith and identity of The United Church. What once was presented in the *Service Book* as a then-now (historic-contemporary) dichotomy between the ancient creeds and "A New Creed," has evolved more recently, since *Baptism and Renewal of Baptismal Faith*, into a they-we (the faith of the whole church-*our* communal faith) division. This extends also to the tenuous inclusion of the classical creeds in *Voices United* and *Celebrate God's Presence*, the most recent liturgical resources, which provide several translations of "A New Creed" but virtually none of the classical creeds—the lone exception being the French version of the Apostles' Creed, which appears in *some* printings of *Voices United*. The message contained in these resources is clear: "A New Creed" has become the statement of faith for The United Church. In expressions of both its order and its liberty, The United Church has turned to the words of "A New Creed" to articulate its theology and identify its faith.

4

"A New Creed" in the Nonliturgical Literature of The United Church

Introduction

In 1996, The United Church Publishing House and Metropolitan United Church, Toronto, published a booklet entitled *We Are Not Alone, We Live in God's World*. Attractively illustrated with colorful, artistic portrayals of Canadian and United Church life, each page is captioned with a line from "A New Creed." Along with its publication information, the inside back cover states, "A New Creed is the Creed of The United Church of Canada." The example of this booklet is highly illustrative of the way that, in a relatively short span of time, "A New Creed" went from being a kind of pressure release valve—intended to provide a mere alternative confession in cases where theological disagreements had become irreconcilable, in the cultural tumult of the 1960s—to the status of "the Creed of The United Church of Canada."

In the nonliturgical texts of The United Church's tradition, we find some longer and more sustained reflections on "A New Creed" than those provided by their liturgical cousins. The aims and types of these various writings are also even more diverse than the admittedly impressive variety of worship settings for which the church has provided formal liturgies. Most telling of all is the way these nonliturgical works give us a glimpse into an array of individual viewpoints found within The United Church.

Despite the variety of texts that refer to "A New Creed," they express a remarkably consistent point of view: while there is significant theological diversity within The United Church of Canada, "A New Creed" articulates the denomination's faith and gives it an identity. For these reasons, this confession is to be celebrated. The significance and viability of these claims appear largely to have been assumed and not subjected to critical reflection. At the very least, alternative confessional possibilities seem not to have been considered seriously.

Somewhat surprisingly, there has not been a mountain of literature produced on the subject of "A New Creed." This may be due to economies of scale. The United Church—like Canadian society as a whole—simply is not a large enough market to be particularly profitable for publishers. It is also the case that there are some sources where one might expect to find a discussion of "A New Creed" but where we do not.[1] It will be the purpose of the following pages to consider, in the chronological order of their appearance, the evidence of some nonliturgical texts that might rightly be called primary sources for the interpretation of "A New Creed" within The United Church.

Nonliturgical Texts

This You Can Believe (1976), by Russell Crossley

Although published privately and now long out of print, copies of *This You Can Believe* have remained remarkably available in the secondary market through the years. This little booklet contains a series of sermons preached by Russell Crossley at Dublin Street United Church in Guelph, Ontario, during the mid-1970s. It is obvious from the booklet's subtitle—*A Commentary on a Contemporary Creed of The United Church of Canada*—that it is going to offer a helpfully detailed analysis of "A New Creed" and its contents.[2] Consistent with those who have gone on to write about it in subsequent years, Crossley turned to "A New Creed" to explain the faith of The United Church, especially its distinctive faith in relation to that of other churches, because it alone expresses *this* denomination's faith. Crossley indicates that his sermon series originated

1. For example, Homewood, *Faith of the Church*.

2. A detailed interaction with Crossley's particularly theological interpretations of "A New Creed" will have to wait until we engage in such an examination in the next chapter.

from his desire to respond to those who say, "The trouble with the United Church is it doesn't believe anything." To the contrary, he asserts that The United Church has a faith—one that simply might not match that of its critics. In order to respond more fully to those who would criticize The United Church, Crossley intended to instruct his hearers (or readers) so that they might be able to express their faith more clearly and give a better representation of The United Church to outsiders. He says,

> Sometimes those outside the United Church do not think we have any beliefs because the members have trouble expressing them. Too often in our church we have used a process of osmosis hoping that people will soak up the teachings of the church just by hanging around the atmosphere. Many in the United Church are fuzzy about their beliefs and it is to help correct this that this short sermon series is directed. I have chosen as an outline a contemporary creed [ie. A New Creed] . . . the essential point is . . . to assist them in articulating the faith to others.[3]

Crossley does stress the flexible nature of belief within The United Church and the highly personal nature of his own presentation. He also acknowledges that neither the creed nor his sermons represent a comprehensive treatment of theology in general or the faith of The United Church in particular. Nonetheless, his clear purpose is to disseminate information to his audience so that they would be able to understand the faith of The United Church and also be able to articulate it to others in a manner better than had hitherto been done. While "A New Creed" is not said to be a comprehensive theological statement, it is described as representing the faith of The United Church.

This United Church of Ours (1981, 1991, 2000, 2017), by Ralph Milton

Among the first places one would likely turn in hopes of learning something about "A New Creed" would be Ralph Milton's wildly successful book *This United Church of Ours*. First published in 1981, it has since gone through three subsequent and expanded editions, in 1991, in 2000, and again in 2017. Notes Catherine Faith MacLean, "Ralph Milton's lighthearted *This United Church of Ours* sold 35,000 copies in eleven printings through the 1980s and 1990s. It 'became the standard text for UCC

3. Crossley, *This You Can Believe*, 1–2.

membership classes across Canada . . . . No other book or publication has been used as extensively for this purpose.' Although it is not an official publication of the denomination, it expressed theological perspectives that were readily received by UCC members."[4] Milton's popular and folksy account has done much over the years to teach people about The United Church and encourage reflection on the sort of everyday things that often get taken for granted. His book tackles diverse subjects ranging from how to choose a seat when you arrive at a church for the first time to the doctrine of the Trinity. Surprisingly, Milton does not mention "A New Creed" in *This United Church of Ours*. The book includes a chapter on theology, "This We Believe," but does not use or refer to "A New Creed." Upon closer examination, this can be explained by Milton's basic approach to the task of theology, which is essentially non-credal. He writes, "What follows is my own *personal* perspective. Each person's theology—their system of beliefs—is as unique as a fingerprint."[5] Milton was content to say that some would agree with his theology and others would not, but he was especially careful not to attempt to define the beliefs of others.[6]

It is worth noting however, that the study guide appended to the third edition of *This United Church of Ours*, prepared by Bev Milton and Norma Goughnour, does refer readers to "A New Creed" as the starting point for a discussion of the faith of The United Church. It reads, "What does the United Church believe about Jesus? Look again at the New Creed (VU918) to start this discussion. Read it aloud together."[7] By contrast, the Basis of Union's original "Twenty Articles of Doctrine" is "not a good place to start," writes Milton himself.[8] Although it is only hinted at here, later editions of the book assume that "A New Creed" expresses in a unique and helpful way the faith of The United Church.

4. Catherine Faith MacLean, "The Triune God," in Schweitzer et al., *Theology of United Church*, 36.

5. Milton, *This United Church*, 150 (emphasis in original).

6. It is important to note that although he does not mention "A New Creed," Milton's approach to theology is somewhat similar to that of its authors. To claim that "each person's theology . . . is as unique as a fingerprint" is to fit comfortably in a tradition whose liturgical confession is intended to be "filled with personal content by those who say [it]" (Milton, *This United Church*, 150).

7. Milton, *This United Church*, 214.

8. Milton, *This United Church*, 151.

This Is Your Church (1982, 1986, 1993), by Steven Chambers

This Is Your Church was first published in 1982 by *The United Church Observer* and eventually printed in a third edition. It had similar aims to *This United Church of Ours* but was much more formal and documentary in approach. Author Steven Chambers offers remarkably little of his own opinion throughout, preferring instead simply to present information about the wider life of The United Church where possible and to provide basic explanation where necessary. In his opening chapter on "The Faith," Chambers provides about three pages of introductory explanation before printing, over the next five pages, the doctrinal section of the Basis of Union. He clearly intended the book as something of a reference work.

In this same chapter, Chambers provides an interesting page and a half of written reflection under the heading "Creeds of the Church." Within this section, he gives a brief definition of a creed as well as two very succinct paragraphs on the historical background of the Apostles' and Nicene Creeds. He then goes on to explain in somewhat more detail the existence of "A New Creed" before concluding the section with its entire text. Virtually no explicit analysis of "A New Creed" is offered. However, some of Chambers' own views are evident upon careful reading in the basic choices he made about what material to document as well as in some of the analysis he offers, sometimes implicitly. In keeping with many others in the denomination, he seems to have contended that "A New Creed" alone expresses the contemporary faith of The United Church, whereas other confessions or doctrinal statements do not. "The continued use of these two ancient [Apostles' and Nicene] creeds in the United Church," we read, "is based on the fact that they are used widely in churches around the world." He does not say that these two creeds are used because people in The United Church believe their contents or that they represent the faith of the denomination as a whole. They are used, rather, because they are important to churches around the world. Chambers knew as well as anyone else that the classical creeds were not really used at all in the contemporary United Church. By contrast, "A New Creed" was "written [by and] for the United Church." Its words alone are then included for the benefit of the reader.[9]

Like the ancient creeds, the Basis of Union's "Twenty Articles of Doctrine" are of essentially historical interest in The United Church. They do not express the faith of the church in modern times. They are "really

9. Chambers, *This Is Your Church*, 10–11.

only a snapshot in time: a document which holds the image in place on paper, while movement and action continue in life." The "Twenty Articles of Doctrine," moreover, "are not intended for use in worship, nor for instruction,"[10] and "we should . . . resist the temptation to use them as a rule book."[11] They are not even the work of The United Church, Chambers asserts, but "the attempt of a yet-to-be-born new church" to write theology.[12] The "Twenty Articles of Doctrine" therefore do not express the faith of The United Church, because they were written prior to the consummation of union. Chambers's perspective is consistent with most others in The United Church as they are presented in this chapter: "A New Creed" continues to articulate the faith of the church, while other confessions do not.

Welcome to The United Church of Canada: A Newcomer's Introduction to "A New Creed" (1986), by Patricia Wells

Welcome to The United Church of Canada is a brief commentary and reflection on the text of "A New Creed" that has been published by the denomination and reprinted several times over the years. Although it seems to provide little conspicuous reflection on the place of "A New Creed" within The United Church, this booklet is significant for our topic because of the unquestioned assumption on which its publication rests. Its title reveals much about the author's perspective and that of the denomination that published it. *A Newcomer's Introduction to "A New Creed"* is made synonymous with the purposes of introducing people to The United Church itself and of articulating its collective faith. That The United Church is itself the publisher signals in clear fashion that "A New Creed" expresses and symbolizes the faith of the denomination.

In its content also, *Welcome to The United Church of Canada* makes the assumption that "A New Creed" gives voice to the faith of the denomination. "A New Creed" is a text that helps explain and interpret The United Church, and the life of this particular denomination is the context that gives meaning to the words of its creed. After attempting to paint a brief but representative picture of "the loneliness of modern life," Wells writes, "It is in the knowledge of all this that the church has the audacity

10. Chambers, *This Is Your Church*, 1.

11. Chambers, *This Is Your Church*, 4.

12. Chambers, *This Is Your Church*, 1.

to say . . . ***We are not alone, we live in God's world.***"[13] We cannot fail to notice the reference to the church. Since none of the words of "A New Creed" are the confession of any other denomination or of the universal church, the referent is clearly The United Church of Canada. In other words, this confession is *the* faith of The United Church. "A New Creed" is no longer held to be an alternative creed for use in select liturgical settings but has become the norm.

Because "A New Creed" gives particular expression to the faith of The United Church and is a key symbol for the church, it is much loved. Its words and phrases often generate enthusiasm among the people of The United Church as little else does. The bold and enlarged typeface of the text of "A New Creed" throughout the booklet presents a striking emphasis to the reader. "A New Creed" is shown to represent the faith of the denomination and provides the church with an identity. Wells's enthusiasm for the subject shines through in the punctuation of the text with an exclamation mark. Her booklet concludes, "***We are not alone. Thanks be to God!***"[14] There are no exclamation marks in "A New Creed." What we find here, as we will see later in Styles, is a text that has been revised with added emphasis by an individual author to convey enthusiasm at the unique faith-identity of The United Church it supports.

"United in Faith" (1990), by Sang Chul Lee

In 1990, The United Church Publishing House produced an attractive coffee table book on the history of The United Church entitled *Voices and Visions: Sixty-Five Years of The United Church of Canada*, edited by Peter Gordon White. Among the contributors to that volume was then Moderator Sang Chul Lee, who wrote the concluding reflection "United in Faith." In this essay, Lee describes his spiritual autobiography through the lens of "A New Creed." Various phrases of "A New Creed" provide the rubrics for the different stages of his life's journey. "We are not alone" captures his experience as a young man enduring political and economic oppression in his homeland, where he was introduced to the teachings of Christianity by United Church missionaries.[15] William Scott in

13. P. Wells, *Welcome to United Church*, 2 (emphases in original).

14. P. Wells, *Welcome to United Church*, 11 (emphases in original).

15. A helpful biographical profile of Lee was written by Jung, "Wanderer with Open Mind."

particular, who was willing to join with the Korean people in their suffering due to his faith, left a lasting impression.[16] "To seek justice and resist evil" describes the impact on Lee of Scott's successful effort to convince The United Church to enter into partnership with the new Presbyterian Church of the Republic of Korea—established by theological moderates and liberals who had been pushed out of the existing, more conservative Presbyterian denomination in that country.[17]

In 1961, aged thirty-seven, Lee came to Canada to pursue graduate study at Union College in Vancouver. While there, he fell in love with the vision of Canadian church union that sought to minister to the nation and to do so in an inclusive, ecumenical way. For Lee, this vision is described fittingly as "called to be the church."[18] Lee returned to Canada permanently in 1965, accepting a call to a largely ethnically Japanese congregation in Vancouver.[19] He soon became active in the governance structures of The United Church, setting a course that would lead eventually to his election as moderator. He articulates his desire to do this kind of work as a call "to love and serve others."[20] During the era of his moderatorship, a dominant theme in world events was the collapse of the Soviet Union. For Lee, this opened up new vistas of possible unity among Christians and indeed for all humanity. From his perspective, this is evidence that "God . . . works in us and others."[21] In concluding, Lee demonstrates how thoroughly "A New Creed" had shaped his thinking with phrases like:

- "The United Church's creed expresses our faith clearly and positively. It says we are not alone. We live in God's world."
- "We are living with many different forms of life on earth . . . about all this, the creed says, 'we believe in God who has created and is creating.'"
- "Our creed says clearly that God came to us in Jesus Christ, and demonstrates the power of reconciliation to make all things new."

16. Lee, "United in Faith," 153.

17. Lee, "United in Faith," 154.

18. Lee, "United in Faith," 154–55.

19. His ability to preach and minister effectively in both English and Japanese made him the uniquely suitable candidate (Jung, "Wanderer with Open Mind," 64).

20. Lee, "United in Faith," 158.

21. Lee, "United in Faith," 159.

- "The creed states also that God is working in us and others by the Spirit."
- "The creed says that we are called to be the church, to celebrate God's presence. This is very important."[22]

The full text of "A New Creed" is then included at the close of his reflection.[23]

That this essay is a sincere expression of Moderator Lee's personal faith and spiritual journey, there can be no doubt. Many in The United Church would be in sympathy with his interpretation of the story of their denomination. Significant is Lee's explicit use of the language and thought forms of "A New Creed" to give shape and meaning to his autobiographical reflection. Explicitly and without qualification, he asserts that "A New Creed" summarizes and expresses the faith and story of The United Church of Canada.

A Faith to Live By (1991), by Frederick A. Styles

In his widely read monograph and study guide *A Faith to Live By*, Frederick Styles provides us with a fulsome reflection on "A New Creed." As with many others in The United Church tradition, Styles is very careful to define faith in both personal and open-ended terms. Yet, with this emphasis on the personal nature of theological interpretation, it is all the more striking when he states clearly that The United Church does have a definite faith and that this faith is expressed by "A New Creed. "Especially noteworthy is his use of the definite article in reference to "A New Creed," calling it in his introduction, "the new creed for the United Church."[24]

Styles moves from his introduction to a brief opening chapter that offers a discussion of creeds and their place in the life and liturgy of The United Church. Though he provides a somewhat nuanced argument about the classical creeds that is alternately praising, critical, and dismissive, Styles leaves little doubt that "A New Creed" is the creed for him and his church. We read, "In 1968 the General Council of The United Church

22. Lee, "United in Faith,"159–60.

23. As it stood, prior to the insertion of "to live with respect in creation."

24. Styles, *Faith to Live By*, v.

of Canada accepted a new creed as the official statement of faith for the United Church."[25]

According to Styles, "A New Creed" falls within the confessing tradition of the classical creeds. Creeds are good, he suggests, but new ones are needed from time to time.[26] He argues further that all creeds are heavily contextual, and no one creed can lay claim to representing the faith of the Christian church as a whole. To this extent, Styles seems to argue for the acknowledgment of the past significance of the classical creeds and the present relevance of "A New Creed"—at least within the context of The United Church. He writes, "We need a new creed from time to time, not so much because we have ceased to believe the old ones, but because new questions have become more significant in the life of the Church and in the lives Christians lead from day to day. And it must also be admitted that language and thought forms change, so that what was once of burning importance for Christians begins to seem terribly irrelevant."[27]

Styles asserts that although the catholic tradition of the church is worth claiming as one's own heritage, the content of the classical creeds cannot even be considered as expressing the faith of The United Church today. The creeds are relics. This sentiment comes through particularly clearly when he draws a comparison between the Christological disputes at the council of Nicaea and the medieval debate about "how many angels could dance on the head of a pin." Regarding the Christology of the Nicene Creed, he writes, "All of this may sound terribly unimportant in our day . . . . But lest we think that the early church leaders had all taken leave of their senses, let's pause to take note of what was really being discussed . . . . Seen in that light, their debate was no more frivolous than

25. Styles, *Faith to Live By*, 1. Many appear not to know that "A New Creed" was rejected by the Twenty-Third General Council, and a revised text was later approved by the General Council Executive. Though this is not necessarily germane to the present chapter, Styles is inaccurate in suggesting that the conciliar acceptance of "A New Creed" was analogous to the process by which the classical creeds gained authority in the early church. Rather, to the extent that the classical creeds relied on conciliar approval, in the case of the Nicene Creed—at the Council of Nicaea (325) and the Council of Constantinople (381)—these ecumenical councils simply affirmed the consensus of confessional language that had already arisen widely from the grassroots across the Christian church. The best history of the classical creeds is Kelly, *Early Christian Creeds*.

26. Styles, *Faith to Live By*, 1.

27. Styles, *Faith to Live By*, 4.

the current belief of many people in star signs, and the popularity of such films as *The Exorcist* and *The Amityville Horror*."[28]

For Styles, the classical creeds are antiquated confessions that do not express the serious faith of any right-minded person today. Confession of faith is a good thing, but these particular confessions have long since passed their best-before date. Christian memory and tradition are good things but only if we are not bound by what Christians used to believe. On the other hand, the words of "A New Creed" stirred the author's passion and evoked his zeal. When quoting "A New Creed," he sometimes punctuates the text with exclamation marks in places where there are none: "We are not alone!" and "Thanks be to God!"[29]

"A New Creed" is the doctrinal confession that gave expression to Styles's own faith and, he argues, that of his church. The language of "A New Creed" helped him shape an understanding of the Christian gospel and the mission of the church within his own context. His reflection on dispensing with the faith of the classical creeds and adopting that expressed by "A New Creed" is revealing: "Such a process can be painful, as we leave behind cherished prejudices and biases that have been part of us for many years. But the call of God to us as Christians is to open ourselves to God's presence, to believe that God is alive and well and living among us, ready to lead us into new truth, new levels of understanding, new dimensions of discipleship. Our response is to be open to one another so that we can share one another's vision, to celebrate the presence of God, and to ready ourselves to follow God's leading."[30] Styles clearly contrasts the prejudices and biases that should be left behind with the vision of celebrating God's presence that should be embraced by Christians today. There is little doubt that for him and for his United Church, "A New Creed" is *the* expression of faith.

Mending the World (1997), by the InterChurch and InterFaith Committee of the General Council

Mending the World: An Ecumenical Vision for Healing and Reconciliation is a document that was produced by the InterChurch and InterFaith Committee and was "affirmed" by the Thirty-Sixth General Council in

28. Styles, *Faith to Live By*, 3.
29. Styles, *Faith to Live By*, 1, 5.
30. Styles, *Faith to Live By*, 5.

1997. Stemming from a belief that "the world is at the centre of God's concern," *Mending the World* seeks to (re)define The United Church's mission according to something called "whole world ecumenism." To understand this phrase in the report requires more explanation because ecumenism does not mean in *Mending the World* what it has meant historically in Christian usage. Rather, as there is a stated desire to see the end of "the estrangement of God's children from one another and from the created order," whole world ecumenism describes its purpose as the elimination of anything that might fit under the rubric of alienation. Such a purpose is articulated more precisely by the authors of *Mending the World*: "We are thus led to speak of 'whole world ecumenism,' naming the search for justice for God's creatures and healing for God's creation as the church's first priority, and joining with other persons of good will in the search for justice, wholeness and love."[31] The InterChurch and InterFaith Committee made a number of recommendations to The United Church regarding the implementation of the principles it advocates in *Mending the World*. The General Council itself also made a number of recommendations regarding the report while affirming it in the strongest possible terms. Among the recommendations of the court was that The United Church resolve to "commit itself . . . to use the *Mending the World* report as a lens through which all the work of the General Council is reviewed on an on-going basis."[32]

For our present purposes, the significance of *Mending the World* is its authors' claim that "A New Creed" provided the theological foundation for their report. The opening words of the creed are cited at the very beginning of the section on theological foundations as a means of alluding to the statement in its entirety. "The new creed," we go on to read, "provides us with a beginning." *Mending the World* establishes the admittedly provisional text of "A New Creed" as the starting point for theological reflection in The United Church, because it uniquely expresses the church's faith.

> It ["A New Creed"] reminds us that we are not orphaned, that we are residents of a place created and owned by God, who came in Jesus and who works still, through the Spirit, to bend the broken creation back into the unity and wholeness for which it was made. The creed reminds us that we, the Church, have been called into being to participate in this healing work, 'to celebrate

31. InterChurch and InterFaith Committee, *Mending the World*, 1.

32. InterChurch and InterFaith Committee, *Mending the World*, 20.

> God's presence,' 'to seek justice and resist evil,' and, in its latest version, 'to walk [sic] with respect in creation.' The Church's task is to discern what this means in our time. To this end the Church turns to its formative story for understanding and guidance, as it seeks to be faithful to its past, and responsive to its present.[33]

This demonstrates that "A New Creed" had come to represent "the beginning" for The United Church. In that sense, the text of "A New Creed" was evidently functioning virtually as sacred Scripture for the denomination. The discernment of its meaning is stated as the primary spiritual goal to which the church should strive. In *Mending the World*, in other words, "A New Creed" is not spoken of as a sister-document written similarly by a United Church committee but virtually as a medium of divine revelation, which we are called upon to interpret. In this remarkable document, "A New Creed" is claimed as articulating the formative story for The United Church.

In its more specifically theological arguments also, *Mending the World* relies heavily on the phrases of "A New Creed," as we might expect in a report that sets its text as foundational. A lengthy discussion of the theological significance of Jesus, in which it is claimed that several different interpretations of the figure or character of Jesus are held in tension, concludes this way:

> What is critical for this paper is the observation that ethical implications for mission arise out of each of these constructed portraits, providing priorities for action that direct us toward a whole world ecumenism. These include the living of God-centred rather than self-centred lives, the priority of right action (whether as sign only, or as transformative action), and care for others.
>
> We believe in God . . .
>
> who has come in Jesus, the Word made Flesh,
>
> to reconcile and make new . . .[34]

Although *Mending the World* holds that different interpretations of Jesus and his significance are both necessary and irreducible, one particular interpretation of his meaning and relevance is used to offer a metanarrative

33. InterChurch and InterFaith Committee, *Mending the World*, 8.

34. InterChurch and InterFaith Committee, *Mending the World*, 9.

or overarching story of the faith of The United Church—that expressed in "A New Creed."

Mending the World moves quickly, in its theological section, to a discussion of the importance of ethics. "The Church affirms," we read, "that God is acting to reconcile and make new," reforming creation back to its original design. God, we are told, has an "initiative," and "the Church's responsibility is to align itself with God's initiatives." "The Christian life," we find, "does not restrict itself to ethical concerns and activity only . . . . However, the ethical component in mission looms large in our time."[35] Because of all the things that people are doing wrong, to others and especially to the natural environment, it becomes imperative for the Christian proclamation, according to the authors, to emphasize the doing of things differently and rightly. Since the sphere of human behavior is almost infinitely diverse and complex as well as immeasurable, ethics needs a formative story. Without such a metanarrative, even those most conscious of the importance of ethics would admit that religion can easily turn into an abyss of unending regulations and a legalistic quagmire. It is not surprising then that we would find the ethics-oriented lines of "A New Creed" concluding and summarizing this section of *Mending the World.*

Mending the World is a crucial text for helping us to understand how "A New Creed" has come to function within The United Church of Canada. While most of the literature examined in this chapter has been the work of an individual or individuals—though much of it has been published by The United Church Publishing House—this document represents the work of a denominational committee. Further, *Mending the World* received remarkably strong affirmation from the Thirty-Sixth General Council. This report claims that "A New Creed" provides both the "theological foundation" and the "formative story" for The United Church, while at the same time the General Council expressed a desire to set this report as a critical lens through which all of its activity should be judged.

The Painted Trunk and Other Stories (1999), by Alyson C. Huntly and Yvonne Cathcart

The Painted Trunk is a collection of brief, illustrated children's stories published in 1999 with the ambitious and worthwhile goal of teaching children about the history of The United Church. "A New Creed"

35. InterChurch and InterFaith Committee, *Mending the World*, 14.

is presented in this volume as the expression of the faith of The United Church and also as symbolic of the denomination's unique identity. One of the short stories in *The Painted Trunk* is called "One Big Family." Like each of the book's other stories, "One Big Family" revolves around the interaction of David, Janine, and Gran—two children and their grandmother. During a communion service in Gran's congregation, when David and Janine are visiting one Sunday, the three discuss the different methods of serving communion that are used in The United Church before reflecting on the idea that this variety reflects all kinds of diversity within the denomination.

> "Well, we are one family, whichever way we do it [serve communion]," said David.
>
> "I think so too," said Gran. "United Churches are very different. Throughout the country, people do things in different ways, but we are all part of one church."[36]

At the conclusion of this story is printed the text of "A New Creed."[37] Given that the story does not mention "A New Creed" or really anything about theology and confession, one might naturally wonder why its text has been included at this point. For an answer, we must turn to the back of the book, where we find a set of brief teaching points for each of its short stories. In this section, we find that "A New Creed" is the faith expression and even the symbol of The United Church par excellence. We read:

> When the United Church began, it blended together many different ways of doing things—ways of serving communion, differences in the order of service, different ways of talking about faith . . . or serving in the world. Even today individual congregations are very different from each other. Even within a congregation, differences are a part of who we are . . . but we are all part of one big family we call The United Church of Canada. Our United Church creed is one way of saying that we are one church, united through our faith in Jesus Christ.[38]

By this account, "A New Creed" is thoroughly "our United Church creed." Although it is said to be only one way of saying "we are . . . one big family we call The United Church of Canada," none other is considered. In this

36. Huntly and Cathcart, *Painted Trunk*, 44.
37. Huntly and Cathcart, *Painted Trunk*, 46.
38. Huntly and Cathcart, *Painted Trunk*, 53.

account, "A New Creed" is presented to children and their families as the most fitting tool for promoting denominational unity.

Jesus 24/7: A Short Course in Faith for the Questing Christian (2008), by David Bruce

Jesus 24/7 is a relatively recent introduction, with a study guide, to the Christian faith. It was written by then United Church minister David Bruce—as his doctor of ministry thesis—and published by The United Church Publishing House.[39] The significance of this work for our current discussion is its use of "A New Creed" as the organizing principle for its introduction to the theology of The United Church and therefore its claim that this doctrinal confession best expresses the faith of the denomination. In many ways, Bruce follows the line of argument used by other writers whose work is considered in this chapter: faith is personal and expressed cautiously. As we read, "*Jesus 24/7* reflects my background as a Canadian, as a minister in The United Church of Canada, and as a father of three children . . . . It reflects my personal journey of faith and my personality that have been shaped by being male, middle-aged, and part of the dominant culture in which I grew up. I have tried to be sensitive to other perspectives . . . but I have probably failed plenty along the way."[40] Bruce contends that The United Church of Canada has a faith that is difficult to describe simply.[41] Yet, "A New Creed" is the text that has come to express uniquely the faith of The United Church. We read, "For a long time I have believed that regular folk in The United Church of Canada needed a short course in the basics of the Christian faith, one that was written just for them."[42] Elsewhere we find, "*Jesus 24/7* is written for use in The United Church of Canada . . . . Its 12 sessions follow the beautiful words of the much-loved 'A New Creed.'"[43] Further, for the purposes of worshipping as The United Church and introducing people to their denomination's faith, "A New Creed" is "the gold-standard."[44] "A

39. David Bruce, a classmate of mine in graduate school at the Toronto School of Theology, has since moved to Roman Catholicism. See Bruce, "Swimming the Tiber."

40. Bruce, *Jesus 24/7*, 1.

41. Bruce, *Jesus 24/7*, 1.

42. Bruce, *Jesus 24/7*, 1.

43. Bruce, *Jesus 24/7*, 3.

44. Bruce, *Jesus 24/7*, 1.

New Creed" is "a description . . . of the Christian faith as talked about by people in The United Church of Canada."[45]

In concert with many others who have written about "A New Creed" or faith in The United Church more broadly, Bruce describes the former as an expression of the latter with a deftness and a subtlety that are especially powerful in providing their own kind of clarity. We read, "Nothing in *Jesus 24/7*, beyond the words of 'A New Creed,' should be taken as the 'official' word of the United Church."[46] As with similar claims found in each of the writings we have reviewed in this chapter, Bruce strives to qualify his assertions by acknowledging personal limitations and religious diversity but nonetheless leaves little doubt about what is being claimed: "A New Creed" contains and expresses the faith of The United Church like no other text does or is able to do. Therefore, "A New Creed" functions as a primary symbol of The United Church's faith and identity.

Who's Minding the Story? The United Church of Canada Meets "A Secular Age" (2018), by Jeff Seaton

Who's Minding the Story? is the published doctor of ministry thesis of Jeff Seaton, a United Church minister from British Columbia.[47] This volume offers an interpretation of the thought and praxis of two celebrity members of The United Church clergy—John Pentland and Gretta Vosper—in light of prominent Canadian philosopher Charles Taylor's analysis of secularization in *A Secular Age*. Taylor argues that the secularization of the West, which we have all experienced over the course of our lifetimes, has been largely misinterpreted. In our culture, the standard explanation of secularization has been that as science and technology have enabled rapid growth in human understanding, religion has become less necessary and less possible. However, Taylor suggests that this is an oversimplification and even untrue. Rather, what we have experienced as secularization is "a move from a society where belief in God is unchallenged and indeed, unproblematic, to one in which it is understood to be one option among others, and frequently not the easiest to embrace."[48] For Seaton, the significance of this claim is that The United Church has tended to embrace

45. Bruce, *Jesus 24/7*, 3.

46. Bruce, *Jesus 24/7*, 5.

47. For more information on Jeff Seaton, see https://www.jeffseaton.com/about/.

48. C. Taylor, *A Secular Age*, 2–3.

the less useful analyses of standard secularization theory. Because the cultural challenges to the church have been misunderstood, misdirected strategies to address them have been adopted. Typifying the ill-advised remedies to misdiagnosed ailments within The United Church in recent times have been the approaches of Pentland and Vosper. In one way or another, in response to secularization theory, Pentland and Vosper have echoed the famous dictum of John Shelby Spong, "Christianity must change or die."[49]

Building further on the arguments of *A Secular Age*, Seaton proposes that the church, rather than laying down its tools, adopt its best posture in order to claim a place, in faithful and loving ways, within a society that, properly understood, is both secular and diverse. This he argued can be done best when Christians draw deeply on the classical, biblical Jesus tradition. "I am persuaded," he writes, "that the 1960s marked an ending and a beginning for the United Church of Canada, that the church born in 1925 did not survive the decade, and that a new United Church was brought to birth, one that survives to the current day." "One symbol of the new church," he continues, "is the United Church's New Creed, born in 1968."[50] Seaton does not focus a great deal on "A New Creed," except generally to amplify this interpretation of its role in the life of The United Church. It is not that he is particularly critical of "A New Creed," but rather, he seems to express regret that it has become something of a crutch for the denomination.[51] He proposes instead what he calls a "progressive orthodox" vision for the denomination, one which would maintain much of the liberal openness of The United Church but which would also "seek to push beyond the limitations of reliance upon only one credal statement, the 1968 New Creed, to recover the challenges and adventure of a broader engagement with the doctrines of the universal church."[52]

"A New Creed" is not a main emphasis of *Who's Minding the Story?* Rather, this confession and its use are noted as a representative characteristic of The United Church's response to the tumult of the 1960s and ongoing response to the challenges perceived by the secularization of the denomination's Canadian context. In one sense, it is more properly a secondary source for our analysis of "A New Creed." Its appearance within

49. Spong, *Why Christianity Must Change.*

50. Seaton, *Who's Minding the Story*, 15.

51. Seaton, *Who's Minding the Story*, 87.

52. Seaton, *Who's Minding the Story*, 118.

The United Church tradition, however, and writing by a United Church author allow it to serve also as a primary source in our study. In *Who's Minding the Story?*, Seaton places himself outside the broad consensus of The United Church in his questioning of the denomination's pervasive use of "A New Creed." In his highlighting of this phenomenon, however, he testifies to the reality of the theological dominance of "A New Creed." A difference between Seaton and the other authors whose work is considered in this chapter is that he interprets this reality from a different, somewhat more critical perspective.

The Theology of The United Church of Canada (2019), edited by Don Schweitzer, Robert C. Fennell, and Michael Bourgeois

In 2012, the anthology volume *The United Church of Canada: A History* was published by Wilfrid Laurier University Press. Under the editorship of Don Schweitzer, the book features a series of chronological and thematic essays by some of the denomination's leading thinkers. Somewhat surprisingly, "A New Creed" is mentioned relatively little in its various chapters. Of much more interest is that book's sequel, *The Theology of The United Church of Canada*, edited by Schweitzer along with Robert C. Fennell and Michael Bourgeois. A more substantial publication than its predecessor, this volume features essays on various theological themes as they have been considered in The United Church's tradition. Two main inspirations seem to lie behind *The Theology of The United Church of Canada*. On the one hand, a key stated purpose is to demonstrate that there is a rich tradition of theological discourse within the denomination—partly in response to an oft-heard criticism over the years.[53] A second driver appears to have been the desire to put into historical context the significant decision of the Forty-First General Council in 2012 to designate The United Church's four major statements of faith as "standards subordinate to scripture." While The United Church's consideration of important theological themes like the doctrine of the Trinity, sin, creation, Christology, ecclesiology, and eschatology are examined across its history, special attention is given in each essay to the important place of the newly minted subordinate standards.

Like Seaton's *Who's Minding the Story?*, *The Theology of The United Church of Canada* is mostly helpful as a secondary source for the study

53. Young, "Introduction," 1.

of "A New Creed." In some instances, its authors provide considerable analysis of this text, historically and theologically. However, it is worth considering this volume as a primary source for the study of the place of "A New Creed" in the denomination, at least insofar as it offers the reflections of persons from The United Church tradition on their own personal and corporate theology. A governing theme of the book I would suggest is the argument that The United Church's theology is expansive. By this, I mean that the denomination's theological affirmations have not just evolved but grown in number and broadened. Therefore, The United Church is held up as a community that is much more interested in affirming than in denying. This interpretation is proposed descriptively and also celebrated. In her chapter on the Trinity, MacLean focuses not on where Trinitarian doctrine can go astray but describes a multiplicity of ways that new and different expressions might help to round out our understandings of God.[54] Similarly, Kervin celebrates the historical move, still ongoing in the denomination, from sexist to nonsexist to inclusive to emancipatory theological language. At the pinnacle of our theological expression, he argues, will be the capacity to describe God in terms as broad and diverse as all human experience.[55] Even in the first and last sentences of the book's concluding chapter, penned by its three editors, The United Church's theology is described as "a work in progress." Depicted as emerging from an ongoing dialectic between sources and contexts, the denomination's theological output is commended for both its quality and its quantity.[56]

Following from this central theme of the book, we can well anticipate how its various authors will assess "A New Creed." Indeed, this briefest of The United Church's faith statements is celebrated, here as elsewhere, for its openness to different and innovative interpretations. It is noted approvingly that the words of "A New Creed" themselves have been allowed to change and grow—and may yet continue to do so into the future.[57] "A New Creed" is said not to be definitive in meaning but "allusive."[58] It

54. Catherine Faith MacLean, "The Triune God," in Schweitzer et al., *Theology of United Church*, 21–49.

55. Kervin, "Sacraments and Sacramentality," 236–39.

56. Schweitzer et al., "Conclusion: . . . a Work in Progress," in Schweitzer et al., *Theology of United Church*, 333–43.

57. Young, "Introduction," 15.

58. Robert C. Fennell, "Scripture and Revelation in the United Church of Canada," in Schweitzer et al., *Theology of United Church*, 58.

"affirms that God works in a variety of ways, perhaps even through other faiths."[59] With "A New Creed," "The doors of acceptance were swung wide open."[60] For Schweitzer, "A New Creed was intentionally drafted so that people across a broad range of theological perspectives could profess it with integrity."[61] It makes room for positions ranging from classical, Christological orthodoxy to the famous, provocative statements of Bill Phipps during his moderatorship in 1997. In these and similar statements, the authors of *The Theology of The United Church of Canada* show that "A New Creed" is the denomination's statement of faith par excellence, not so much for the theological clarity of its individual words and phrases but for what together they symbolize.

Conclusion

In her superb history of The United Church, Airhart refers to "thousands of United Church congregations" that believe "themselves 'called to be the Church,' as the New Creed put it 'to celebrate God's presence.'" "A New Creed" and the cultural upheaval of the era it was written to address have "forced (or freed)" The United Church, she writes further, to reconsider its faith.[62] Beardsall adds elsewhere that "A New Creed" "remains . . . beloved and well-used."[63] Indeed, over the five decades or so of its existence, "A New Creed" has risen from being originally conceived as "a possible alternative to the Apostles' Creed" to becoming the normative statement of The United Church's theology. From this brief but representative study of the nonliturgical literature of The United Church tradition since the 1970s, a clear consensus has emerged. While generally qualified with admissions of personal subjectivity and acknowledgments of the denomination's theological diversity, "A New Creed" has been consistently asserted to be the one confession that above all enables the people of The United Church to express their faith together.

59. Hyuk Cho, "Practising God's Mission Beyond Canada," in Schweitzer et al., *Theology of United Church*, 261.

60. Adrian Jacobs, "The Holy Spirit," in Schweitzer et al., *Theology of United Church*, 168.

61. Schweitzer, "Christology of United Church," 137.

62. Airhart, *Church with Soul*, 299.

63. Beardsall, "And Whether Pigs Have Wings," 113.

Considering the frequent acknowledgments of theological diversity in The United Church's theological tradition, however, views that are more critical of "A New Creed" are conspicuous by their relative rarity. Seaton's moderately critical interpretation, directed not so much at the text itself but at its surprising pride of place, is evidently an unpopular one. Acknowledgments of theological diversity, which have appeared often in the denomination's nonliturgical literature, do not qualify the utility of "A New Creed" as a statement of faith. Rather, such recognitions bolster its status. Precisely because its language is ambiguous, and deliberately so, this text has been celebrated for preserving a common identity that might otherwise be extraordinarily difficult to sustain across an institution as diverse as The United Church of Canada. "A New Creed" has come to be heralded because it is seen to be an especially successful attempt to manage the breakdown in theological consensus that, since the mid-1960s, has clearly been a defining feature of the denomination's existence.

5

A Close Reading of "A New Creed"

Introduction

Much of the discussion of "A New Creed" in The United Church has addressed the same issues considered so far in this study: where its text came from and what its place in The United Church is. In other words, "A New Creed" has rightly been viewed within the big picture of The United Church of Canada's story. While there has been much quoting of, allusion to, and celebration of its individual words and phrases, there has been relatively little theological reflection on the contents or message of "A New Creed." In historical context, this is a bit surprising. *This Is Our Faith* (1943), by John Dow, provides a significant exegesis of "A Statement of Faith" (1940). R. C. Chalmers's *See the Christ Stand* (1945), a revision of the author's doctoral dissertation at Emmanuel College, offers a study of The United Church's theology, particularly in respect to what we now call the "Twenty Articles of Doctrine" (1925). The former volume especially was a commercial success. The relative lack of detailed analyses of the text of "A New Creed" over the last fifty years is also surprising, in that theological discussion and debate were central to the work of the Committee on Christian Faith in writing it. It is the purpose of this chapter to engage in a close reading and critical, theological assessment of "A New Creed." So far we have been looking at the forest; now it is time to examine the trees.

The present discussion will offer a perspective that is intentionally literary and theological, as well as historical, in approach. For the conviction that these three disciplines belong together for the study of a sacred text, which "A New Creed" undoubtedly is in The United Church, I draw upon the methodology articulated by N. T. Wright in *The New Testament and the People of God.*[1] In a sympathetic summary of Wright's lengthy discussion of method, I assert that these three considerations—literary, theological, and historical—need to be held in appropriate tension in order to craft the most fruitful analysis. In the study of a religious document, they are a bit like the legs of a tripod: with even one of them missing, our interpretations and understandings are not likely to be grounded as firmly as they ought.

In the first section, we will look at the body of the text. Contrary to common assumption, we will see that the words of "A New Creed" do not articulate, or perhaps even allow, if the point were pressed further, a classical vision of the Christian faith. In other words, "A New Creed" is not an updated rendering of the theology of the classical creeds or "a creative liberal restatement of the faith for contemporary purposes."[2] "A New Creed" was not written to express any corporate theology. Rather, it serves primarily to facilitate subjective, personalized religious expression. I would argue that this approach to language undermines corporate confession and community—two features essential to the founding of the Christian movement. Had they even considered the possibility of such an approach, I suggest the Christians of earlier centuries would have thought it left the subject of theology devoid of meaning. In section 2, we will look specifically at the title "A New Creed" to see what it conveys, what its significance is, and whether it is a descriptively helpful or appropriate moniker for this text. I will show that while a case can be made for its assumed label, this seemingly accidental title is actually somewhat misleading.

Commentary

Introduction

I have argued that, contrary to popular assumption, "A New Creed" does not articulate a particular theological vision. Rather, its purpose is

1. N. T. Wright, *New Testament*, 14.
2. Kervin, "Sacraments and Sacramentality," 244.

to enable a certain kind of approach to theological confession. "A New Creed" seeks to allow individuals to mean almost anything they want in their own minds as they utter its words with their lips. Seen in that light, its function has been to manage the breakdown of consensus in The United Church as a distinctly Christian community of faith. Few seem to acknowledge this explicitly, but it is implicit in many of the ways "A New Creed" is discussed. I suspect its usefulness in this politically oriented role may lie behind much of its institutional prestige within The United Church, if at times subconsciously so. Precisely because it is felt to hold together a consensus of sorts amidst an irreducibly diverse denomination, it is held up and celebrated by many in positions of leadership. Through a broadly historical approach, this has been demonstrated clearly to be the intent of its authors—the Committee on Christian Faith—which could reach no theological consensus in the process of attempting to write a modern creed for The United Church. In the pages that follow, we will engage in a close reading of "A New Creed" and comment on it briefly, line by line and word by word. In so doing, it will become especially clear that, from a slightly different angle, "A New Creed" deals not in particulars and concretes but in generalities and abstractions. As such, though its legacy has benefited from a kind of political utility, we can unfortunately conclude that this text invites confusion and disagreement, passing on to present and future generations the theological and sociocultural difficulties and conflicts of the turbulent age in which it was written.

Before going on, it is important to note that my intent is not to label "A New Creed" as being too liberal (or too conservative).[3] No doubt there was something of a liberal impetus for attempting to write a creed for The United Church that would serve to replace the classical creeds in sacramental contexts. While "A New Creed" appears to be more accommodating to theological liberalism than the classical creeds are, and while many theological liberals do indeed cherish this text for that reason, we should resist the temptation to so categorize it. It is also possible, at a reach, to argue that this is an orthodox creed.[4] While it is clearly not a catholic

3. No doubt the "too liberal" label is the criticism most often uttered, though quietly and by the very few, among Evangelicals in The United Church. See Zachar, "Renewal/Reform Groups," a term paper completed at Ontario Theological Seminary (now Tyndale Seminary) in 1997.

4. I anticipate this response to the argument of this book. Indeed, this seems to be a common theme of the various writers in *The Theology of The United Church of Canada*. However, if classical Christianity were consistent with such an existentialist or individualistic approach as embodied in "A New Creed," any of its representative

expression of the faith, that does not therefore make it automatically a liberal statement. It was designed to be neither liberal nor conservative but somehow also both. (Keep in mind: its writers were highly intelligent individuals who painstakingly considered every word of "A New Creed" and knew exactly what they were doing.) In stating it this way, I acknowledge the contrary argument that is often implied, which holds that this feature is precisely the genius of "A New Creed." In a sense, it is. However, I view it a problem that this text communicates in a deliberately unclear way and celebrates the individual conscience at the expense of seeking to foster community and understanding. Kervin was on to something in his proposal that the text's "vocabulary and syntax [have] become . . . cultural-linguistic touchstones of ecclesial identity."[5] However, it is inherent to this text that it does so precisely in ambiguous ways that hollow out the foundations of that very identity. It does this not just in keeping with the Congregationalist strain of The United Church of Canada's heritage but in a markedly more hyper-individualistic way that actually hinders the development and strengthening of community.

Structure

It is important to say something about the literary structure of "A New Creed." As with any other text, it has a structure—explicitly and implicitly. The structure of "A New Creed" seems somewhat unique. It does not conform to a predetermined pattern, including the Trinitarian, three-stanza structure of the classical creeds—to which it was said to be analogous. We do not have a label—comparable to other forms of literature identified largely by their structure like novel, sonnet, or haiku, or even creed—that is clearly appropriate to it. As we saw in the historical account of its writing, the final version of the text evolved slowly from a prototype drafted by Mac Freeman, which had a very loose, basically point-form outline. Structure does not seem to have been a generating influence in the production of "A New Creed." That is, it was not inspired by or crafted to fit an existing form—despite the committee's stated desire to produce a text that would be "concise" and "formal." However, we need to be open to the possible ways that structure influences our understanding of the text.

---

articulations would seem subject to such a vast array of interpretations that it would be impossible to know of what the belief system fundamentally consists.

5. Kervin, "Sacraments and Sacramentality," 244.

My humble contention is that the best literary framework for understanding "A New Creed" is that of poetry. Obviously, that is a hugely generalized statement. Poetry is an inherently broad category. But it is probably a good starting point to say that "A New Creed" is much more suitably described as poetry than as prose. Like most poetry, "A New Creed" is brief, and there is an "intense unity" about its various phrases, which stems from a plot-like internal logic. It also relies heavily on rhythm both to communicate and to please.[6] While there is not a strict rhythmic pattern to "A New Creed," we notice how it varies short, sharp-sounding phrases of four or five syllables with longer and more flowing lines of seven or more syllables. Within these longer lines, it is not just that there are more syllables in total but that longer, multisyllabic words are employed. The effect of the short and sharp phrases, which are inserted at key intervals in the text, is especially striking and gives us important clues about what is being emphasized in the text: we are not alone, we live in God's world, we believe in God, we trust in God, we are called to be the church, God is with us, we are not alone, and thanks be to God. These stand out as having an almost staccato-like feel. By contrast, the longer phrases are somewhat more descriptive. They are meant to qualify the force and message of the shorter statements and are grouped together within the two main stanzas of the creed. The combination of these two, complementary phrasing techniques is what, I suggest, gives "A New Creed" its appealing poetic ring.

In what sense might we be able to pin down the literary structure of "A New Creed" any further? Since it was written to fit no preexisting or really any particular pattern, we can return here briefly to some historical aspects of its composition to grasp something of its implicit structure. The Committee on Christian Faith, following Mac Freeman's prototype, had two ultimately constructive objectives for its creed: to speak to an existential experience of their contemporaries in general and to speak to the existential condition of loneliness in particular. We can see how the shorter, sharper phrases are used at the beginning, middle, and end of the creed to emphasize just these notions. R. C. Chalmers criticized precisely some of these phrases for being redundant. However, that seems actually to have been their point, whether the authors of "A New Creed" intended it explicitly or not. In the bulk of the two main stanzas, which feature the longer and more flowingly descriptive phrases, we see two

6. W. Harmon and Holman, *Handbook to Literature*, 398–99.

other desires of the committee played out. First, there was a clear desire to de-emphasize the literal expression and significance of the biblical story of salvation as classically understood. Whereas the Apostles' and Nicene Creeds have entire stanzas that name and summarize the identity and work of each of the Father, the Son, and the Holy Spirit, "A New Creed" offers only three phrases in its attempt to cover its Trinitarian bases. We see this in the first major stanza, beginning "We believe in God." Second, the committee wanted to emphasize the ethical, practical, and experiential aspects of Christian living. Over and against the classical creeds, which are more implicit in this area, we see this clear emphasis of "A New Creed" reflected in the stanza that begins "We are called to be the Church." In taking the briefer and more forceful phrases as our cue, further, we can find a more sophisticated sense of structure in the form of a chiasmus—from the Greek letter *chi*, meaning *x*-shaped. Now, the reality and significance of chiasmus is controversial. Some look for and find it almost everywhere, while others are more suspicious and believe it usually to be read in to a text. The value in chiasmus is in demonstrating the relationship between the beginning (introduction), middle (climax), and ending (conclusion) portions within a given text. That being the case, it is not surprising that any piece of literature might begin in a certain way—say, by suggesting a problem to be resolved—move to a climax, and then conclude in a manner that moves back to reflect on the initial problem—either in success or failure.[7] Taking the shorter phrases as our cues, we might plot "A New Creed" chiastically:

7. For a helpful discussion of chiasmus, see W. Harmon and Holman, *Handbook to Literature*, 90–91, and Gorman, *Elements of Biblical Exegesis*, 82–84.

A We are not alone,
A1 we live in God's world.

B We believe in God:
B1 who has created and is creating,
B2 who has come in Jesus, the Word made flesh, to reconcile and make new,
B3 who works in us and others by the Spirit.

C We trust in God.

D We are called to be the Church:
D1 to celebrate God's presence,
D2 to live with respect in Creation,
D3 to love and serve others,
D4 to seek justice and resist evil,
D5 to proclaim Jesus, crucified and risen, our judge and our hope.

A2 In life, in death, in life beyond death, God is with us.

A We are not alone.
E Thanks be to God.

Notwithstanding the final "Thanks be to God"—which, as we will see below, some committee members wanted to leave out for precisely the kinds of structural reasons I am suggesting—we find that both the beginning and the end of "A New Creed" introduce the key thesis of the text: we are not alone. The committee felt strongly that this was an existential condition that they wanted to address. In the middle, at the crux of "A New Creed," we find a corresponding existential emphasis on the key faith decision, or response, of the Christian: to trust in God. Fitting within this general framework, we find descriptions of the *relatively* less important details of particular beliefs and actions suggested.

Line by Line Commentary

For the purposes of a close reading, I have assigned line numbers to the phrases of "A New Creed." To my knowledge, this text has not been published with line numbers previously. However, in its deliberations, the Committee on Christian Faith did use such a system internally.[8] While

8. Evans, "Possible Revision of Creed."

the creed has been modified grammatically to make its language inclusive in 1979–1980, and then another line was added in 1995, this scheme corresponds closely to that used originally by the committee:

(1) We are not alone, we live in God's world.
(2) We believe in God:
(3) who has created and is creating,
(4) who has come in Jesus, the Word made flesh, to reconcile and make new,
(5) who works in us and others by the Spirit.
(6) We trust in God.
(7) We are called to be the Church:
(8) to celebrate God's presence,
(9) to live with respect in Creation,
(10) to love and serve others,
(11) to seek justice and resist evil,
(12) to proclaim Jesus, crucified and risen, our judge and our hope.
(13) In life, in death, in life beyond death, God is with us.
(14) We are not alone.
(15) Thanks be to God.

This is obviously not quite how "A New Creed" is laid out on paper today. In *Voices United* and elsewhere, the lines frequently run over. For example, line 4 appears as "who has come in Jesus, / the Word made flesh, / to reconcile and make new." In other words, the text runs more vertically on the page.[9] Interestingly, the lines were originally not quite as divided when they were published in the *Service Book*. There, for example, line 5 reads "who works in us and others by his Spirit" rather than "who works in us and others / by the Spirit," as it does now.[10] The *Service Book* was a fairly small volume, and when one looks at "A New Creed" in it, one gets the sense that those lines that ran over did so in large measure due to the sheer narrowness of the page. The width of the text in relation to the page in *Voices United* looks a little less attractive to my eye. In seeking to understand the meaning of the words and phrases in "A New Creed," it makes sense to consider entire phrases as the Committee on Christian Faith originally conceived and numbered them, rather than the individual clauses that have been given their own lines since the publication of *Voices United*.

9. *Voices United: Hymn and Worship Book*, 918.

10. *Service Book for Use of People*, 310.

(1) We are not alone, / we live in God's world.

This opening phrase, with its emphasis on addressing the human condition—according to one interpretation—is the most distinctive part of "A New Creed," at least in comparison with the emphases and language of the classical creeds. It read originally, "Man is not alone, he lives in God's world." As we saw earlier, this unique opening was featured in a prototype drafted by Mac Freeman in late 1967. In subsequent years, Freeman remembered having found his inspiration for this first phrase and overall theme in an article by John C. Bennett, although at least one other committee member later recalled hearing a clear echo of Abraham Joshua Heschel's famous book *Man Is Not Alone* (1951). Freeman felt at the time that there was an urgency to speak to the "loneliness of modern man." He later remembered, quite rightly it seems, that his initial draft "caused a creative explosion within the group."[11] The committee affirms Freeman's instincts and also declares its sense of the importance of beginning the creed without the traditional "I believe" or "We believe." They write, "The preliminary stress on man's state should not be mistaken as a displacement of God from the centre of this expression of faith. The creed was so designed by the Committee to make contact with contemporary persons beset by questions about man, lostness and loneliness on the one hand and man's self-sufficiency in world affairs on the other. The opening statement speaks to both these questions in one clear affirmation."[12] As we read in the final "Report on Creeds" to the General Council Executive, "There was general agreement within the committee that the creed should start with man."[13]

This first line of "A New Creed" is well liked by many. It represents for them a break with the Christian credal tradition that has ceased to satisfy and a unique identity marker for The United Church. However, not all have thought this a good or appropriate way to begin a creed. Some prominent figures in the denomination rose to speak against the proposed confession at the Twenty-Third General Council, in Kingston, leveling at it the criticism that it did not begin with "I believe" or "We believe." The United Church historian Clifford articulates this view when he writes:

11. Telephone interview with Mac Freeman, 7 Dec. 2009.

12. Standing Committee on Christian Faith, *Creeds*, 17.

13. Standing Committee on Christian Faith, "Report on Creeds."

> The most distinctive feature of the 1968 Creed was its beginning. It began with the human condition rather than God and thereby abandoned the starting-point of the ancient creeds and the majority of the Reformed confessions. The committee was aware that this was unusual and they justified it by pointing out that . . . it was designed . . . "to make contact with contemporary persons beset by questions about man . . ." Some fifteen years later, however, the committee's justification of this departure from its own tradition and that of ecumenical Christendom, fails to be entirely convincing and it is difficult to avoid the conclusion that it marks the New Creed as a product of the "culture of narcissism" which characterized many aspects of North American life in the late sixties and early seventies.[14]

The question of whether any creed, or at least a good creed, ought to begin with "I believe" or "We believe," or in any particular way at all, is an interesting one and will be considered in section 2 of this chapter.

For now, we simply acknowledge that this is how "A New Creed" does begin and examine what its opening words mean in context. The obvious place to begin is with the published interpretations of this phrase that have been offered within The United Church tradition. Moderator Lee put it this way: "The United Church's creed expresses our faith clearly and positively. It says we are not alone. We live in God's world. That sounds to me as if we are not alone because God is with us always."[15] Other commentators, such as Patricia Wells and David Bruce, have in similar ways seen in the phrase an apologetic against atheism. Bruce, in particular, considers that "We are not alone, we live in God's world" could be an appropriate expression of philosophical, moral, or experiential explanations for God's existence.[16] For Robert C. Fennell, the God of "A New Creed" is the God of classical Christianity.[17] Similarly, Catherine Faith MacLean states that this God is unmistakeably the Triune God.[18] By contrast, Harold Wells emphasizes the distinction between what he sees as the vision of "A New Creed" and what he calls "classical theism." Whereas the historic classical theism portrays an invulnerable God, he

14. Clifford, "United Church of Canada," 18.

15. Lee, "United in Faith,"159.

16. P. Wells, *Welcome to United Church*, 2–3, and Bruce, *Jesus 24/7*, 7–12.

17. Robert C. Fennell, "Scripture and Revelation in The United Church of Canada," in Schweitzer et al., *Theology of United Church*, 57–58.

18. Catherine Faith MacLean, "The Triune God," in Schweitzer et al., *Theology of United Church*, 33.

argues, the God of "A New Creed" is with us by coming alongside.[19] For virtually all contemporary United Church commentators, the use of inclusive language in the current edition of "A New Creed" is appreciated. Members of the Committee on Christian Faith, as noted above, wanted to open with such a phrase in order to "make contact" with their contemporaries. In that sense, we can perhaps summarize the intended function of this opening line as attempting to address the potential concerns both of atheists and those who conceived of God as impossibly distant.

As Clifford acknowledges, the opening line of "A New Creed" represents a notable departure from the ecumenical creeds and the majority of doctrinal confessions of the wider Protestant tradition. In this sense, it is a very different *kind* of faith that has been professed by the people of The United Church in recent decades. In its purposefully plural and expansive language of suggestion, "A New Creed" has invited ambiguities. Although framed with a clear purpose by the Committee on Christian Faith—"to make contact with contemporary persons beset by questions about man"—uncertainty around its meaning has characterized this well-known phrase, as it is really left up to each individual reciting it to decide upon his or her own personal and private interpretation. To my way of reading, it seems on one level to be saying that we are not alone *because* we live in God's world. In other words, it is distinctly God's presence that prevents us from needing to feel lonely. Yet grammatically, this is not a necessary inference. "We are not alone" and "we live in God's world" can be taken as two thoughts not necessarily dependent on each other. Quoted above, Lee demonstrates as much when he goes on to write in his interpretation of the opening words of "A New Creed," "And people are with us always, because God's world is the world full of the people. We are living with many different forms of life on earth, creatures of land and water, living plants and living air. We are living in a world of diversity but this diversity is a blessing and comfort for us."[20] Similarly, HyeRan Kim-Cragg writes, "Humans desire relationships because God made us this way. This truth is most strongly captured in the first words of A New Creed: 'We are not alone.'"[21] In her learned analysis, Airhart argues that this phrase of "A New Creed" has "resonated with and beyond the spirit of the times with its opening words that captured a longing for fellowship

19. H. Wells, "Good Creation," 77–95.

20. Lee, "United in Faith," 159.

21. HyeRan Kim-Cragg, "What Are People For? In Christian Life, Discipleship, and Ministry," in Schweitzer et al., *Theology of United Church*, 204.

in defiance of existential loneliness."[22] Why does "A New Creed" not have in its opening line the word "because"? While God's presence may be our implied comfort, there could be other possibilities. Between the clauses of this opening line there may be correlation but not necessarily causation.

(2)–(3) We believe in God: / who has created and is creating,

Mac Freeman's prototype of October 1967 contained the seminal version of the phrase: "God has created and is creating us." For several successive revisions, the direct object of God's past perfect and present tense acts of creating was always "us." Only very late in the committee's work was "us" removed as the direct object of God's creating activity and the phrase made indeterminate. Having grown up in The United Church, I had always thought this phrase was crafted to accommodate such popular scientific ideas as Darwin's theory of evolution and the evidence for our expanding universe. I was fascinated to discover in the archival records of the Committee on Christian Faith that the early drafts of the creed were not intended to address these issues at all but were meant rather to continue the emphasis of the opening line on the human condition: "We believe in God: who has created and is creating *us*." Since the approved text has evolved to become less explicitly existential in purpose and orientation, the question is worth asking, how are the words "has created and is creating" functioning in "A New Creed," and what sorts of things have people taken them to mean?

By the conclusion of its task, the Committee on Christian Faith intended primarily with this line to make mention of God's creating activity as a reference to the work of the first person of the Trinity. Along with the next two lines, which refer to God's coming in Jesus and God's work "by the Spirit," it was to suggest the confession of belief in the Triune God. In *Creeds*, the committee says that this stanza was "a witness to the Trinitarian God."[23] This is echoed in the assessment of MacLean.[24] In their final report to the General Council Executive, the committee writes that, "The Trinitarian structure of the creed is brought out by the roughly-equal lines

22. Airhart, *Church with Soul*, 274.

23. Standing Committee on Christian Faith, *Creeds*, 17.

24. Catherine Faith MacLean, "The Triune God," in Schweitzer et al., *Theology of United Church*, 33.

(3), (4) and (5)."[25] As such, "We believe in God: who has created and is creating" is intended as a liberal or perhaps nonsexist restatement of the Apostles' Creed's "I believe in God . . . *maker of Heaven and Earth*." Most later commentators so interpret the words "has created."

"And is creating," on the other hand, remains more of a theological puzzle. Typically, those commenting on "A New Creed" take "is creating" in a different way, that is as having nothing to do with the verb "to create" at all. Crossley writes, "The United Church believes not only that God is creator but that He is still creating. We mean by this that God created the world and retains His interest in it. He continues to care and communicate with His creation."[26] Patricia Wells writes similarly, "It is this God who, by the processes of birth, growth, healing, by the life-giving energy which flows in all things, continues to sustain the universe through every moment of its existence. It is that God who by the designs of evolution, the events of history, the promptings of each individual soul *continues* to mould, shape, and form this creation."[27] Harold Wells also sees in this statement a sense of the ongoing interconnectedness of God with creation, in contrast to classical theism, which has helped The United Church move toward an ecotheology.[28]

There are two key things to note about this phrase. First, the Committee on Christian Faith wished to emphasize the placement of these words within a threefold structure, and so to align their confession with classical Trinitarian Christianity, at least in some sense. Second, the "is creating" clause, a holdover from an earlier and more explicitly existentialist draft of the creed, has sometimes been interpreted in The United Church as meaning something semantically different from "has created." Both elements signal challenges for the meaning of "A New Creed." For one thing, this phrase is not properly Trinitarian. In fact, the inherent modalism of its language has been acknowledged by even some of its sympathetic readers.[29] If a mere restatement of classical Trinitarianism was the goal, this is a problem. "A New Creed" does not refer to three persons, with names appropriate to personhood, but to three functions.

25. Standing Committee on Christian Faith, "Report on Creeds."

26. Crossley, *This You Can Believe*, I.ii.

27. P. Wells, *Welcome to United Church*, 3 (emphasis in original).

28. H. Wells, "Good Creation."

29. See Catherine Faith MacLean, "The Triune God," 33, and Kervin, "Sacrament and Sacramentality in the United Church of Canada," 234–39, both in Schweitzer et al., *Theology of United Church*.

One former committee member described this section of "A New Creed" as "Trinitarian, but not in-your-face-Trinitarian."[30] The doctrine of the Trinity holds however, that God is *both* one *and* three, in being and identity, for all eternity. While impossible to comprehend, the Trinity is very simple to state. The doctrine of the Trinity, at least in my view, is also not especially open to expansive readings. It both affirms and denies. As such, it is not sufficient to list three functions of God. Due to the nature of the proposition, a theological statement is either Trinitarian or it is not. As has long been realized, attempts to explain away the tensions involved actually dissolve the concept. As such, this portion of "A New Creed" describes a theological vision that is subtly but significantly at odds with the faith it has been claimed to restate.

Another conceptual difficulty is raised by the language "is creating." In what sense is God's ongoing activity analogous to the once-and-for-all work of creation? While some have seen this simply as an accommodation to theories of evolution and of an ever-expanding universe, which may have begun with a big bang, others have argued that "is creating" does not mean "is creating" but something like "is at work" or "is still present with." To say one thing, such as "is creating," while suggesting another is a questionable use of confessional language. This would be a metaphorical strategy, but it does not appear that metaphor is what the authors were going for.[31] It could also be argued that the analogy between the act of creation and God's ongoing involvement with creation serves as much to de-emphasize God's stunning creativity *ex nihilo* (from nothing) as it does to inspire awe and wonder. Committee member W. O. Fennell later admitted to being "somewhat regretful" of this phrase as it exists in "A New Creed." He thought it would have been better and more consistent with popular belief to say "God is sustaining" or "God is upholding" creation.[32] I contend that Fennell was correct in his assessment. "A New Creed" would be a much clearer and more catholic statement of faith if it featured one of his retrospective suggestions.[33]

30. Telephone interview with Gordon Nodwell, 15 Dec. 2009.

31. Perhaps the best definition of metaphor has been provided by Janet Martin Soskice, a "figure of speech whereby we speak about one thing in terms which are seen to be suggestive of another" (Soskice, *Metaphor and Religious Language*, 15).

32. Telephone interview with W. O. Fennell, 7 Dec. 2009.

33. Another possibility would have been to express the New Testament's theme of new creation, as in "If anyone is in Christ—new creation!" (2 Cor 5: 17, author's translation).

(4) who has come in Jesus, / the Word made flesh, / to reconcile and make new,

With this phrase, we move to the second line of the stanza that is intended to suggest belief in the Triune God. The reference here to Jesus is intended to convey the sense of what classical Christian theology has known as the second person of the Trinity—the Son—who became incarnate in Jesus of Nazareth. Of this we find in the Apostles' Creed, "I believe . . . in Jesus Christ, his only Son, our Lord." This Jesus is the primary figure of the New Testament, the central character of the four New Testament Gospels, and the one around whom, and in light of whom, the Christian church took shape. The teaching and preaching of the church about his life, ministry, death, and resurrection—no matter how widely interpretations of these events have differed nor how hotly contentious such interpretations have been—have formed the foundation for an ongoing Christian community in the last two millennia. It is obvious that any Christian doctrinal confession has to say something about Jesus, and "A New Creed" does.

One of the interesting things about the reference to Jesus in this particular phrase is that it is so significantly different from what was originally written by the Committee on Christian Faith in the late 1960s. Originally, the approved text read, "who has come in the true Man, Jesus, to reconcile and make new." An interesting aspect of the crafting of this original phrase was the heated debate among committee members over whether the words "true" or "man" should be capitalized. Despite the intensity with which certain members held views on that issue, the phrase was to be torn down and rebuilt just a few years later, in a move to introduce inclusive language. Clifford expresses surprise that the initial text was not more forward-looking in this regard. He writes, "The New Creed . . . did not reflect, in spite of the fact that for the first time the drafting committee included two women, the concerns of the new feminist movement which was just beginning to make the presence of women felt within the churches."[34] Yet, when it did come time to review the language of "A New Creed" in the late 1970s for the purposes of making it "inclusive in its language," this phrase was rather fundamentally rewritten. Indeed, Schweitzer goes so far as to argue, "The Christology of A New Creed changed when it was revised in 1979–80."[35]

34. Clifford, "United Church of Canada," 18.

35. Schweitzer, "Christology of United Church," 137.

As with others in this text, the language of this phrase may allude to traditional Christian belief, but it also invites private confession among individuals who understand, by the same words, radically different ideas. As with the preceding line, we find an emphasis on a second work of God, rather than on the personhood of the Son. It is simply "God . . . who has come in Jesus." The identity of Jesus is then explained further and amplified in a second portion of the phrase. Jesus is "the Word made flesh" (previously "the true Man"). According to its writers, the original phrasing was first employed to strike a chord similar to "Luther's 'proper man' or the modern expression 'the man for others.'"[36] The modified text, approved by the General Council Executive in 1980, draws on John's Gospel in describing Jesus as "the Word made flesh." The Gospel of John's prologue famously describes Jesus as *lógos* in Greek. In English Bibles, this *lógos* has typically been translated as Word with a capital *w*.[37] The most obvious foundation for the particular wording in this line of "A New Creed" is John 1:14, "And the Word became flesh and dwelt among us." In this sense, "Word" draws on the context created by the opening verses of the chapter, "In the beginning was the Word, and the Word was with God, and God was the Word. This one was in the beginning with God."

There is clearly the hint of a high, orthodox Christology in this line of "A New Creed." Ironically, the more recent edition of this line is more traditional than its earlier rendering "the true Man." That said, a striking aspect of both phrases in the context of this confession is their popular obscurity. Having served in The United Church's ministry for fifteen years, in a variety of congregational settings, I suspect a high proportion of United Church members would not know where this notion of the Word comes from—the *lógos* incarnate of John's Gospel—and would have little idea what it means theologically. There are many others who are theologically educated enough to know about the *lógos* of the fourth Gospel who yet interpret this phrase in surprising ways. Patricia Wells writes, "Jesus is God's *Word*, God's *speaking* to us." This is a helpful theological statement. Yet, while affirming with the classical Christian tradition that Jesus was "fully human, one of us," the most she says of his relationship to divinity is that "Jesus was uniquely filled with God's Spirit."[38] Thus, we can see how easy and comfortable it is for many in The United Church

36. Standing Committee on Christian Faith, *Creeds*, 17.

37. For further discussion of this point, see Bromiley, *Theological Dictionary*, 513–14.

38. P. Wells, *Welcome to United Church*, 3 (emphasis in original).

to interpret this phrase in a more liberal way. Tellingly, Schweitzer asserts that the famously controversial 1997 remarks of then Moderator Bill Phipps "were in keeping with A New Creed."[39] It is apparently easier for theological liberals to describe Jesus-as-Word as simply "God's speaking to us" than to swallow the two-natures conception of Chalcedonian Christology. As Peter Wyatt notes in an essay on inclusive language and baptismal formulae, theological liberalism is more comfortable talking about "the Economic Trinity"—God's relationship to the world—than it is "the Immanent Trinity"—God's eternal, internal relationships.[40] This phrase of "A New Creed," then, functions subtly and cleverly. While hinting at something like orthodox belief, its language also serves to obscure, in order to allow alternative interpretations. Indeed, we will see in our discussion of line 6 below that precisely in its existentialist orientation, "A New Creed" is not interested in the transcendent reality of God but God only insofar as God encounters us. It is not a coincidence that Schweitzer is able to observe, "New here was a lack of insistence on Jesus as the sole source of salvation."[41]

Before moving on, it is important to look briefly at the second half of the present line, "to reconcile and make new." Here again, we find further emphasis in the Christological phrase not on personhood within the immanent Trinity but on a second work of God. The purpose of God's coming in Jesus, we find, was "to reconcile and make new." This is lovely but vague. What has been reconciled? What has been made new? At first blush, this might seem to be an allusion to the work of Christ in atoning for sin and in bringing about new creation, two key elements of Christian orthodoxy. On closer examination, there is also the possibility that the phrase can be interpreted without any sense of these things at all. One early draft of "A New Creed" deviated radically from traditional Christian understanding when it spoke of the God who "reconciles himself to us" in Jesus.[42] Conversely, it is just as possible grammatically, and perhaps more likely in context, that the intended reference could be to reconciliation in human relationships alone and to renewal in a psychological or existential sense.

39. Schweitzer, "Christology of United Church," 143.

40. Wyatt, "Ministering with High Doctrine."

41. Schweitzer, "Christology of United Church," 136.

42. Standing Committee on Christian Faith, "Meeting Minutes" (11 Dec 1967, box 6).

(5) who works in us and others / by the Spirit.

This is the concluding phrase of the opening stanza. As we learned from looking at those that precede it, this line was meant by the authors of "A New Creed" to round out the Trinitarian aspect of the confession. In the originally authorized version of "A New Creed," the wording was only marginally different and the meaning entirely identical to that we see today. It read, "We believe in God . . . who works in us and others by his Spirit." Traditionally, the third person of the Trinity has been known as the Holy Spirit. As noted in the second chapter, R. C. Chalmers offered a critique of the move to "the Spirit" in response to the original presentation of "A New Creed" to the Twenty-Third General Council. It is difficult to know exactly what lay behind the making of this distinction. A good guess might be the committee's desire that their creed be, according to one of its former members, "Trinitarian, but not in-your-face Trinitarian."

Interpretive questions remain regarding the phrase "who works in us and others." First, there is the declaration that the Spirit "works." This seems to be a repeated emphasis on the economic Trinity, shading into modalism. The question remains, what does the Spirit do? The claim made is strikingly open-ended and ready "to be filled with personal content by those who say the creed."[43] Patricia Wells understands that the Spirit is "a 'comforter' and a strengthener," working also in "people of other religions and people of no religion. . . . To identify these actions and events specifically as works of the Spirit," she goes on, "is risky."[44] Others have also emphasized the possibility that the Spirit works outside the Christian church.[45] Grammatically, the only limit placed on God's work "by the Spirit" in this line is that this work is located "in us and others." It is unclear to whom this refers, as even the French translation "*Confession de foi de l'Église Unie du Canada*" says something different here.[46] Even the denomination's leading thinkers often preserve such uncertainty in their

43. Standing Committee on Christian Faith, *Creeds*, 18.

44. P. Wells, *Welcome to United Church*, 5.

45. Hyuk Cho, "Practising God's Mission Beyond Canada," 261, and Robert C. Fennell, "Scripture and Revelation in the United Church of Canada," 58, both in Schweitzer et al., *Theology of United Church*.

46. The "*Confession de foi de l'Église Unie du Canada*" says something fundamentally different: that God "*travaille en nous et parmi nous par son Esprit.*" Translated back into English, it reads that God "works in us and *among us* by his Spirit." We know that this is not something that got lost in translation because *les autres* ("others") is used later in the *Confession*, in the phrase "*pour aimer et server les autres.*"

interpretations. While "A New Creed" is ambiguous about in whom the Spirit works, it is silent on the nature of the Spirit's work. Argues Wells, "*Wherever* there is a true striving for justice and peace, the evidence of love and wholeness, there the Spirit of Christ is at work."[47] It could be suggested that the work being enabled is defined in the remainder of "A New Creed." However, this is does not seem grammatically indicated, and no United Church interpreters appear to have suggested this.

A challenging question remains. Is God, through the work of the Spirit, inspiring some people to believe in the Lordship of Jesus and, at the same time, inspiring others to deny it? Christians have traditionally believed that God was at work in them, allowing them to become children of God, heirs of the promise made to Abraham, crying "Abba, Father" (Gal 4:6). According to classical Christian tradition, the work of the Holy Spirit involves creating, sustaining, and renewing the universal church. To the extent that God has been thought to work outside the church, it is work that has been seen typically as for the spiritual good and growth of the church, the furtherance of God's kingdom, and the conversion of nonbelievers. Of course, it is possible to articulate an alternative theological position to this, but "A New Creed" does not exactly do so. Patricia Wells writes, "To identify . . . actions and events as specifically works of the Spirit is risky . . . . We could be mistaken. But to be silent—or vague—is a failure to take God's presence in the world seriously."[48] Unfortunately, the grammar of "A New Creed" and the expositions of its most learned interpreters suggest precisely that it is problematically vague in this statement.

(6) *We trust in God.*

This is another of the key, brief lines of "A New Creed" that gives us clues about its structure and intentions. Isolated between the two major stanzas of the text, it is perhaps easy to pass over. Crossley does not comment on it at all in his sermon series. Wells does in her booklet, but with brevity. Yet, this is an important phrase for helping us to understand "A New Creed," because it signals the climax of its existential message. The existentialism of "A New Creed" is demonstrated incontestably by its opening and closing emphases on the human condition, with the words "We

47. P. Wells, *Welcome to United Church*, 5 (emphasis in original).

48. P. Wells, *Welcome to United Church*, 5.

are not alone."[49] In its final report to the General Council Executive, the Committee on Christian Faith writes that there was no question among the members that their creed should be existential in approach; the only question had been around what existential conviction to express.[50]

Existentialism is a very broad topic, even within the limited sphere of Christian theology. However, the authors of "A New Creed" have helped by pointing us specifically to the existential concerns they wished to address and by emphasizing trust in God as the primary human response needed. In using religious language to stress God's place as being in relation to us and the trust-response, "A New Creed" demonstrates the ultimate importance of encounter for the existentialist. The first person perspective is the starting point and foundation, while God's reality is significant only as it *encounters* us. It is analogous to the old question: if a tree falls in a forest, and no one is there to hear it, does it make a sound? In terms of existential theology, if God doesn't encounter us, does God matter, or does God even exist? For many, the answer would be no. It should be clear that this kind of approach is especially useful when certainty of belief is diminished. Of what value is the Bible, for example, if its words are useless as history? Of what use is the Christian faith if its traditional tenets are thought to be false? The existential approach tries to redeem the Bible and Christianity from thoroughgoing skepticism by suggesting the possibility of a positive impact on people's lives. Rudolf Bultmann, the most famous exponent of theological existentialism in the twentieth century, puts it much better. He writes, "With this we come back to the assertion that for modern man the idea of a God above or beyond the world is either no longer viable or is perverted in a religiosity which would escape from the world . . . . Only the idea of God which can find, which can seek and find, the unconditional in the conditional, the beyond in the here, the transcendent in the present at hand, as possibility of encounter, is possible for modern man."[51] In that case, the important things are not precisely who God is, whether Triune or not, for example, but whether trust in God leads one to a better life—in an ethical or experiential sense—personally and in relationship with others.

49. Standing Committee on Christian Faith, "Meeting Minutes" (16 Oct. 1967, box 6). In his prototype, Mac Freeman put even more emphasis on this perspective, and he concluded his text with these words: "I trust God and commit my existence to his purpose."

50. Standing Committee on Christian Faith, "Report on Creeds."

51. Bultmann, *Translating Theology*, 93–94.

Within the literary structure of "A New Creed," we can see the existential meaning and function of this brief phrase. It concludes and brings to a climax the first major stanza and the focus on what is stated about God. The presence of this line, when seen in combination with the brief statements about God in the preceding section, shows us what is most important—not what is believed about God but how we encounter God and what that experience evokes in us. In another sense, this phrase provides a link with the second stanza, which states the appropriate practices that stem from God's encountering us through call and our trust-response.

(7) We are called to be the Church:

This line begins the second major stanza of "A New Creed." Whereas the first addresses the nature of God, this one is taken up with ethical matters—what we ought to do as a consequence of our belief. It has been one of the criticisms of the classical creeds, especially in the period of theological modernity under the influence of existentialism, that they do not say much about how Christians should be living. "A New Creed" was meant to take this critique into account, and thus it spends a relatively high percentage of its words on the nature of Christian practice. We see the seeds of the present line sown as early as Mac Freeman's prototype where we read, "God has called and is calling us into the company of Jesus with whom we are chosen to be servants, by whom others are also set free."[52] Though the line has been revised significantly, this idea of God's calling people into a community of action is one that has remained constant at approximately this place in the creed. When "A New Creed" was originally approved by the General Council Executive, the phrase read, "He calls us to be his church: to celebrate his presence." The modifications made in the 1980 version were the replacement of the gendered pronouns "he" and "his" with "we" and "the," as well as the necessary switch to the passive form of the verb. Though obviously problematic for many with its "he" for God, the previous language had the benefit of referring the act of calling and the lordship of the church more clearly back to the God who was spoken of in the first major section of the creed. "We are called to be the Church," unfortunately, leaves the connection ambiguous, and something of the continuity of "A New Creed" has been lost.

52. Standing Committee on Christian Faith, "Meeting Minutes" (16 Oct. 1967, box 6).

One of the criticisms levelled at the committee's creed, as originally presented to the General Council, particularly by R. C. Chalmers, was that "to be his church" should be "into his church," giving the stronger sense that the church is God's, not ours. However, the committee felt very strongly about this point, and it retained "to be." We read an interesting piece of reflection on this point in the committee's report to the General Council Executive:

> The committee noted the criticism of "to be his church" and the suggested alternative of "calls us into his church." It was suggested that the form "to be" implied that we ordinary men decide to club together and form a voluntary association called "the Church," but this argument ignores the line "He *calls* us . . ." "To be" is deliberately kept to indicate an activist sense of church membership, rather than a passive relationship to an institutional entity. Further, it provides a better introduction to the succeeding lines, which explicate what is involved in "being the church."[53]

The committee goes on in its published booklet *Creeds* to express this thought somewhat differently. "The rightful response of Christians to God," we read, "is to be his church. The activist sense of church membership is here stressed and spelled out: in worship we celebrate God's presence: in loving and serving others we follow Jesus in his mission as servant and reconciler: this also entails political-social involvement against evil, on behalf of just treatment for all people."[54]

This line has been the cause of much gratitude in The United Church tradition, but it does not seem to have been the subject of intense reflection. "We are called to be the church" has been taken often as a justification for the existence of the church. Crossley writes, "There are many who would reckon themselves religious who would reply, 'But I don't need the church . . . I can worship God at my cottage or on the ski slopes.' The question is, do they?"[55] Patricia Wells declares, "With the growing popularity of mutual help groups—Weight Watchers, Stroke Recovery, Alcoholics Anonymous—it may be more evident that, in order to live our faith effectively, we need one another."[56]

53. Standing Committee on Christian Faith, "Report on Creeds."

54. Standing Committee on Christian Faith, *Creeds*, 17.

55. Crossley, *This You Can Believe*, IV.ii.

56. P. Wells, *Welcome to United Church*, 6. Ironically, she goes on to qualify this peculiar claim by saying, "The danger with any longstanding institution is that its original purpose can so easily be muddied."

(8) to celebrate God's presence,

This phrase has been taken widely in The United Church simply as a shorthand reference to worship. This is especially evident in the title of the most recent service book of the denomination, *Celebrate God's Presence*, a resource that provides worship orders and service materials for all kinds of community gatherings, large and small, including many that no one would naturally associate with celebration—such as the funeral service of a child. Though anyone of theological sophistication will acknowledge that worship is not always celebratory, celebration is still presented as the underlying principle of worship. Lament, for example, can be a celebration of the presence of God, even though it does not feel festive.

Worship is a response to the grace of God. Wells writes of worship, perhaps echoing the Westminster Shorter Catechism, "But essentially we are there to enjoy God."[57] Chalmers expressed his confusion to the Committee on Christian Faith, thinking the reference here was specifically to the Lord's Supper, and asked why there was not a reference to baptism also. The committee then illuminated their intent in writing the phrase by echoing their Reformed forebear John Calvin. "We celebrate the presence of God," they wrote, "this suggests the proclamation of the word and Christ's saving presence through the sacraments."[58] An unanswered question remains left over from the first stanza about how God is present with us. The classical answer, at least in Western Christianity, is that it is Jesus who is in our midst, as we gather in his name, by the Holy Spirit—who proceeds from the Father *and from the Son*. Another option might be of a more Eastern or Pentecostal emphasis, that it is, namely, the Holy Spirit by whom God is present with us. It is not a problem to say that we celebrate God's presence, but the creed is not as clear about this as it might be. Of course, in striving to be brief, its authors could not explicate every possible detail.

(9) to live with respect in Creation,

This line is by far the most recent addition to "A New Creed." While every other word was authorized by the General Council Executive, either in 1968 or in 1980, these appeared only in 1995. In 1994, a motion

57. P. Wells, *Welcome to United Church*, 7.

58. Standing Committee on Christian Faith, "Report on Creeds."

was brought to the Thirty-Fifth General Council that "A New Creed" be amended to include a phrase within its ethical section that would "explicitly acknowledge our responsibility for the integrity of creation and our place in it."[59] By early 1995, the Theology and Faith Committee had crafted the present line and proposed it for insertion at this point, and this change was approved by the General Council Executive in March of that year. The approval of this change was timely in that it allowed for the inclusion of the revised text to appear in *Voices United*, published in 1996.[60]

That "A New Creed" has been added to with a line that makes reference to environmental concerns is no doubt one reason many are so fond of it. In contrast with so much of the Christian tradition, which can seem like it is fossilized at a distant point in the past, "A New Creed" has been expanded by a denomination that has been not only willing but eager to modify its confession to keep up with the times. It would seem that there could hardly be a clearer way for a church to appear, and perhaps be, more current than to take the massive social concern that exists around the environment and to incorporate it into its most prominent statement of faith. While there is much to be said for a church to keep up with its times, there is always the danger that it will be blown about by every wind of change and get caught up in short-lived fads. In this case, however, the health of our biosphere will doubtless continue for many generations to be a key concern.

A difficulty with this line of "A New Creed" is the uncertainty of its meaning. "Creation" is not the object of the verbal clause "to live with respect." Grammatically, it seems our respect can be of any kind and directed toward anything or anyone, as long as creation is understood as the context. Other statements were considered for inclusion at this point in the text. "God calls us . . . to be good stewards of creation" might have been a good option. "'To care for the earth,'" however, "was felt to be too anthropocentric, failing to acknowledge the interrelationality of humankind and the earth," writes Harold Wells.[61] This conclusion indicates that by the mid-1990s, the existentialist impulse of the denomination had changed—"too anthropocentric" would not have been a critique coming from such a perspective as held by the original framers of "A New Creed." For Harold Wells, the addition of "to live with respect in creation"

59. *Record of Proceedings*, Thirty-Fifth General Council, 526–27.

60. H. Wells, "Good Creation," 91.

61. H. Wells, "Good Creation," 91.

signalled The United Church's move towards an ecotheology.[62] His wife Patricia Wells demonstrates that this is a form of panentheism (God-is-in-everything). She writes:

> God is present in every creature, every part of creation, and it is the divine Spirit . . . which constantly sustains it. To violate it is to violate God. To respect it is to fulfil the first commandment.
>
> [To live with respect in creation] will give us the opportunity to again be enchanted with the creation . . . from the most distant star to the ant on our garden walk.
>
> [Jesus] was God's "Word made flesh," and flesh in biblical terms goes beyond the human realm. It implies all flesh.[63]

As we can see, the present phrase could be read as having nothing to do with the consequences of our behavior on the environment, as creation is not explicitly prescribed as the recipient of our respect. At the same time, it can be interpreted in a pagan way, with even adherence to the first commandment—"I am YHWH your God, who brought you out of the land of Egypt . . . you shall have no other gods before me" (Exod 20:2)—hinging on our reverence for creation, thereby blurring the distinction between God and what God has made. A curiosity about this line is its capitalization of "Creation." Even the "presence" of God in the previous line is not so articulated. Perhaps Wells and Wells understand this line as its crafters intended.

(10) *to love and serve others,*

As with many other lines in this confession, the origins of this statement can be traced back to Mac Freeman's prototype of late 1967. His draft reads, "God has called and is calling us into the company of Jesus with whom we are chosen to be *servants*."[64] We note here the importance of service within the overall calling of the Christian. The Committee on Christian Faith goes on to elaborate in *Creeds*, "The activist sense of church membership is here stressed . . . in loving and serving others we follow Jesus in his

62. H. Wells, "Good Creation," 91.

63. P. Wells, *Welcome to United Church*, 8.

64. Standing Committee on Christian Faith, "Meeting Minutes" (16 October 1967, box 6; emphasis in original).

mission as servant and reconciler."[65] The strengths of the phrase, as it now exists, are that it places love centrally within an overall Christian ethic and that it links love with service. Patricia Wells reminds us of both when she calls our attention to Jesus's answer to the question in Matthew 23, "What is the greatest commandment?," to which Jesus famously responded, "You shall love the Lord your God with all your heart and soul and mind . . . and you shall love your neighbor as yourself."[66]

However, the nature of the love and service being called for is not entirely clear. Wells herself highlights the possibility of confusion on this point. She writes, "'Love' must be one of the most fluid words in the English language . . . . We say variously, 'I love my car—my job—my girlfriend.'"[67] Service is often connected closely with each of these loves, and the possibility of serious confusion is real indeed. Looking to the literature of The United Church tradition, we find little to illuminate the situation. Lee writes, "The presence of God enables us to love and serve others."[68] Crossley clarifies little when he claims, "When you and I act compassionately we are being the church." Yet, he later demonstrates the dangers of this ambiguity. "Can we not," he asks, "expand our definition of the church to include any deed of mercy and kindness?"[69] This doesn't seem like it would leave us with a meaningful definition of the church, but nothing in the grammar or syntax of this line would preclude such an interpretation.

(11) *to seek justice and resist evil,*

In *Creeds*, the Committee on Christian Faith elaborates on the present phrase by stressing the necessity of "political-social involvement against evil, on behalf of just treatment for all people." This is consistent with the sentiment that this stanza is meant to stress, that is "the activist sense of church membership."[70] Later interpreters of "A New Creed" have emphasized the note of political activism. Crossley writes, "Righteousness is a virtue until someone asks us to sign a petition or boycott a product or

65. Standing Committee on Christian Faith, *Creeds*, 17.
66. P. Wells, *Welcome to United Church*, 9.
67. P. Wells, *Welcome to United Church*, 9.
68. Lee, "United in Faith," 160.
69. Crossley, *This You Can Believe*, IV.iii–iv.
70. Standing Committee on Christian Faith, *Creeds*, 17.

buck the crowd.... But what is the gospel unless it includes the prophetic word."[71] Wells sees the target of this kind of righteousness as "policies and institutions" and the goals as "attempting to make social change," as well as "changing the world in response to both human and ecological needs."[72] Lorraine MacKenzie Shepherd argues, "It omits any reference to personal sin, saying that we need only resist evil, implying that it is external to us."[73]

In their interesting volume on doctrinal preaching, MacLean and Young see in this line an empowering manifesto for the church.[74] The United Church tradition seems more broadly to have taken it this way, if implicitly so. In 2010, a short film about the history of The United Church entitled *Dare to Be: Remembering Our History* was distributed to pastoral charges on the occasion of the denomination's eighty-fifth anniversary. It spends a great proportion of its time recounting the historic political positions that have been taken by our United Church forebears in response to contemporaneous issues such as the Great Depression or the Vietnam War. The United Church generally seems to consider such activity prophetic. An ongoing challenge to the language of seeking justice or resisting evil is that it can manifest in mere virtue-signaling. Jesus is reported to have said, "Do not resist an evildoer" (Matt 5:39). In the biblical story, prophecy must flow from the righteousness of the prophet, even if this brings suffering upon the person of God. This is why the prophetic command is to *do* justice and to *oppose* evil. We see this most clearly in one of the more well-known prophetic verses in the Hebrew Bible: "He has told you, O mortal, what is good. And what does YHWH seek from you but to do justice, and to love loving-kindness and to walk humbly with your God?" (Mic 6:8) In the case of justice, it is something we are literally to do. God, whose justice and justness are the foundation of these very concepts (and commands to us) in the Bible, is the one who seeks these things from us. Far from being an isolated example, this famous verse seems to represent the consensus of Christian Scripture. We can find examples among English versions of the imperative "seek justice," such as in some translations of Isaiah 1:17. However, even in that

71. Crossley, *This You Can Believe*, IV.iv–v.

72. P. Wells, *Welcome to United Church*, 10.

73. Lorraine MacKenzie Shepherd, "The United Church's Mission Work within Canada and Its Impact on Indigenous and Ethnic Minority Communities," in Schweitzer et al., *Theology of United Church*, 296.

74. MacLean and Young, *Preaching the Big Questions*, 157.

example, the main emphasis is on what each of us is to do rather than on what we are to promote in others' actions. Based on the well-known structure of parallelism in Hebrew poetry that is employed, this phrase is clearly a restatement and elaboration of "learn to do good," which precedes immediately in the text of Isaiah.

Similarly, "resist evil" finds relatively little support. Evil is not simply to be resisted but opposed, renounced, and even hated. Psalm 97:10 reads, "YHWH loves those who hate evil." Likewise, we find in Romans 12:9 Paul's instruction to "hate evil." Throughout much of the history of the Christian tradition, a key question put to baptismal candidates has been "Do you renounce evil (or the devil)?" In seeking through an existential approach to encounter modern people where they are, "A New Creed" has eased the call of God by locating sin entirely externally. Evil becomes someone else's problem, and our call is to make commentary upon it. R. C. Chalmers pointed out in 1975, "The center of all our trouble is human sin, with personal and social dimensions."[75] "The church," he writes, "in order to be a witness for Christ in these days of revolution must not only speak the prophetic word. It must also live according to its precepts and principles. Love of neighbour must be seen by men in action as well as in words."[76]

(12) *to proclaim Jesus, crucified and risen, / our judge and our hope.*

The history of this line is one of the more interesting in "A New Creed." In the draft that was presented to the Twenty-Third General Council, it read simply, "We proclaim his kingdom." In fact, this paucity of reference to Jesus was one of the key reasons the creed was initially rejected. Therefore, the committee focused much of its subsequent effort in trying to revise it according to this criticism. Following the 1968 General Council, Donald Evans proposed as an alternative "to proclaim the risen Jesus, our judge and our hope." After further deliberation, the committee settled on the present wording. The justification of the current language is very significant and deserves to be quoted at length:

75. Chalmers, *Happy Science*, 196.

76. Chalmers, *Happy Science*, 193.

> This revised line attempts to do several things in line with criticisms which have been made:
>
> To be even clearer concerning the importance of evangelism, of Christian witness. In the original the "We proclaim his kingdom" seems to be a summing up of the previous lines and could seem a mere summing up, as if the celebration of various moral activities *in themselves* constituted proclamation . . . .
>
> Also, to be more specific in reference to the central content of the Christian proclamation; not "his kingdom" but "the risen Jesus, our judge and our hope." "His kingdom" suggests to modern ears mainly a social rule of God especially when it comes after [the previous line].
>
> To be more explicit in expressing the conviction that Jesus is alive, and leave open the possibility of various interpretations of the Resurrection.
>
> To be sure that the central event of Christ's life, the crucifixion, is specified.
>
> To emphasize the element of judgment . . . .
>
> To include an eschatological element . . . . Various interpretations as to the way in which the risen Jesus is our hope are left open.[77]

The Christian tradition has often been somewhat reticent about making absolutist claims around certain areas of theology, such as the atonement. The reality of the atonement has generally been asserted, but not always a particular theory of how Jesus's death on the cross effected the forgiveness of sin and the reconciliation of humans to God. One belief about which the Bible and orthodox tradition have been clear is the bodily resurrection of Jesus. By contrast, the committee sought to leave open various interpretive possibilities around the resurrection. N. T. Wright's exhaustive study shows convincingly that there is one historical conclusion to be drawn about Jesus's resurrection from both biblical and extra-biblical evidence: following his literal bodily death, Jesus was raised from his deathly slumber into new life, with a new and transformed resurrection body. This shocking event was seen by its earliest witnesses as an anticipation of what will happen to all of God's people at the dawn of a new creation, when there will be formed a new heaven

77. Standing Committee on Christian Faith, "Report on Creeds."

and a new earth.[78] Common misunderstandings of the biblical view of resurrection sometimes confuse it with a more generalized afterlife or a curious assertion that the followers of Jesus would use the language of bodily resurrection to speak of his coming alive, though remaining dead, in their hearts and minds.

It is interesting that Crossley and Wells say nothing about the crucifixion and resurrection of Jesus in their commentaries. They focus entirely on "to proclaim" in arguing that Christians do not simply *live* their faith but *tell* it as well. It cannot escape our attention that the mention of Jesus's death and resurrection (as well as his eschatological judgment and glorious return) are declared by "A New Creed," according to its structural logic, to be part of our proclamation rather than our belief. This well-known view of the existentialist par excellence Rudolf Bultmann—that Jesus was raised not in actuality but in the *kērygma* (in the New Testament, alternately the act of proclamation and the message heralded by the apostles)—is expressed tellingly in this line of "A New Creed."[79] "The modesty of A New Creed's eschatological claims," writes Bourgeois, "well reflect the sobered expectations of many late-twentieth-century Christians in the global North."[80] As Beardsall observes similarly, the "softening" in this line "no doubt contributed to warm acceptance [of 'A New Creed']."[81]

(13) *In life, in death, in life beyond death, / God is with us.*

Like several others in the text, this phrase can be traced back to Mac Freeman's prototype. His original reads, "In life, in death, in life beyond death we are in the presence of God."[82] The close relationship between that initial attempt and this final language is obvious. In some ways, the emphasis of "A New Creed" on the ever-presence of God is a helpful one theologically, when trying to express the Christian view of death. The promise that God is with us in life, in death, and beyond can be a great

78. N. T. Wright, *Resurrection of the Son.*

79. Bultmann, "Primitive Christian Kerygma."

80. Michael Bourgeois, "The End of the World as We Know It (Eschatology)," in Schweitzer et al., *Theology of United Church*, 325.

81. Beardsall, "Sin and Redemption," 114.

82. Standing Committee on Christian Faith, "Meeting Minutes" (16 Oct. 1967, box 6).

truth and comfort. However, "A New Creed" again suffers somewhat from a lack of clarity. When explaining that God is with us in death, Crossley describes not death per se but the process of dying—as if to say that God is with us after we discover that our disease or condition is terminal. He then goes on to say, "No one knows what the afterlife is really like . . . . Beyond death, we do not know anything in the way of details."[83] By contrast, Wells reads this line in a more traditional way. She cites Romans 8:38–39 as foundational to this promise of God's caring for us in death—that is, while we are dead. She also quotes Isaiah 9:7 and Revelation 21:4 to emphasize the eternal nature of the God on whom we rely. She is explicit in naming the confident hope we have of "new, resurrected bod[ies]" in God's promised future.[84]

(14) *We are not alone.*

Based on our discussion of the literary structure of "A New Creed," we can conclude that the impact of this particular phrase comes as a result of its placement. Being a restatement of the opening line, it tells us nothing new. No interpreter in The United Church tradition, to my knowledge, has published commentary upon it. As a repetition of the opening words of the creed, it reemphasizes the main theological theme of the text and addresses again its primary existential concern. Structurally, it brings to a conclusion the thesis of "A New Creed"—in a way not unlike a piece of music that a composer has started and finished with the tonic. In other words, it summarizes the statement and gives the reader (or reciter) a clue that the confession has reached its appropriate resolution. In this sense, it reminds us of the opening line, but it also links that sentiment in a very artistic way with the phrase immediately preceding (even though there is a period at the end of that prior line): "In life, in death, in life beyond death, / God is with us. / We are not alone." Another feature of the present line that makes it effective, according to the purposes for which it was written, is its brevity. Amidst all "A New Creed" has claimed, this is the thing worth repeating, for it is what is held to be most important. It is very likely the rhythmic force of its brevity, emphasized again in the next

83. Crossley, *This You Can Believe*, V.iii–v.

84. P. Wells, *Welcome to United Church*, 11.

line, which lead Wells and Styles to punctuate the text with an exclamation mark in their works.[85]

(15) Thanks be to God.

This final line of "A New Creed" provides something of a historical curiosity. As we saw in the second chapter, these words were not in the draft that was presented to the Twenty-Third General Council. This line found its way into the text only at the very last moment, and then only tentatively. When the Committee on Christian Faith made its final presentation to the General Council Executive in November 1967, at the last possible moment to have "A New Creed" included in the forthcoming *Service Book*, this line was marked with a double asterisk and was said to be "still under consideration as a possible addition." Though it was curiously presented finally as "still under consideration," "A New Creed" appeared in the *Service Book* with no indication that this line was optional or included only tentatively. Explanations are not evident in the available records. While "several members" of the Committee on Christian Faith, we learn, valued this late addition, "other members felt it better to end with [the previous line] as a 'reverse echo' of line (1)."[86] Apparently, this tension was not resolved within the committee before the completion of its work on this project. The General Council Executive's minutes do not offer additional clarity.

More than any of the other of the lines of "A New Creed," this derives its meaning from the act of saying it, rather than from any information it conveys or ideas to which it alludes. As such a speech-act, there seems to be no reason why it might not be a legitimate conclusion to a confession of faith. It is certainly right to give God thanks. By way of comparison, the classical creeds have traditionally concluded with the word "Amen."[87] Amen is an anglicized Hebrew adverb that means "truly." In other words, saying amen carries the implication that we truly meant what we just said.

Other possible ascriptions, such as "praise be to God" or "to God alone be the glory," are well attested in the Christian tradition. An ancient

85. P. Wells, *Welcome to United Church*, 11, and Styles, *Faith to Live By*, 5.

86. Standing Committee on Christian Faith, "Report on Creeds."

87. This is the case in the ecumenical editions (English Language Liturgical Consultation) of the Apostles' and Nicene Creeds as printed in *Voices United: Hymn and Worship Book*, 918–20, and *Celebrate God's Presence*, 218–19.

communion liturgy includes the phrase "It is right to give God our thanks and praise." A final amen or an ascription of glory and/or praise to God might suggest more of an emphasis on the transcendent reality of God. The choice of "thanks be to God" seems more likely to be grounded in the existentialist orientation of this particular text, which seeks to emphasize the importance of encounter for religious experience.

Conclusion

The foregoing section has attempted to provide some critical reflection and commentary on the text of "A New Creed." This has involved discussion of the structure of the confession as a whole, as well as its individual words and phrases. We have discovered that although "A New Creed" had its genesis in a rejection of the classical creeds by theological liberals, it is not necessarily to be judged a liberal confession. There is the possibility in individual interpretation that it can give expression to a more traditional vision of Christianity. However, its orientation seems best plotted on a different axis altogether. Specifically in its existentialist idiom, "A New Creed" is primarily individualistic, as it encourages private understandings of meaning, grounded in a privileging of personal encounter. In its corporate, plural grammar, the high degrees of generalization and abstraction employed appear to serve a helpful political purpose in the context of a theologically fragmented denomination.

The Title: "A New Creed"

Introduction

"A New Creed" is an almost accidental title. As we saw in the third chapter, "A New Creed" appeared first as a proper name with the publication of the *Service Book*. Prior to that, the document was referred to during internal deliberations variously as "a new creed," "A Creed," "the new creed," "The United Church Creed," and with other labels as well. In *Creeds*, initially published in 1969 but then reprinted in a second edition in 1975, the text appears under the heading "A New Creed Prepared by the Committee." In other words, the title was not seen as definitively set by the committee that wrote it, either at the time of its initial approval or even years after its publication. As we continue to notice incidentally throughout this study, scholars in more subsequent years do not always treat "A New Creed" as the document's inviolable title either. However, in the publication of more recent liturgical resources such as *Voices United* and *Celebrate God's Presence*, and especially with the adoption of this text among The United Church's four major statements of faith as subordinate standards in 2012, "A New Creed" is most definitely now a formal title.

The word *creed* is a powerful one in the Christian tradition. Throughout most of the church's history, creeds have been tremendously influential. To label a recent statement of faith a creed is to claim for it a high degree of theological authority. Of such authority in the Protestant tradition, prominent British theologian Alistair McGrath writes:

> Protestantism regards the Bible as being of supreme authority and understands the creeds to be reliable, communal statements of faith that are subordinate to the Bible. The creeds set out the beliefs of Christianity; confessions set out the distinctive beliefs of a specific form of Protestant Christianity. In terms of a hierarchy of authority, the situation can therefore be represented as follows: Bible → creeds → confessions.[88]

With its unique moniker, "A New Creed" is clearly intended to claim a level of authority, at least within The United Church, that is analogous to that of the Apostles' Creed and the Nicene Creed. We know that it was written with the intention of replacing the Apostles' Creed in services of baptism. More recently, in the *Celebrate God's Presence* service book, "A New Creed" has been printed alongside the ancient creeds under the common heading "Historic Creeds."[89] In the literary tradition of The United Church, "A New Creed" is often presented as the creed of the denomination, which, though like the classical creeds in significant ways, also surpasses them in contemporary theological relevance.

However widely spread such assumptions may be within The United Church, some voices have questioned the credalness of "A New Creed." In his learned book on baptismal liturgies, Kervin often refers to the text as "the so-called A New Creed" or alternatively "the United Church 'Creed.'"[90] Victor Shepherd states, "Needless to say, the 'creed' is no creed at all, since it has failed to find ecumenical consensus."[91] Given McGrath's

88. McGrath, *Christianity's Dangerous Idea*, 234.
89. *Celebrate God's Presence*, 218.
90. Kervin, *Language of Baptism*, 158, 217.
91. Shepherd, "Testimony of Dr. Victor Shepherd," in Zung, "Bermuda Trial."

contention, the issue of whether "A New Creed" is actually a creed is not moot. Although the language of the text itself is more significant for us than its title, the word creed is such a meaning- and value-laden term within Christianity that the title provides an important context in which the words of "A New Creed" are read or recited. Having engaged in a detailed reflection on the words and phrases of "A New Creed," we will now consider its title.

The Meaning of Creed

"A New Creed" was created in the mid-1960s because some members of the Committee on Christian Faith were not happy with the proposed use of the Apostles' Creed in baptismal services and wished "to formulate a modern credal statement" for The United Church.[92] Intending to write a creed of its own, the committee sought a definition of creed in order to guide its work. For this purpose, they turned to *The Oxford Dictionary of the Christian Church (ODCC)*, which defines creed as "a concise, formal and authorized statement of important points of Christian doctrine." The committee went on to clarify in *Creeds* that brevity, formality, appropriate authorization, and an emphasis on only the essentials of Christian doctrine were, in its understanding, the hallmarks of a creed.[93] It is fair to say that they understood the definition supplied by the *ODCC*. To the brief definition quoted in *Creeds* is added in the *ODCC* itself only, "the classical instances being the Apostles' Creed and the Nicene Creed." "A New Creed" seems to fit this so-called dictionary's definition for the most part, being concise, formal, and, in some sense, authorized. The question remains for us, however, whether these features are sufficient for the identification of a creed. I would suggest that they may not be, and that despite its connection with the Oxford brand, the *ODCC* provides a thin and inadequate definition of a creed. It is surprising that its editors, taking the Apostles' Creed and the Nicene Creed as their classic examples, do not also identify such characteristics as antiquity, direct summary relationship to the biblical story, an opening of either "I believe" or "We believe," or even ecumenical use as fundamental marks of a creed. If anything, these features would seem to be even more significant marks of the classical creeds than their relative length and so-called formality.

92. Standing Committee on Christian Faith, *Creeds*, 5.

93. Standing Committee on Christian Faith, *Creeds*, 6.

If we really want to define the word creed as well and fully as we possibly can, we do far better to look at the multivolume *Oxford English Dictionary (OED)*, perhaps the most extensive and authoritative dictionary of the English language. Though its definitions also deserve critical analysis, the *OED* is thorough enough to form at least the foundation of a more fulsome reflection. In its entry for creed, there are essentially two main definitions. The first is:

> A form of words setting forth authoritatively and concisely the general belief of the Christian Church, or those articles of belief which are regarded as essential; a brief summary of Christian doctrine: usually and properly applied to the three statements of belief known as the Apostles', Nicene, and Athanasian Creeds. (the Creed, without qualification, usually = the Apostles' Creed.)

This is offered as the primary meaning. Clearly, creed stems from the Latin *credo* ("I believe") and came into English due to the liturgical use of the Apostles' and Nicene Creeds. This sense of the word is shown in the *OED* to have entered the English language by AD 1000 at the latest. The second definition of creed has been abstracted from this original meaning and refers to belief-in-general. It reads, "An accepted or professed system of religious belief; the faith of a community or individual." To this is also added a sub-definition, "A system of belief in general; a set of opinions on any subject." In modern vernacular, this is the definition that seems to be implied in this kind of phrase: "Employers may not discriminate on the basis of race, creed, or gender." These are the *OED*'s two basic meanings of creed.

It is clearly the first, essentially ecclesiastical definition that was drawn upon by the editors of the *ODCC* and thereafter used by the Committee on Christian Faith. Key differences, however, between the *ODCC* and the *OED* are the reference to ecumenism—"the general belief of the Christian Church"—in the latter and also the emphasis of the *OED* on the "proper" referents to creed being the Apostles', Nicene, and Athanasian Creeds. While "A New Creed" might fit the definition of the *ODCC*, it does not seem to fit the definition from the *OED* quite as well. That said, the *OED* does offer two sub-definitions under this main heading that may offer more possibilities. One is "A repetition of the creed, as an act of devotion," while the other is "More generally: A formula of religious belief; a confession of faith, *esp.* one held as authoritative and binding upon the members of a communion." This latter especially seems to be an excellent fit for "A New Creed," though it is authoritative but not necessarily binding within The United Church. Before suggesting that either definition might offer the prospect of an endorsement for the title of "A New Creed," however, we need to look critically at the examples given in their defence. Of creed as an act of devotion, the two examples refer seemingly to an act of penance and to ritual use of the rosary. In each case, the obvious reference is to the Apostles' Creed or possibly the Nicene Creed. Of the second, more promising sub-definition, we find four examples from English usage. However, two of these clearly refer to the classical creeds—therefore being better examples of the first main definition—and one, conversely, refers to such a general sense of belief that it is actually more suited to the second main definition. The only example that does seem to refer to any "formula of religious belief" is one the *OED* culled from the *Manual of Congregational Principles* (1884). It reads, "Nor is it consistent with Congregational principles for a particular church to draw up a Creed and to require its acceptance by candidates for membership." However, even here, the reference is not to any document that actually exists but only to a hypothetical one.

In contrast to the *ODCC*, the second edition of the *OED* tells us that creed is "properly" meant to refer to the ancient creeds of Christianity. Although creed can also refer simply to "a formula of religious belief," this seems a less well-attested definition. That said, the existence of "A New Creed" and its description as a creed within The United Church tradition are doubtless a use of the word creed that itself could bolster this definition in future editions of the *OED*.

In order to bring this discussion to a close, we must return to our initial question, is "A New Creed" a creed? Accepting that matters are not always so black-and-white, we might ask instead, is "A New Creed" a helpful title for this text? Generally, we tend to think of a given word's meaning as drawing on etymology and usage. Etymologically, "A New Creed" is poorly described as a creed, since it does not begin with "I believe" or "We believe." The case is weakened further, since we know that the word creed is properly and primarily applied to the classical creeds of Christianity. In terms of its actual use in the language, however, "A New Creed" is possibly described as a creed. As almost anyone will tell us, usage trumps etymology in a better understanding of a word's meaning. That "A New Creed" is so referred to as a creed, at least within The United Church, is therefore something of a self-authenticating definition. That said, I wish to argue that there is a third consideration, which has the real value of telling us whether we should use a given word in a certain way. That is that many words, regardless of how they are used or intended by a certain writer or speaker, carry one or more implications. Any reflection on a word's meaning, as a result, must take into consideration the implications of its being used. The word "negro," for instance, was used commonly in times past as a label for persons of color from African descent. "The Negro Leagues" of baseball is an example of this usage, and Negro was the term advocated by black leaders in North America up to and during the civil rights era, as opposed to the terms African American or Black, which predominate today.[94] Martin Luther King Jr. uses it self-referentially in his famous "I Have a Dream" speech. This has a sound etymological foundation: it derives from the Latin for black, *niger*. It also has a historically well-attested usage. However, the word has since fallen out of favor and is no longer used. Today, because it is out-of-date, it would possibly be heard with racist overtones from the past and therefore is avoided.

I want to be clear: "A New Creed" is in no way a racist or prejudiced text. The foregoing illustration simply shows how important are the implications of a word's meaning, which is not just its referent but its significance. Creed is a word that claims authoritative significance in Christianity. Based upon their antiquity, their extensive ecumenical use, and their value for understanding in summary the biblical story of salvation, the classical creeds are exceptionally important for the Christian tradition. The title of "A New Creed" lays claim to a share of that kind of authority. "A New Creed" was first envisioned as an alternative to the Apostles' Creed. In today's United Church, it has attained membership among the historic creeds. In that "A New Creed" is concise, formal, and authorized, it may be a kind of creed. Unlike the Apostles' and Nicene Creeds, however, it is neither ancient nor ecumenical. It does not begin with "I believe" or "we believe." In its underlying philosophy of language, moreover, it is not able to attempt the same kind of theological articulation as do those texts universally acknowledged to be creeds. As such, "A New Creed" is not really the same kind of thing as the classical creeds, though indeed it shares some characteristics with them. In so labeling it, I would suggest that The United Church has fostered some confusion.[95]

94. Bryson, *Made in America*, 155.

95. I once served a congregation that used a computer-generated overhead projection system in the sanctuary. In preparing for Sunday worship, I would send all the service materials to a designated individual who would then prepare a slide show of all

Broadly speaking, confession or statement of faith might be more fitting terms within a formal title for this text.

Conclusion

The United Methodist Church in the United States has included in its hymnal a selection of "Affirmations of Faith." Among these affirmations are the classical creeds, as well as a selection of modern faith-statements from that denomination's ecumenical partners. One of these is the text of "A New Creed."[96] However, we see in this appearance that "A New Creed" is not so titled. Rather, the *United Methodist Hymnal* refers to it as "A Statement of Faith of The United Church of Canada." From our foregoing discussion, it is clear that this is a more suitable title for this text. Realistically, it is the kind of label that is going to be much more acceptable in ecumenical context than is the somewhat presumptuous title "A New Creed." Even within The United Church tradition, there is some acknowledgment that the "*Confession de foi de l'Église Unie du Canada*" is not the same kind of text as *Le Symbole des Apôtres*. The making of this distinction would be helpful in the English-speaking United Church as well.

Conclusions

In previous chapters, we have noted the prevailing perceptions and presentations of "A New Creed" within the life and literature of The United Church. We have seen that "A New Creed" is thought widely to be The United Church's confession of faith par excellence. Through a close reading in this chapter, we have examined the possible meanings of the text itself. In considering the overall structure of "A New Creed," as well as its individual words and phrases, we have observed that its existentialist impetus led to the replacement of clear and concrete theological claims with expressions of a different kind intended to enable a sense of subjective

---

the prayers, hymn texts, etc. One week, I had decided to include the Apostles' Creed in the upcoming service of worship. That Sunday morning, I arrived to find that the text of "A New Creed" had been inserted in its place. When I asked the person, she said, "I thought you meant the new Apostles' Creed." She was not being subversive; she just did not know any better. This is an instance of the unfortunate educational consequences of "A New Creed" for the people of The United Church.

96. *United Methodist Hymnal*, 883. This version does not include the line "to live with respect in Creation."

encounter by individuals. Beyond a shared existentialist impulse, the Committee on Christian Faith agreed on little. Their commitment to promoting subjectivity held the additional benefit of allowing the writers of "A New Creed" to sidestep their fundamental divergence in many areas of belief. Subsequently, the text has been understood to brace a denomination whose political reality involves seeking to maintain a broad and at times fragile consensus. Moreover, the assumed title of "A New Creed" has served to bolster the institutional aims of The United Church and strengthen the authority of this text within it.

6

Moving Forward

Introduction

As we have seen, "A New Creed" is a prominent, authoritative, and influential text in The United Church of Canada. This is evident especially in comparison with the other confessions and doctrinal statements available in the denomination's tradition. As Seaton notes, The United Church has come to rely "upon only one creedal statement, the 1968 New Creed."[1] This adoption of a somewhat sectarian confessional stance would seem unexpected, given the ostensibly ecumenical nature of The United Church project. Sufficient, critical reflection on this phenomenon is conspicuous only by its relative absence.

Before drawing ultimate conclusions about "A New Creed" and its use, we need to consider the meaning of creeds within the church. In the first section of this chapter, three possible interpretive lenses for the phenomenon of credal confession will be examined. Regardless of their particular contents, message, or wording, there is no universal agreement about the value or importance of creeds in general within the Christian tradition. At issue is whether this subject of creeds is important and, if so, in what way(s). Having determined that credal questions are significant ones, we will consider in the second section the reflection of scholars from outside The United Church who have advocated for a retrieval of

1. Seaton, *Who's Minding the Story*, 118.

helpful and healthy practices of credal confession within their own denominational traditions.

The Significance of The United Church's Adopted Confession

Introduction

There exists today, as has existed historically, significant diversity across the Christian church about the meaning and value of credal confession. In fact, there remain broad spectra of assumptions about the relative importance of doctrinal confession and to what extent credal texts are helpful within the life of Christian community. This section will consider three compelling interpretive lenses for the use of creeds or doctrinal confessions in general. These possibilities are of particular relevance in assessing the unique situation of "A New Creed" in The United Church of Canada. Some dissenting voices have arisen specifically from within The United Church to suggest that all formalized confession may be inherently unappealing, as a potential hindrance or even as an affront to the religious experience of the individual conscience.

Possible Meanings of Creeds

Creeds are not fundamentally important—
Gretta Vosper and Northrop Frye

In practice, "A New Creed" has replaced alternative confessions of faith within The United Church—particularly, although not exclusively, in worship. One possible way of responding to this reality is to downplay the significance of formally articulated theological confession. Broadly speaking, such an approach has been taken by two writers from within The United Church tradition, Gretta Vosper and Northrop Frye. I do not mean to suggest that these two individuals have said the same things or that their work is of the same kind or quality—it is not. However, both Vosper and Frye are examples of those who have tried to deemphasize the significance of doctrine, and of doctrinal diversity, within and beyond The United Church. Instead, they have preferred to underscore the importance of ethics and experience within the realm of human spirituality. In their respective generations, this has allowed them to craft nontraditional visions of Christian theology while staying within the fold of the institutional church. In both writers, we can see an eagerness to discard classical Christianity and confessionalism more generally, while attempting to minimize the significance of so doing.

In recent years, Gretta Vosper has served as an ordained minister of The United Church who came to prominence by writing a controversial book, *With or Without God: Why the Way We Live Is More Important Than What We Believe*. As this title suggests, her argument is that Christianity is essentially an ethical venture and one that is not rightly or properly grounded in classically Christian belief. She describes her vision:

> What the world needs in order to survive and thrive is the radical simplicity that lies at the core of Christianity and so many other faiths and systems of thought—an abiding trust in the way of love as expressed in just and compassionate living. Out of the multitude of understandings of religion, spirituality, and faith; out of the varying views of the origins, nature, and the purpose of life; out of the countless individual experiences of what might be called divine; out of it all may be distilled a core that, very simply put, is love.[2]

We can understand her perspective more quickly and easily when we see that it is essentially that of today's Western, post-Christian culture, at least insofar as it is interested in spiritual matters. That is to say, religious (supernatural) beliefs are not relevant, but you can hold them as long as you do not suggest they are important for anyone but yourself. What really matters and what everyone is really getting at, whether they know it or not, is the importance of being a good person. In contrast to the traditional interpretation of the biblical story, Vosper has opted for a different metanarrative—a story or argument that seeks to explain all others. Despite claims to the contrary, however, this narrative is equally prescriptive. It claims the universal necessity of love.

The late Northrop Frye, also an ordained minister of The United Church, spent most of his career as a professor of literature at Victoria College, in the University of Toronto. One of the most celebrated intellectual figures of The United Church tradition, he was also one of the twentieth century's leading literary theorists. Frye did not propose so crass a dismissal of God as Vosper, though he steadfastly refused to assign any

2. Vosper, *With or Without God*, 4.

concrete referent to the words of the Bible. Instead, he insisted that myth and metaphor are the Bible's natural genres, which often makes it difficult to discern what it is he wanted us to think about the reality of God. Unlike Vosper, however, he did not intend to collapse Christianity into the ethical but rather into the experiential. What matters is not the historical or metaphysical realities of the Christian gospel, which were utterly inaccessible and even undesirable for Frye, but their transformative impact on us. To take the Bible as descriptive history is mere "literalism," he contended, and "the letter that kills."[3] He wrote further, "The reason for basing kerygma on mythical and metaphorical language is that such a language is the only one with the power to detach us from the world of facts and demonstrations and reasonings, which are excellent things as tools, but are merely idols as objects of trust and reverence."[4]

Frye's take on theology and the Bible is perhaps most quickly and easily sensed by the quip "If a passage of scripture fails to transform me, is it still true?"[5] His religious perspectives are demonstrated throughout his writings but perhaps most clearly in *The Great Code* and its sequel, *Words with Power*. His final book, *The Double Vision* (1991), is especially relevant for us because it addresses the contemporaneous situation of The United Church. In response to a critic who had called The United Church agnostic, Frye asserts, "The United Church is agnostic only in the sense that it does not pretend to know what nobody actually 'knows' anyway."[6]

Both Vosper and Frye have been content to leave classical Christianity behind, because neither has been interested in the concrete reality of either Scripture or any kind of rule of faith, including the ancient creeds. These texts may be potentially useful if they point us to the kind of actions or experiences we desire, but they do not have a kind of intrinsic value based on their literal interpretation or concrete referents. The essential qualities of true and meaningful religion transcend the literal reality or historical veracity of biblical claims. Returning to our efforts to interpret the role of "A New Creed" within The United Church, it is reasonable to draw on the writings of both Vosper and Frye to suppose that the text's prominence in The United Church may not be overly significant. If the classical creeds do not have an inherent value, from their

3. Frye, *Double Vision*, 14.

4. Frye, *Double Vision*, 18.

5. Frye, *Double Vision*, 20.

6. Frye, *Double Vision*, 20.

perspective, then neither do any such texts. Confessional documents can be used well or badly; what matters is the quality of the life that flows from their recitation and study.

A benefit of the interpretations of Vosper and Frye is that these interpretations guard against both an idolatry of paper and ink and an abstract, ethereal understanding of Christian faith. The authors have placed their emphases on ethics and experience respectively—that is, the living out of the Christian message. These can be helpful emphases. A challenge for their downplaying of doctrine and, at least by implication, credal confession is that neither Vosper nor Frye seem to have been entirely consistent in their suggestions that the essence of faithful Christianity can be found simply in either ethics or experience. In my view, neither author is convincing in the claim to be relatively uninterested in the reality of theological discourse or in the referent of theological language. Vosper writes, "To be a Christian is not to say specific words [or] believe in a certain set of doctrinal beliefs."[7] Yet, you would hardly get this impression from reading her work, which is filled with overt criticisms of classical Christianity, such as that God, the Bible, and the whole package are totally made up. In an open letter to Moderator Gary Paterson in 2015, Vosper labels faith in a "supernatural being" an "idolatrous belief."[8] In this instance, she seems to have been quite intent on advocating a particular theological or ideological perspective.

For his part, Frye was less willing to relegate theology to the fringes of Christian understanding than he claimed. Experience was without doubt the key thing for him. Yet, this claim itself rests on what appears to be its own theological presuppositions. A literal-historical reading of the Bible is not only "the letter that kills"; it is possibly "demonic."[9] Although he claims not "to deny or belittle the validity of credal, even a dogmatic, approach to Christianity," this is precisely what he seems to do in stating that "creeds and dogmas quickly turn malignant."[10] If experience in and of itself is so central to Christianity, properly understood, why would it be necessary for Frye to have insisted that Scripture and doctrine must always be mythical and metaphorical? In that case, interpreting the Bible would be quite beside the point. At best, different interpretations would

7. Vosper, *With or Without God*, 197.

8. Vosper, "Letter to Gary Paterson."

9. Frye, *Double Vision*, 18.

10. Frye, *Double Vision*, 17.

be more or less helpful, but ultimately, the experience of the individual would determine that subjectively.

As we have seen from this brief examination of the thought of Vosper and Frye, emphases on ethics and experience can be insightful and helpful. However, it is evidently difficult to be consistent in claiming to downplay the content of belief or the importance of doctrinal confession at the expense of other aspects of the Christian life. Such themes as we find exemplified in their writings have not been shown as ultimately successful appeals to an understanding of the Christian faith abstracted from its own theological tradition. It is difficult to imagine similar efforts at sidestepping the critical importance of confessional language for the church being more successful.

Creeds might be significant, but maybe more superficially—Peter L. Berger

A second option for interpreting the importance of doctrinal confession would be more middling: formal theological expression could be significant, but not fundamentally so. A variation on this theme is one that might see "A New Creed," given its symbolic importance for The United Church, as something of a marketing tool. In other words, the denomination's decision to use and elevate "A New Creed" so prominently could be, at least implicitly, something of a promotional strategy by which it has attempted to set itself apart from its competitors. I have stated this too clumsily. To aid in a more articulate consideration of this possibility, we can draw on the work of prominent twentieth-century sociologist Peter L. Berger. A much-cited author in the field of sociology, Berger's range of interests was broad. Himself a Lutheran Christian, one of his areas of scholarly focus was the sociological study of religion, especially in North America. His arguments, as they pertain to our question, are found in a fascinating 1963 article, "A Market Model for the Analysis of Ecumenicity."[11] In his market model, Berger seeks to understand the coexistence of ecumenism and denominationalism, two seemingly contradictory phenomena, within North American Christianity. In light of this paradox, his perception was that most scholars had interpreted denominationalism as an evil barrier to be overcome on the path toward

11. A similar article of Berger's, co-authored with Thomas Luckmann, is "Secularization and Pluralism."

the eventual unity of the visible church. Without offering a value judgment of this position, he shows that it does nothing to explain the *existence* of the paradox in the first place. What is needed, he argues, is a "macro-sociological model of interpretation" that can make sense of the odd interrelationship between denominationalism and ecumenism.[12]

In order to arrive at a satisfactory model, Berger sets out to examine the experience of those churches, primarily the mainline, middle-class denominations that are often participants and partners in ecumenical dialogue and venture—even outright mergers—and, at the same time, also compete amongst themselves quite intentionally. Looking at the historical situation of the mainline Protestant churches, he argues that the separation of church and state (in the United States) has led to "a pattern of denominational pluralism" and that a) these mainline churches have "an increasingly homogenous middle-class population" (and therefore a very class-specific "potential membership"); b) that inflationary pressures are making it incredibly expensive to operate congregations, due to escalating staff salaries, as well as the rising costs of the construction and maintenance of suitable buildings; and c) that tax-exemption laws are allowing denominational bureaucracies to accumulate wealth independently of the broad membership and therefore to act more independently and in more economically rational ways. The result of these combined forces is that while competition between denominations for "the interest, allegiance, and financial support of their [common] potential clientele" is becoming too expensive, central bureaucracies are also able to rationalize their operations, thus creating a "cartelization" process. "Cartelization," he argues, "rationalizes competition by reducing the number of competing units by amalgamation and also by dividing up the market between the larger units that remain."[13] As this happens, "the phenomenon of product standardization occurs." In order to differentiate between their "brands" in such a scenario, churches are forced to seek "marginal differentiation," meaning "functionally irrelevant embellishments and packaging of the product."[14] Given the many and varied similarities that exist between the mainline Protestant churches, and the resulting focus on "programming . . . ministers' personalities . . . and the aesthetic accoutrements of

12. Berger, "Market Model," 79.

13. Berger, "Market Model," 87. "It is evident, however," Berger writes further, "that there is a point beyond which rationalization through mergers will not go, if only because of the vested interests of the bureaucracies in charge of its administration."

14. Berger, "Market Model," 88.

the 'church plant'" in order to attract new members, Berger argues that, "denominationalism . . . can be thus understood through the concept of marginal differentiation."[15] He concludes by saying that such a market model is able to account for "the paradox of the coexistence of ecumenicity and denominationalism."[16]

Although Berger was primarily conscious of and therefore addressing the situation in the United States, there is no apparent reason why his analysis would not be largely applicable to the mainstream Protestant churches in Canada as well. In fact, the post-war United Church would seem to present an excellent case study—not only as the product of an ecumenical merger from its founding but as a denomination that continued to engage in serious merger talks with the Anglican Church in Canada, the Disciples of Christ, and the Evangelical United Brethren in the 1960s and 1970s. Berger's market model does not address creeds specifically, but it does make room for a consideration of a denomination's theology. He argues, "Theology has a legitimating function with respect to the process of marginal differentiation," meaning that a denomination is likely to overemphasize minor theological differences against a backdrop of general similarity.[17] This claim makes reference to a denomination's public representation of its theology to the wider society and therefore is of interest for our study of the importance of "A New Creed" for The United Church.

So the question raised is, might The United Church have been so emphasizing "A New Creed" as a way of promoting itself amidst a sea of competitors among whom there is very little real difference? There does seem to be a sense in which this is the case. After all, The United Church is very similar in theological outlook, political orientation, and demographic makeup to such other mainstream denominations as the Presbyterian Church in Canada, the Anglican Church of Canada, the Evangelical Lutheran Church in Canada, and perhaps others as well. Further, "A New Creed" has often been used in The United Church's marketing and promotional materials. It is also argued with some frequency that "A New Creed" is one of the few things that is different, unique, and special about The United Church.

15. Berger, "Market Model," 89. He goes on to say, "Denominationalism can thus be understood as highly functional in a situation where one wants to remain competitive in spite of product standardization."

16. Berger, "Market Model," 90.

17. Berger, "Market Model," 90.

Still, such an interpretation of events as suggested by Berger's market model would not tell the whole story or sufficiently explain the place and use of "A New Creed" within The United Church. For one thing, a church's doctrinal confession is not "functionally irrelevant embellishment" or mere "packaging." It goes right to the heart of what kind of community a church is and is not analogous to "programming" or "the minister's personality." As Berger himself acknowledges at the close of his essay, "'theological factors' may also play a part within the limits of what is rationally possible and may even upon occasion transcend these limits."[18] In other words, beliefs and their formal articulation have the real potential of breaking open the model. That seems to be the case here. Secondly, the promotion of "A New Creed" need not imply, as it tends to do in current practice, the rejection of other possible confessions by The United Church, especially in its liturgy. Thirdly, The United Church has many other things that it might use to promote itself, over and against similar denominations—such as its uniquely ecumenical and Canadian story. Finally, the replacement of other confessions in The United Church by "A New Creed" has functioned largely to serve those already in the denomination, rather than as a marketing tool addressed to outsiders. Although Berger's model is a helpful one for us and does explain some aspects of our subject, it is in the end not fully adequate for understanding the place of "A New Creed" within The United Church of Canada. Given what we have seen more broadly about the importance of "A New Creed" for the denomination—both in its practices and its self-understanding—we need a deeper explanation.

Creeds are fundamentally significant to a church's identity—Mary John Mananzan

In order to reach a more satisfactory understanding of the unique role of "A New Creed" in The United Church, it is clear that we need to gain a better sense of how it is that creeds actually function within a Christian community. Our best attempt to grasp the significance of this particular text for The United Church will draw upon the work of Mary John Mananzan, a linguistic philosopher and prioress from the Benedictine Order of Roman Catholicism. Known widely as a theologian of liberation and as an advocate for women in her native Philippines and elsewhere,

18. Berger, "Market Model," 93.

Mananzan's work is important for our present subject due to her relatively unknown but uniquely relevant book *The "Language Game" of Confessing One's Belief: A Wittgensteinian-Austinian Approach to the Linguistic Analysis of Creedal Statements*. Although she is hardly the first or only author to have considered the use and meaning of religious language, hers is the best and most detailed study of the way credal statements function linguistically within Christianity. There is something in her work to inform almost every element of the current subject. For the moment, we will focus particular attention on her argument that the act of "confessing one's faith" has meaning not in abstraction or isolation but as a corporate act that takes place only in the context of a particular believing community. As a result, we will see that since "A New Creed" relies on the life of The United Church for its significance, its special role as this community's distinctive and sole liturgical confession means that the denomination sets itself apart from others that, however similar they may be in other ways, use fundamentally different texts to express their belief. By implication, The United Church of Canada has separated itself from the wider church in the nature of its use of "A New Creed."

In the 1960s, The United Church was encountered by the reality that many of its people were no longer willing to express their faith using the words of the classical creeds. For a variety of reasons, these ancient confessions had lost their value for many—including those in teaching and leadership roles. In much the same era as "A New Creed" was written, Mananzan set out to examine the classical creeds—their being the authoritative confessions in her Roman Catholic tradition—from the perspective of the discipline of linguistic philosophy. Within her academic field, those providing the stiffest challenge to the ancient creeds were the logical positivists, such as A. J. Ayer and Antony Flew. They were arguing that all religious language—especially about God or other supernatural things—being neither verifiable nor falsifiable, was without meaning in a scientific age. Mananzan identifies three groups of scholars who had responded to the challenge of logical positivism in different ways. The first response she names "non-cognitive." Advocates of this position accept the premise of logical positivism but argue that the value of religious language is found not in literal truth anyway but in the sort of ethics and experiences such language can enable. While she praises this group for identifying an important aspect of religious language—the non-cognitive aspect—she rightly argues that the a priori rejection of truth claims "would prove most fatal not only for theology but also for religion."[19] The second type of response she identifies is the "cognitive." Its advocates reemphasize the intellectual value of religious speech, especially through a typically Thomist "analogy of being." While this is presented as a more constructive approach, Mananzan finds this group of scholars too caught up with metaphysics and technical terms.[20] The final approach described is one she labels "functional-situational." Tracing this approach backwards through the likes of Dallas High to the later writings of Ludwig Wittgenstein, Mananzan commends these scholars for their willingness to look at religious language not in terms of preconceived categories but rather as it is actually used in particular communities.[21] In essence, it is this Wittgensteinian approach that shapes her thesis.

Unlike the earlier Wittgenstein, who had assumed a one-to-one correlation of the meaning of a word to its particular referent, the later Wittgenstein came to associate meaning with use. That is to say, the correct use of language involves adherence not only to the rules of grammar but also a sensitivity to the relationships, behaviors, and presuppositions that provide its context. Used properly, that is contextually—in the fullest sense of that term—words can be meaningful within a great diversity of speech-acts or "language games." In making use of this macroassumption, Mananzan also draws heavily on the work of J. L. Austin, the Oxford philosopher whose detailed analysis allowed her to take also a microperspective on the Christian creeds as they are actually used. In particular, two of Austin's theories are of special importance to Mananzan. The first is perfomative theory, which seeks to delineate speech that is significant primarily through the very act of speaking from that which depends essentially on the truth or falsehood of the words spoken. Second is force theory, which distinguishes even further between language that seeks to inform (locutionary), that which is essential to an act (illocutionary), and, finally, that which can claim meaning in its effect on others (perlocutionary).[22] Going on to examine Christian creeds, she argues that while they do inform (locution), the inner dynamic of the creeds is more about the *act* of confessing one's faith (illocution) and even the effects, such as encouragement, that that act has on others (perlocution).

19. Mananzan, *"Language Game" of Confessing*, 21.
20. Mananzan, *"Language Game" of Confessing*, 31.
21. Mananzan, *"Language Game" of Confessing*, 38.
22. Mananzan, *"Language Game" of Confessing*, 74.

This Mananzan argues with particular reference to the phrase "I believe," which has as its primary purpose not passive assent to factually true statements, but rather an expression of trust, confidence, and commitment.[23]

In the final phase of the study, Mananzan looks closely at "the Christian life" as the context of Christian credal confession to see what such a setting might tell us about the confessing act of Christians—individually and collectively. She suggests that there are two central presuppositions of the Christian life. First, there is the metaphysical presupposition that God exists. Second, there is the Christological presupposition, that God is revealed in history, in Jesus Christ of Nazareth. Christianity is *Christian*, therefore, in its *theo*logy and its *Christ*ology. It is also, of necessity, credal in its foundational setting upon revelation rather than investigation, and upon testimony rather than evidence. In short, the Christian life is grounded in a "faith activity." Crucially, it is also a social endeavor through participation in the church, as well as a missionary endeavor, due to the universal claim of its salvific message, and a liturgical endeavor through its central act of corporate worship.[24] In a helpful concluding paragraph, Mananzan summarizes the significance of her study of "confessing one's faith" with Christian creeds, arguing that such an act "offers enough appeal to man's faculties—rational, emotive, and volitional, to warrant its being taken seriously and its being chosen as the utterance of one's existence. It does not have the coercive force of the obvious nor the inescapable consequence of logical necessity. To engage in Christian religious discourse remains a free choice, but a choice which is neither arbitrary nor irrational, but a decision based on acceptable grounds."[25]

The significance of Mananzan's argument for this study of "A New Creed" is twofold. First, she was responding to the same sorts of sociocultural challenges to the confession of Christian orthodoxy as were the people of The United Church at the time "A New Creed" was written. In contrast to the approach followed by her contemporaries in The United Church then or since, however, who have chosen to write and rely on a whole new kind of creed in recent decades, she found superb justification for the traditional language of Christian confession through an in-depth linguistic analysis of the classical creeds.

23. Mananzan, *"Language Game" of Confessing*, 80.

24. Mananzan, *"Language Game" of Confessing*, 130.

25. Mananzan, *"Language Game" of Confessing*, 149.

Second and more importantly, Mananzan shows that religious language of whatever kind finds its meaning not on the premises of logical positivism or other fundamental criticisms or a priori rejections of religious language, but rather in the contexts of accepting and trusting the special revelation of God-in-Christ within the believing community. If this suggestion is correct—and I believe that it is—we see that "A New Creed" has meaning as a faith-statement within the context of its use by The United Church. Conversely, it does not have meaning for churches that do not use it to confess their collective faith. Following this, it would be correct to say that creeds tell us something important about the communities that use them to confess their faith. That the universal church has tended to hold in common the confession of the classical creeds, and more importantly the historic rule of faith they articulate—though I acknowledge the oversimplification of this—while The United Church has created its own unique confession of a different kind, tells us that the United Church has itself become a different kind of faith community, one that is distinct in a key way from the "one, holy, catholic, and apostolic church."

Conclusion

A great many people in The United Church of Canada love "A New Creed." This realization prompts the question, so what? Implicitly, its words and phrases derive their meaning not just from the broad tradition of Christian theology but from their particular arrangement within, and use together as, a confessional document. Assumptions about what a creed is in general will therefore shape our interpretation of "A New Creed" in particular. The most fully articulated reflection on the meaning and linguistic function of creeds within the modern Christian tradition has been provided by Mananzan. Understood most helpfully as a speech-act, or language game, we can see that one consequence of The United Church's pervasive use of "A New Creed" is a separation from the wider church. Moreover, the linguistic presuppositions of this text have become highly influential on the inner dynamic of The United Church of Canada.

A Way Forward: Some Constructive Proposals

Introduction

In both the liturgy and literature of The United Church tradition, "A New Creed" has widely come to be portrayed as expressing *the* faith of The United Church. However, we have seen that "A New Creed" does not actually attempt to define that faith clearly or give voice to any collective theological vision. Rather, this text invites individuals to hold virtually any theological position, however personally or idiosyncratically, and it encourages them to fashion a private religious encounter in whatever way they wish. Yet, it is more than simply a theological monument to the individualism of post-1960s Western society; "A New Creed" begs to be seen within the context of the longer story of The United Church. Against that backdrop, we realize that "A New Creed" is not so much a celebration of the individual before God but a diplomatic text aimed at managing the breakdown of The United Church's consensus as a community of faith.[26]

Since it is the doctrinal statement of only one small segment of the Christian church and lacks ecumenical acceptance, the pervasive usage of "A New Creed" has subtly divided The United Church from the rest of the universal church in a meaningful way. Contrary to some views, "A New Creed" is not simply one relatively recent set of words that also happens to express the faith that is held in common by Christians across different parts of the wider church and that reaches back into antiquity.[27] "A New Creed" was written precisely because some, perhaps many, within The United Church of the turbulent 1960s could no longer accept the theological vision of classical, catholic Christianity. As such, we must recognize that "A New Creed," particularly in the context of its wholesale adoption by The United Church, has become a schismatic text that is presently dividing the body of Christ.

26. To some extent, this move might be judged to have been not only necessary but also successful. See Seaton, *Who's Minding the Story*, 101–2. Seaton cites the argument of Airhart, *Church with Soul*, 292–300.

27. On this point, I disagree with the claim of Wilson et al.: "'A New Creed' of the United Church emerged out of a recognition that the church in every age needs to reaffirm its faith in contemporary thought forms and language." In fairness, they also acknowledge rightly, "It could be argued that ['A New Creed'] is not a replacement for the classical creeds which are universal expressions of Christian faith" (Wilson et al., *Guide to Sunday Worship*, 56–57).

It is also clear that "A New Creed" was written in a tumultuous period of social upheaval in which the members of a small committee of one denomination could not find, even amongst themselves, theological agreement. Feeling, probably rightly, that their lack of consensus reflected the theological state of The United Church at the time, they crafted an intentionally ambiguous statement of faith whose words were expressly intended "to be filled with personal content by those who say the creed."[28] Given the vague nature of this confession and its rise to prominence, the people of The United Church remain unlikely to arrive at a common faith. As Kervin notes, "A New Creed" has become fundamentally "a new kind of language for UCC theology."[29] The widespread adoption of this language and its accompanying thought-forms within the denomination may preclude us from coming to a theological consensus. The use of "A New Creed" in current practice creates a null curriculum with a powerful message: a particular set of shared beliefs is not central to Christianity, and therefore, the church is not essentially a faith-community.[30] As a consequence, it appears self-evident that this text undermines the fostering of such community—not just for The United Church in relation to the holy, catholic church but within its local congregations as well.

My motivation for undertaking this study came originally from historical curiosity. Having noticed the widespread and unquestioned use and even celebration of "A New Creed" within The United Church, I decided to try to find out where this text came from and why it was written. In my initial research, I discovered that, despite its prominence, very little scholarly attention had been given to "A New Creed." What written histories existed at that time provided no more than a page or two of summary material, and the information in these examples had been gleaned mostly from *Creeds*. On a theological level, I also noticed that published reflections on "A New Creed" had been limited largely to devotional or promotional materials aimed at popular audiences. Having taken the opportunity to engage in a detailed analysis of "A New Creed"—historically,

28. Standing Committee on Christian Faith, *Creeds*, 17.

29. Kervin, "Sacraments and Sacramentality," 244.

30. The highly publicized Gretta Vosper affair is not worth considering here. However, Seaton makes the helpful point that "Vosper's position is merely a logical next step on a trajectory that connects back" to 1960s theology and, to my mind therefore, "A New Creed," which was meant to accommodate such theology. A dominant current within United Church theology and ecclesiology, Seaton argues, seems to stand in an uncomfortable tension between what the 1960s bequeathed theologically and the conclusions to which Vosper has taken it (Seaton, *Who's Minding the Story*, 103–4).

theologically, and literarily—I argue that it should not continue to be used in the same manner and to the extent it has come to be. Mananzan shows that the significance of a creed lies not just in *what* it says but even more importantly in *how*, *when*, *why*, and *by whom* it is said. The content of a creed and the roles it plays in a given community help determine what kind of community is going to be formed by it.[31] As Christians, if we wish to confess the faith as testified to by the apostles and in the canon of Scripture—acknowledging that while there is obvious diversity in this tradition, there remains an identifiable core—we must adopt a different approach to our confession of the faith. My wish in saying this is not to emphasize the negative, nor is it to be critical of any individuals on a personal level. I do not begrudge anyone their spiritual journey. Both individually and collectively, however, I do advocate the consideration of a more historically and biblically informed Christian faith for the people of The United Church, as well as the richer experiences of that faith that would doubtless follow.

In this section, I wish to propose two constructive solutions to the theological and confessional problems that are presented by the manner of usage of "A New Creed" in current United Church practice. First, I will argue that the use of "A New Creed" should be significantly reduced, while also suggesting some ways that it might still be used within a more appropriate theological framework. Second, I will contend that the Apostles' and Nicene Creeds ought to be used more frequently and in a greater variety of situations in The United Church. A model for such reclamation of these confessions might perhaps be the way(s) "A New Creed" is presently used in the denomination. That is to say, I don't suggest the classical creeds be imposed on anyone or be used as tests. Rather, I encourage my fellow United Church Christians to find joy and a sense of identity in the beauty of their words, as well as the good news they convey. In making this case, I will draw especially on the work of two scholars—one Baptist (Steven R. Harmon) and one Roman Catholic (Luke Timothy Johnson)—who have articulated well the need for more and better use of these classical creeds within their own traditions.

31. Just recently, while finishing work on the manuscript for this book, I was on a Zoom meeting with some fellow United Church folk during which one person asserted confidently, "We know that we have a biblical mandate to seek justice and resist evil." I found this a fitting example of the shaping influence of credal language and practices.

What to Do with "A New Creed"

An evangelical leader in The United Church was once supposed to have said, "[A] New Creed [is] sub-Christian and implicitly heretical." This person defended that statement by arguing that this text represents a deliberate turning away from two cornerstones of traditional orthodoxy: the Trinity and the two natures of Christ.[32] It is clear that its use of "A New Creed" has demarcated The United Church from the wider church that overwhelmingly does not use this confession or recognize it as a creed. Moreover, the philosophy of language that provided the foundation for its writing has given rise within The United Church to atypical, nontraditional interpretations and expressions of Christianity. Even so, is it right to label "A New Creed" as heretical? Would this not be a display of unkind and inflammatory rhetoric? No doubt, words like heresy, heretic, and heretical are out of favor in contemporary church and society. They conjure up disconcerting and embarrassing images of medieval (or early-modern) inquisitions and witch hunts. Such events in church history are indeed tragic, and we need to repent of them, not repeat them. However, the use of language has become so sloppy and poor throughout our culture today that it is now difficult to say many things clearly and to assume a common understanding. Conversely, if we do use our words plainly and precisely, the biblical *haíresis*, from which the later heresy word group originated, can become a possible designation for a group that would define its faith exclusively by the words of "A New Creed"—based on the assertion that it is not a catholic, or universal, expression of Christianity. To determine in what ways this move would be helpful or not, we will now turn to a more thorough consideration of heresy and its often discussed relationship to something called orthodoxy.

Orthodoxy and Heresy

Orthodoxy and heresy are typically understood as representing two opposite ends of an ideological spectrum: right belief and wrong belief. They have been paired inseparably in modern discourse, as exemplified famously in Walter Bauer's *Orthodoxy and Heresy in Earliest Christianity* (1934 in German and 1972 in English translation). Based on the

32. This view was attributed to Graham Scott in Michael Riordan, *First Stone*, 90, and quoted in Zachar, "Renewal/Reform Groups." I do not know how reliably attributed this quotation is. However, it is clearly the case that someone said it.

assumption that there were many different Christianities from the beginnings of the Jesus movement, Bauer argues in that seminal work that the triumph of orthodoxy over so-called heresies was essentially a political one, with no sure footing in biblical interpretation, history, or theology. A cornerstone of Bauer's argument is that if there were many different forms of Christianity in the so-called patristic period—each with claims to antiquity, biblical understanding, and possibly even the Jesus tradition itself—a particular set of identifiable and articulated beliefs must not be the key thing about Christianity. Therefore, the traditional claims—that belief is fundamental to Christianity, that the church's faith is uniquely apostolic, and that conciliar orthodoxy is the norm of belief from which others depart—are held to be false. While not wishing to engage Bauer in all the details of his historical argument, I wish to point out the irony that his position has seemingly become that kind of orthodoxy within the context of modern religious studies. As a result, the often unquestioned assumptions in academia are that belief is not fundamental to Christianity and that the so-called orthodox party of the early Christian centuries created a right belief-wrong belief dichotomy in order to mask what was basically a political power grab. If such a maneuver did in fact occur—which it did not—it could be characterized quite distastefully. Indeed, this is how classical Christianity has come to be viewed by many today.

Though there may be some insight contained in Bauer's history, I think it is an anachronism to suggest either that Christianity did not have identifiable beliefs from its genesis as a movement or that some kind of belief-action or belief-politics dichotomy is at all suited to an analysis of the early church. These represent modernist ways of thinking, which would have been foreign to the early Christians. It must also be said that such assumptions as currently predominate in the academy and much of the liberal church in the West make the same sort of moral and political judgments of which they accuse the so-called orthodox party in Christian antiquity.[33] But the church need not always accept the premises of its detractors. Both belief and the articulation of particular beliefs were always important to the early Christians and fundamental to their identity as such. The early Christians would not have conceded that a theological dispute could be viewed apart from the whole of one's life or the web of one's social-political relationships. Ironically, it was in the institutional church's adoption of such modernist perspectives that abuses

33. A helpful and accessible treatment of the early church's history and beliefs is Kelly, *Early Christian Doctrines*.

like inquisitions and witch hunts could take place in later centuries. It is only in suffering from such cognitive dissonance that Christians could do violence to others in the name of right belief.

Thankfully, we can recover a better understanding of the intimate connections between belief and action as well as belief and relationships by reconsidering the challenging words orthodoxy and heresy. Of course, we must keep in mind and be sensitive to the abuse of these terms in historical context. If we can get over the hurdles involved, however, the resulting discussion can be thought-provoking and insightful. To begin, I propose that orthodoxy is best conceived of not as right belief or thought but right praise. I realize that this may be a bit unconventional. After all, a verbal form of the term was coined by Aristotle in the *Nicomachean Ethics* in the fourth century BC with the meaning of having the right opinion.[34] Since the early fourth century of the Christian era, noun and adjectival variants have been somewhat commonplace in theology, often with a similar connotation. Yet although the Greek verb *dokéō* means plainly "I think" in the secular sense, I would point out that the related noun *dóxa* ("glory") and verb *doxázō* ("I glorify") have different emphases, especially in the Bible. In the Septuagint and in the New Testament, uses of this *dox-* word group tend to derive their meaning from the biblical Hebrew for glory (often of God), *kāḇôḏ*.[35] For that reason, I have always been of the mind that Christian ortho*doxy* is more akin to *dox*ology—commonly understood as words of praise—as is the case with well-known doxologies like the *Gloria Patri* or "Praise God from Whom All Blessings Flow." Belief and praise are related, of course, but are not synonymous. Belief is easily turned into an abstraction.[36] Praise, on the other hand, implies belief but is faith put into action. Beliefs can be merely held, but praise must be enacted. It is an irresistible response to the gracious and loving God of Scripture. The most important thing for Christians is not to have perfect theological comprehension but to praise God, to the best of our Spirit-filled abilities. Existentialism of the kind that influenced the writing of "A New Creed" was in part an attempt

34. Liddell, *Intermediate Greek-English Lexicon*, 567.

35. Bromiley, *Theological Dictionary*, 178–81. Bromiley writes, "It thus becomes a biblical term rather than a Greek one."

36. It is interesting to see the difference between English and German here. Bauer's original title is *Rechtgläubigkeit und Ketzerei im ältesten Christentum*. Notice *Rechtgläubigkeit*, rendered literally "right belief."

to correct an overemphasis on the importance of right belief. In my view, however, it was an overcorrection.

Even if, as I contend, orthodoxy might legitimately be imagined as denoting something other than right belief, I acknowledge that it is often employed with this meaning. Regardless, however, heresy is certainly not wrong belief. In this misunderstanding, widely assumed, we see similarly a false distinction between belief and the rest of life. In truth, heresy is related much more significantly to actions and to relationships than it is to beliefs in the abstract. Whereas orthodoxy is not a biblical term, our English heresy comes from the Greek New Testament's *haíresis*, a word that the Bauer, Danker, Arndt, and Gingrich *Greek-English Lexicon* (BDAG) defines primarily as "*a group* that holds tenets distinctive to it," such as a "sect," "party," "school," or "faction."[37] The noun *haíresis* is related to the common verb *hairéō*, "I take," or *hairéomai* (in the middle voice), "I choose." Our word heresy comes from this latter sense of a choice—but what kind of choice(s)? If we look at how *haíresis* was most commonly used in early Christian literature, we see that the key orientations were relational and/or ethical. A heretical group—being synonymous with heresy—is one that had chosen to form a sect, faction, party, or school that was distinct from the whole to which it rightly belonged. This group may have hived itself off for ideological (including theological), interpersonal, or ethical reasons. In ancient Christian sources, it is striking how often the latter two were especially emphasized. In Galatians 5:19–21, Paul lists *haíresis* as a work of the flesh. In his Letter to the Ephesians (6:2), Ignatius of Antioch contrasts *haíresis* with "living according to the truth."[38] Of course, all of this implies a kind of moral judgment that is influenced heavily by one's perspective.[39] Realizing that objectivity and neutrality are yet more modernist ideals difficult to sustain, there is nothing to hinder the holding of a perspective or the making of judgments by any group, Christians included. The argument of Bauer and his school notwithstanding, there seems no reason to hold a bias against the theological assessments of the early church in this regard and therefore to conclude that the beliefs and lifestyle of the so-called orthodox group were not deliberately drawn from the tradition first handed down by the apostles or that their preferred ideas and practices did not come to

37. Bauer et al., *Greek-English Lexicon*, 27–28 (emphasis added).

38. Holmes, *Apostolic Fathers*, 141.

39. Christians themselves were accused of being a heresy within Judaism (Acts 24:5).

dominance except through their popularity. Indeed, this seems not just to be a reasonable possibility but the conclusion indicated by an overwhelming preponderance of historical evidence. However, let it suffice to say that heresy is neither wrong belief nor the opposite of orthodoxy.[40] In fact, it is somewhat like orthodoxy as a term, in that its significance is grasped only from an ecclesial perspective. While orthodoxy can point us to the importance of praise over abstract belief, heresy derives its utility from the conviction that God's people belong together and that factionalism is a sign of the present evil age. We read of the threat posed:

> There is from the outset a suspicion of *haíresis* within Christianity itself, not through the development of orthodoxy, but through the basic incompatibility of *ekklēsía* and *haíresis* (cf. Gal. 5:20; 1 Cor. 11:18–19). In 1 Cor. 1:10ff *haíresis* has a sifting purpose. In 2 Pet. 2:1 it affects the church's very basis; a *haíresis* creates a new society alongside the *ekklēsía* and thus makes *ekklēsía* itself a *haíresis* and not the comprehensive people of God. This is unacceptable.[41]

Because it attempts to communicate a different *kind* of faith than do the classical creeds or the ancient rule of faith on which they are based, because it implies a different practical expression of Christian community than has historically been characteristic of the church, and because it is a confession of no ecumenical stature, "A New Creed" *in its pervasive and exclusive use* can both lead to and be a symptom of such *haíresis*. I acknowledge that the heresy–heretic–heretical group of terms in English derivation is widely misunderstood and, worse, often misused. Even with the best of intentions, it carries negative connotations. If employed at all, its variations need to be used with great precision, care, and sensitivity in every instance. It can never be used appropriately as a slur. Indeed, I do not so use it with respect to the individuals who wrote or who continue to enjoy reciting "A New Creed." Instead, I suggest that, according to its biblical usage, consideration of the New Testament's concept of *haíresis* may be illuminating for The United Church of Canada. It can offer a helpful,

40. In light of the negative connotations of heresy and its not actually being opposite to orthodoxy, some have preferred heterodoxy ("other praise"). While the latter is clearly a better parallel to orthodoxy, heterodoxy does not sidestep the challenge. For there to be an other, there needs to be a norm. Since heterodoxy offers no better argument to either the church or to its opponents, its meaning has not warranted fuller discussion.

41. Bromiley, *Theological Dictionary*, 28.

prophetic critique of the denomination specifically in the ways *we have chosen to use* "A New Creed" in recent decades—as our sole confession of faith in worship and as perhaps our primary source of symbolic identity.

Of course I remain aware of the important distinction I highlighted in the previous chapter, during a discussion of the word creed, between a word's referent (the thing to which it refers) and its meaning (the significance of its use). One thing this distinction highlights for us is that, in some cases, a word's use can be accurate or technically correct but simultaneously unwise or unhelpful. If, for instance, I tell a story in a sermon about a time I slipped and fell on my "backside," I might get a chuckle. If from that same pulpit I were instead to say that I fell on my "ass," it would likely get a far different, more negative reaction. If told in the setting of a coffee shop, even amidst the same group of people, the two variations of that story might be heard yet differently again. In each case, the words would accurately refer to the same thing, but their meaning—that is the significance of their use—would be different. Different relationships and contexts often can and do alter a word's meaning. Though given pause by the possibility that interpretations of my aims may be clouded by negative connotations surrounding *haíresis*, its translation, and cognates, my purpose here is constructive. I hold that a biblically informed understanding of the *ekklēsía*, and therefore of the relationship of the *ekklēsía* with *haíresis*, can deepen our understandings of both the church and the gospel, while warning us where we can go astray. Given The United Church's historic tradition of explicit ecumenism and the General Council's 2012 declaration that even "A New Creed" is a standard "subordinate to the primacy of scripture," I hope there may be an openness to this suggestion within the denomination.

It is worth taking a chance with the terminology because, whatever labels we choose to use, the implications of the use of "A New Creed" in the current practice of The United Church are the same. The text divides unnecessarily what ought to be united—the one church over which Jesus is Lord. As we see in Paul's repeated use of the body of Christ metaphor, the church is inestimably weaker when it does not have all of its parts working together as they were intended to do. Since "A New Creed" facilitates a sort of dismembering of the body, its usage ought to be reconsidered by the people of The United Church. Although many love this text and enjoy reciting it, personal attachment is not a sufficient reason for The United Church to continue its current privileging of "A New Creed" as its sole or even primary liturgical confession. Though experience is an important lens through which to view theological understanding and expression, one must be careful to avoid conclusions based on experiences that have not historically been and are not now shared widely within the worldwide Christian community. Since The United Church has no sound basis historically or ecumenically for adopting this confession as its sole doctrinal expression within its liturgy, the current employment of this text as such seems to be a work of the flesh (in contrast to the fruit of the Spirit) and a sign of the present age (in contrast to the age to come).

There is no question that "A New Creed" is used widely in worship, at the constitution of courts of the church, in Christian education classes, as a sacramental symbol, in formal documents of the General Council, and in promotional materials produced by The United Church Publishing House. However, I urge my fellow United Church Christians to reconsider their current usage of "A New Creed." As it is presently deployed, this text undermines Christian fellowship both beyond and within the boundaries of The United Church. Moreover, it does not present an adequate summary of the biblical story. A consequence of this is that many in The United Church lack the basic theological knowledge required for the assurance of their salvation. This perspective may not be widely held in the denomination today, but it does make good sense of the evidence and therefore needs to be shared.

How to Hold On to and Recast "A New Creed"

All of these things having been said, I do not wish to be a historical revisionist. I do not argue that "A New Creed" ought to be stricken from memory or that it can never be used without benefit. While its current use does need revision, "A New Creed" is a significant part of the history of The United Church and could helpfully be retained for occasional use. Its connection to the history of The United Church makes "A New Creed" an important text. As with any denomination, The United Church needs its people to know about and be interested in its history. "A New Creed" can (and probably should) be used from time to time to further that purpose.

In *Creeds*, the Committee on Christian Faith make a number of recommendations about how the classical creeds might continue to be used in The United Church. They agree that "the classical creeds (i.e. the Apostles' and Nicene Creeds) will continue to be useful especially for instruction," that "the responsible use of the classical creeds implies preparatory instruction," and that "appropriate introductory formulae should be provided for use with the classical creeds in public services."[42] In order to retain the use of a text with such problematic features as we have identified in "A New Creed," we should take as our model this framework that was proposed in the 1960s for the use of the classical creeds. "A New Creed" can continue to serve as a tremendous teaching tool about the history of The United Church. On occasions when it is appropriate to remember the unique history of this denomination or to celebrate the distinctiveness of our tradition, heritage, and identity, it would be appropriate to recite "A New Creed." This could provide an excellent opportunity to learn about theological existentialism and the spiritual crises of the late twentieth century that were manifested in The United Church. The responsible use of "A New Creed" also ought to include preparatory instruction and an introductory formula that qualifies its significance for the life and faith of the denomination. "A New Creed" should not be held as the sole confession of The United Church or promoted as its key sacramental symbol. On these or similar terms, "A New Creed" might be used profitably within The United Church of Canada.

A practical way to express this shift in understanding and to facilitate a changed role for "A New Creed" would be to revise its title. Fortunately, we can draw upon a resource that already exists within The United Church tradition. I speak of the French liturgy of *L'Église Unie du Canada*. Though in English we have one word—creed—for the Apostles' Creed, the Nicene Creed, and "A New Creed," modern French suggests a helpful distinction between the ancient ecumenical *symbole* and the later denominational *confession*. It is well known that symbol (*symbolum* in Latin, *sýmbolon* in Greek) was a word used commonly in Christian antiquity—initially for the threefold question put to candidates at their baptism and then for the formal creeds into which they evolved, in liturgical as well as other contexts. Though the precise reasons for the initial choice of this term are unclear—mostly likely the creed's being the symbol of the presence of the Triune God with whom the individual was being united in baptism—there is no doubt that it was the term used universally for what in English we today label creeds.[43] In contemporary English idiom, symbol has been all but lost as a term for baptismal confessions. Yet in

42. Standing Committee on Christian Faith, *Creeds*, 6.

43. Kelly, *Early Christian Creeds*, 52–61.

French, it has been retained. United Church liturgical resources *en français* refer to *Le Symbole des Apôtres*. This is perhaps a legacy of Roman Catholicism and its once cultural dominance in francophone Canada, particularly in Quebec. In that kind of social context, it would be understandably bizarre to think of "A New Creed" as commensurate with the ancient creeds and to be labeled *Le Nouveau Symbole* or *Un Nouveau Symbole*. Rather, a clear distinction has been made in *l'Église Unie* between the ancient *symboles* and the "*Confession de foi de l'Église Unie du Canada*." It is my contention that the continued but circumscribed use of "A New Creed" within The United Church ought to be based on recognizing this distinction throughout the denomination. Historical consciousness seems to require this. "A Confession of Faith of The United Church of Canada" is a much better and more descriptive title for this "We are not alone" text than is "A New Creed." Considering that the United Methodist Church has included this confession in its hymnal under the title "A Statement of Faith of The United Church of Canada," there may even be some opportunity for its limited use within an ecumenical framework, were it to be entitled and contextualized more appropriately.[44]

A Retrieval of the Classical Creeds

Paul Scott Wilson is a recently retired professor of homiletics who taught at The United Church's Emmanuel College in Toronto. A successful author of many influential books in his field, Wilson has been one of the denomination's more well-known figures within the theological academy and among the clergy across North America. In a 2009 sermon to Toronto's prominent Eglinton-St. George's congregation, he said, "In the United Church we often feel uncomfortable repeating the Apostles' Creed, even though it is in our hymnbook. The language may seem archaic. It needs interpretation, just like the Bible. In fact it is a summary of what the Bible says and more important, it is the one creed that all Christian denominations have in common. Should we discard its truths, we would cease to be ecumenical, we would become a cult."[45] It is noteworthy that these comments caused some controversy at the time. A former member of the

44. *United Methodist Hymnal*, 883. Another possible title might simply be "We Are Not Alone."

45. Wilson, "Let Go and Let God." I thank Professor Wilson for providing me the text of his sermon.

Committee on Christian Faith who was present on that occasion told me that some people "wouldn't shake [Wilson's] hand at the back door" after the service.[46]

Now, I probably would not have used the word cult. Yet, Wilson's characterization of the significance of reciting the Apostles' Creed, and therefore the consequences of steadfastly refusing to recite it, is surely correct. As I. Howard Marshall of the University of Aberdeen writes, "As historically used, 'Christian' refers to the kind of belief enshrined in the Apostles' and Nicene Creeds which speak of Jesus as the Son of God. Those creeds may be wrong in what they say; the beliefs stated in them may be false and untenable, but the creeds define what is meant by *Christian* belief."[47] It would be possible to compile a long list of quotations and arguments that would make precisely this point: Christianity is properly understood as the set of theological beliefs expressed by the Apostles' and Nicene Creeds, and the faith embodied in the retelling of the story those creeds summarize. The narrative framework they provide is the one that helps make the best sense of the Bible as a whole. Their message evidently represents a standardization of that first proclaimed and handed down by the apostles. Therefore I argue that The United Church would be much better off if it could recover a glad and willing use of these classical creeds in many areas of its life and liturgy. To see more clearly just how and why this would be a benefit, we will draw upon the work of two scholars—Steven R. Harmon and Luke Timothy Johnson—who come from outside The United Church but who have argued compellingly for a better use of these ancient confessions within their own denominational traditions. In this, we will see that the problems it faces are not unique to The United Church and that the solutions it needs can be achieved in concert with similar efforts being undertaken in other parts of the worldwide Christian community.

Creeds in the Baptist Tradition—Steven R. Harmon

Steven R. Harmon is a Baptist theologian who teaches at The School of Divinity at Gardner-Webb University in Boiling Springs, North Carolina. A patristics scholar by training, much of Harmon's recent research and writing have been in two related areas: tradition as a source of theological

46. Telephone interview with Gordon Nodwell, 15 Dec. 2009.

47. Marshall, *I Believe*, 67–68 (emphasis in original).

authority for Baptists and ecumenism. As a practicing ecumenist, he has been involved in ecumenical dialogue on behalf of the Baptist World Alliance, the National Council of the Churches of Christ in the U.S.A., and the World Council of Churches.[48] As a pastor-professor, he has sought to help his fellow Baptists appreciate the richness of the whole Christian tradition and also to advance the visible unity of the church through a common reclaiming of that tradition by diverse segments of the worldwide Christian community. One of Harmon's stated desires is to see an increase in the proper and regular use of the Apostles' and Nicene Creeds. What makes his advocacy of the classical creeds interesting is that he comes from an ecclesiastical context—Baptist life in the United States—in which, like The United Church, those creeds are seldom used and widely scorned. He writes, "A few Baptist congregations in the United States on occasion include corporate recitation of the ancient ecumenical creeds in their services of worship, but at present the practice is neither frequent in these few congregations nor widespread in Baptist life in North America."[49]

The reason for this scarcity of the classical creeds within such a large section of the Christian church (the Southern Baptist Convention [SBC], for example, is the largest Protestant denomination in the world, and yet it is only one of many Baptist groups in the U.S.A.) is the commitment to a radical form of *sola scriptura*, expressed in the oft-heard phrase, "No creed but the Bible!" But, as Harmon shows, this axiom was coined outside the Baptist tradition, was not intended to refer to the classical creeds as such, and, interestingly, has been repeated by Baptists in only one country (the United States) for a brief portion of Baptist history (approximately one hundred fifty out of four hundred years).[50]

With a number of like-minded contemporary Baptist theologians, Harmon has made a series of nuanced arguments in favor of reclaiming a regular usage of the classical creeds within that denominational tradition. Though many do not realize it, he argues, all Christians—Baptists included—have received their faith from the passing on of tradition from one generation to the next. No matter how strongly one feels about the principle of *sola scriptura*, it is practically impossible to escape tradition as a source of theological authority. No reading of the Bible in whole or

48. For more information on S. Harmon, see his blog at http://www.ecclesialtheology.blogspot.com/.

49. S. Harmon, *Towards Baptist Catholicity*, 36.

50. S. Harmon, *Towards Baptist Catholicity*, 164.

in part is likely to take place without the interpretive influence of some tradition or other. That is to say, no one comes to a passage of Scripture as a blank slate. Rather, one must try to understand the words of the Bible within some kind of narrative or interpretive framework. Readers of the Bible then have only two real options: to have their understanding informed by a more helpful or a less helpful tradition. With some irony, Harmon notes that Baptists in the United States have in fact not abandoned extra-biblical tradition at all and have often written doctrinal statements—some intended precisely for "coercive uses," such as the SBC's "Baptist Faith and Message" (2000).[51]

Having exposed the common misunderstanding that tends to accompany a confused application of *sola scriptura* among Baptists in the United States, Harmon moves on to present for his readers the many positive implications that can stem from regular use of the classical creeds. In particular, he names three main benefits to Christian communities that can flow from regular recitation of the Apostles' and Nicene Creeds in worship. First, the creeds help to form both individuals and communities in the story of salvation of the God whom they are worshipping. The classical creeds, he writes, "are not lists of doctrinal propositions to which people are compelled to give assent; they are summaries of the biblical story of the Triune God, drawn from the language of the Bible itself." Moreover, these creeds allow assembled believers to

> declare the story to which Christians committed themselves in baptism. Reciting the creeds regularly renews the baptismal pledges of worshippers. Reciting the creeds invites worshippers to locate afresh their individual stories within the larger divine story that is made present in worship, for credal recitation is a form of "symbolic" participation not only in the story of the Triune God but also in the very life of the Triune God that the story references and rehearses. . . . Reciting the creeds impresses upon worshippers again and again the overarching meaning of the Bible and so shapes their capacity for hearing and heeding what specific passages of Scripture have to say to them.[52]

In other words, the proper and regular use of the classical creeds can help mold worshippers into the people God wants them to be, while also providing a powerful vehicle for worship itself through enabling the kind of relationship for which God created us.

51. S. Harmon, *Towards Baptist Catholicity*, 34–35.

52. S. Harmon, *Towards Baptist Catholicity*, 164–65.

The second and third benefits of regular credal recitation require less explanation but are no less important. Namely, the creeds foster fellowship between Christians and God and also between the individual believer and his or her fellow Christians throughout time and space. "Reciting the creeds invites worshippers," we read, "into diachronic solidarity with the saints gone before who for two millennia have confessed this story with these same words." We find also there is tremendous benefit that accrues from the fellowship that is expressed between Christian believers of different stripes today. Harmon notes, "Reciting the creeds declares the worshippers' synchronic solidarity with sisters and brothers in Christ in other denominations who today embrace the story of the Triune God."[53] Indeed, what a powerful expression of God's reign on earth, that Christians around the world are seen to be standing side by side in their confession of God's salvation in Jesus the Messiah! Harmon's argument culminates with the assertion that regular use of the classical creeds in worship, contrary to popular assumption, is a very Baptistic thing to do. "Having no fixed or mandated liturgy," he wrote, "Baptist churches are free to adopt whatever worship practices they find beneficial. Freely choosing to experience the benefits of rehearsing the divine story by confessing the ancient, ecumenical creeds is a most Baptist thing for free and faithful Baptists to do. Regular recitation of the creed as an act of worship may be the single most important means by which Baptists can retrieve the patristic interdependence of theology and worship in their own weekly rehearsal of the Christian story."[54] In *Towards Baptist Catholicity*, Harmon presents a number of practical steps that can be taken by Baptists in order to reap the practical and spiritual rewards that can come with a community life more informed by the tradition of the universal church. Yet, it is telling indeed that he suggests a reclamation of the Apostles' and Nicene creeds in Baptist worship to represent the most important and potentially most significant of these steps.

Though the many and varied manifestations of Baptist life in the United States represent a different context from that of The United Church of Canada, there are many similarities between these two traditions that make Harmon's work applicable for our purposes. In particular, the place of the classical creeds in Baptist life, where they have been rarely used and often scorned in recent decades, is very similar to that found in

53. S. Harmon, *Towards Baptist Catholicity*, 165.

54. S. Harmon, *Towards Baptist Catholicity*, 165.

The United Church. Though The United Church was founded on an ecumenical vision and though its constitution recognizes the authority of the ancient creeds, the Apostles' and Nicene Creeds have all but disappeared in contemporary practice. As in the Baptist circles addressed by Harmon, a key consequence of this is that the people of The United Church have merely replaced the catholic theological tradition with a less helpful and more sectarian one. As with Baptists, the people of The United Church could find their faith-experience enhanced by regular recitation of the Apostles' and Nicene Creeds. Not only would such a practice aid in the development of a better understanding of the biblical story of salvation, it would immensely deepen their relationship with the Triune God, as well as their fellowship with all the saints—past, present, and future. Moreover, we could easily modify Harmon's paragraph, quoted above, and say that given the history of The United Church and the liturgical liberty enjoyed by its congregations, freely choosing to reap the benefits of regular use of the classical creeds would be a very appropriate thing for the people of the denomination to do.

Creeds in the Roman Catholic Tradition—Luke Timothy Johnson

Luke Timothy Johnson has been one of the more well-known New Testament scholars in North America over the last fifty years. A former Benedictine monk who left the priesthood in the 1970s and later married, he has been associated for many years with the Candler School of Theology at Emory University in Atlanta, Georgia. Unlike Harmon, Johnson comes from an ecclesiastical tradition—Roman Catholicism—in which the Christian faith is regularly confessed corporately with one of the classical creeds—often weekly.[55] Yet, though the Nicene Creed in particular is frequently used by Roman Catholics in the United States, Johnson asserts that it is not used nearly well enough. Addressing especially those in his own church, Johnson wrote *The Creed: What Christians Believe and Why It Matters* with the hope that they, and other readers from different traditions, might experience the richness of the creed more fully. Though in many ways his context is quite unlike that of The United Church, his arguments nonetheless offer significant insight for those who wish to make good use of the classical creeds within other denominational settings.

55. Unlike the Roman Catholic Church in Canada, which more often uses the Apostles' Creed, use of the Nicene Creed predominates in the United States.

Johnson begins *The Creed* in an interesting way. Acknowledging the widespread disdain of creeds generally within post-Enlightenment culture, Johnson states that his arguments are not aimed at Christianity's "cultured despisers." Such people, he claims, would not likely read his book and, if they did, would not agree with it anyway. Instead, his intention is to address those Christians who "sleepwalk through the words they memorized as children" and also those who privately alter the creed in recitation due to personal offense and lack of understanding. He writes, "My aim is to make the creed controversial for Christians who say it but do not understand it and therefore do not grasp what a radical and offensive act they perform when they declare these words every week in a public assembly."[56] For Johnson, the vast majority of Christians in the United States do not realize that their worldview has really become that of modernity rather than that of classical Christianity. To the extent they actually are Christians, he argues, they have tried to cram the Christian faith awkwardly into the mold of modernity. Therefore, Johnson seeks to inform his readers of how genuinely countercultural and subversive is the Christian faith, while strongly encouraging people both to believe in and to live out this revolutionary Christian vision of reality.

Johnson suggests that one of the best things the church can do both to impress upon its members the radical nature of Christian faith and to promote the effectiveness of its witness to the world is to use the Nicene Creed more regularly and more fully in various aspects of its life. He writes, "I am not so foolish as to think that the Nicene-Constantinopolitan Creed is the prescription for all Christianity's contemporary ills. But I am firmly convinced that Christianity today would be healthier—and far more interesting—if it actually believed what the creed says, and acted in a manner that expressed that belief."[57] In particular, Johnson notes a number of benefits that can accrue to the church from its use of the creed. One is that the creed works "as a clear and communal statement of the community's faith. The creed is clear, it is not ambiguous or complicated . . . . And it is communal." Next, he suggests that the creed challenges each Christian, calling us to a faith and practice that are beyond us as mere individuals. Third, the internal logic of the Nicene Creed provides a framework, or worldview, in which it becomes possible to discern what are properly Christian actions and attitudes. Further, the creed serves to

56. Johnson, *Creed*, 7.

57. Johnson, *Creed*, 323.

center Christians on what is essential to the faith so that, though free to speculate on other details, they do not become bogged down in or separated from the wider community by nonessentials. Finally, Johnson states that in defining the community's center, without one misguided emphasis or another, "the creed opens possibilities for Christians of all sorts to grow together within a framework of their essential and shared agreement."[58] In so understanding their use of the creed, Christian congregations can avoid two pitfalls that have ensnared so much of the contemporary church: the creation of sectarian boundaries within fundamentalism and the disavowal of a distinctly Christian identity among many so-called theological liberals.

In believing what the Nicene Creed says and in desiring to say it in concert, the church will find itself "able to speak a prophetic word clearly to the world."[59] Johnson states quite bluntly that the worldview of modernity and the language that conspires with it is leading to dreadful misery for millions of people around the planet. Left unchecked, it will eventually lead to ecological annihilation for all. What is needed both for and from the church-in-the-world, he contends, is the clear presentation of reality as God sees it. For the church to understand itself and to fulfill its mission, it needs the Nicene Creed. "The Creed is remarkable," we read, "for its concise rendering of the Christian story and the structure of the Christian vision of reality. It is an instrument that can at once define the community of faith and challenge alternative stories and visions of reality."[60] Further, it "expresses a view of reality that is profoundly counter-cultural, not in some small point of style or other, but in its whole perception of the world and how humans are to act in the world."[61] There is nowhere else, he argues, for society to turn, if it wishes to avoid the self-destruction that lies inevitably at the end of its current course. Essential to the global claims of "authentic creedal Christianity," we find, "is the conviction that the creed is not simply 'an alternative view' as if it were another opinion offered for consideration . . . . Christians offer what they believe to be the truth about the world in every respect. It is not only 'true for them' . . . but true for all."[62] It is only by proclaiming the faith

58. Johnson, *Creed*, 301–2.

59. Johnson, *Creed*, 302.

60. Johnson, *Creed*, viii.

61. Johnson, *Creed*, 302.

62. Johnson, *Creed*, 305.

expressed by the Nicene Creed that the church can do for the world what God has always intended as its mission.

Beyond the virtues of community self-definition and prophetic witness in the world, Johnson argues that a key function of the Nicene Creed is to serve as a "Rule of Faith." Drawing on the ancient Christian understanding of the *regula fidei* that antedated the formation of formalized creeds, he suggests that the Nicene Creed provides "a story or myth for Christians," which can guide the people of God in the daily practice of their faith—especially in regards to the reading and interpretation of Scripture. Though most Christians agree that the Bible is the key source of theological authority for the church, there are many divergent perspectives on its interpretation. Particularly troubling in Johnson's eyes is the virtual chasm that has come to exist between the conservative-fundamentalist reading of Scripture and the liberal-modernist one. Both, he claimed, have abandoned the Christian view of the Bible in favor of a commitment to categories bequeathed by the Enlightenment. Conversely, the creed can help Christians unlock the power of narrative or myth and therefore enable the finding of truth both within critical historical understanding and beyond it as well.[63] The creed-as-rule-of-faith has implications for other areas of the Christian life also and can assist God's people in the practice of those things which are particularly consistent with their faith—including "hospitality, worship and the sharing of possessions."[64]

Johnson laments the state of institutional Christianity in his native country: "One could argue that there is no church in America." For him, the visible church has become like a club for the many who wish to join it on their own terms. Meanwhile, many others desire to call themselves Christians yet without any real connection to a local faith-community, often preferring to watch a church service on television. This is to say nothing of the countless Christians who consider their faith a matter of purely private and personal piety, having no implications for their relationships with other people or the world as a whole. The Nicene Creed, however, "offers the church a clear framework for discerning the proper standard for Christian practices."[65]

At the conclusion of *The Creed*, Johnson offers five steps toward what he calls "reclaiming the creed," a process by which Christians of all

63. Johnson, *Creed*, 308.

64. Johnson, *Creed*, 309.

65. Johnson, *Creed*, 309–11.

different stripes can be encouraged to use the Nicene Creed regularly and to use it well. The first step he suggests is to see if and how it is presently used in the life of the local church—whether in worship, in preaching, in catechism, and so forth. The second phase is to devote the time and effort necessary for serious study of the creed. He contends that it is crucial for Christians to know the history of the text and of its emergence in the life of the early church, as well as to know what its individual words and phrases mean. In so doing, they will come to understand the proper relationship of the Nicene Creed to Scripture (as a summary of the biblical story) and tradition (not as a coercive use of ecclesiastical authority but as a joyous expression of common faith), as well as to appreciate the force of its meaning. Third, local communities must reflect on their study to see in what ways they are comfortable with the creed and in what ways they are not—moving eventually to a strong sense of how the creed might be used within their life together. Fourth, communities must begin using the creed, not only occasionally on sacramental occasions but as a regular element in worship, in the instruction of both converts and the young, as well as in outreach and in group discussion, as a lens through which to view all aspects of Christian living. Fifth and finally, Johnson proposes the celebration and defence of the creed, both inside and outside the local church, in order to preserve the integrity of the community on an ongoing basis.[66]

It is my contention that Johnson's analysis of the Nicene Creed has important implications for The United Church of Canada. Though the Nicene Creed is used regularly in his tradition, unlike the current situation in The United Church, he suggests that Roman Catholics in the United States need to start virtually from scratch in their effective reclamation of this ancient confessional text. In the first instance, his arguments provide a useful response to the criticisms that have been aimed at both of the classical creeds within The United Church since the 1960s. Though many on the Committee on Christian Faith argued that "the classical creeds are now unintelligible" for that creature known as "modern man," Johnson shows that the Nicene Creed is "clear . . . not ambiguous or complicated. It can be understood and affirmed by children as well as by adults."[67] Whereas the Committee on Christian Faith wished to write a new creed because the words of the classical creeds were seen as implausible or offensive to the individual conscience, Johnson shows that the church is properly defined

66. Johnson, *Creed*, 323–24.

67. Johnson, *Creed*, 301.

by the faith expressed in the Nicene Creed and that, moreover, this faith becomes truly alive precisely in the challenge it presents to competing worldviews. If some people in The United Church are offended by the faith of the creeds, it may be a signal to them that the prophetic critique contained in these texts is speaking a word in their direction. The idea that a particular group of people known as a church can simply band together and cleverly replace the theological vision of the classical creeds, or of the rule of faith from which they evolved, is an offense of its own kind. If only Johnson's book had been published forty years earlier, there may have been an opportunity for a more faithful and critical reflection within The United Church on the idea of creating a modern credal confession to replace those that have been used for centuries.

More positively, Johnson's *The Creed* provides a rich and nuanced reflection on the many benefits that accrue to a church from the regular use of the Nicene Creed in different aspects of its communal life. Johnson shows how this simple text allows the community to define itself in a proper and healthy way, how it enables the community to have a genuine prophetic voice in the world, and how it governs the internal life of the church in functioning as a rule of faith. Though the Nicene Creed is scarcely used in The United Church, all of these arguments are essentially applicable to our situation, and we would benefit greatly from heeding Johnson's call.

Another helpful feature of *The Creed* is found at the very end of the book, where Johnson suggests a series of steps that might be taken by a local church that wants to take a genuine look at making more and better use of the creed. Though a congregation might not follow his five steps precisely, one gets no sort of impression that Johnson intended them to represent a rigid process anyway. Rather, they are simply an aid to beginning a conversation about the practical implications of his arguments within a congregational setting. If one were to modify Johnson's presentation for the context of the contemporary United Church, it might be to say that the Nicene Creed could be used alongside the Apostles' Creed. While no doubt the Nicene Creed is a jewel of the Christian tradition, the Apostles' Creed has a valued place in that tradition as well. Especially in the Western church, it also has a powerful message made effective by a coherent internal logic and is interwoven in the historical practice of local communities of all stripes.

Conclusion

At present, the recitation of one or the other of the classical creeds is a rare event in The United Church, occurring in a very small number of local churches and then only irregularly. A central constructive thesis of this book is that The United Church would be better off in virtually every way if congregations and other of its manifestations made use of the Apostles' and Nicene Creeds. As we ponder the perspective on creeds that currently dominates in The United Church, as well as the possible steps that might be taken to effect change, it is instructive to consider the situation in other denominations. Here, we have looked at the writings of Harmon and Johnson, two scholars whose works attempt to identify the challenges facing their respective Baptist and Roman Catholic fellowships, as well as to present their suggestions for meeting those challenges. Though their two contexts are in some ways different from that of The United Church of Canada, and again quite different from one another, both show convincingly that their denominations would be stronger and healthier if their local communities regularly recited the classical creeds with faith and understanding.

Harmon and Johnson take slightly different approaches in their advocacy for more and better use of the classical creeds by the church. On the one hand, Harmon has written broadly in the areas of ecumenism and the recovery of a catholic understanding of tradition within Baptist life. One of his key ideas is that Baptists should reevaluate their commitment to a somewhat misguided sense of *sola scriptura*. Realizing that Scripture is going to be read through one lens or another and that some type of narrative framework must predominate in biblical interpretation and theological reflection, he makes a strong case that Baptists ought to embrace those tools made available by classical, orthodox Christianity—especially as mediated through corporate recitation of the Apostles' and Nicene Creeds. Moreover, he argues that the regular use of these creeds in worship helps to form the mind of the church in light of the biblical story of salvation, enables participation in the life of the Triune God, and promotes fellowship with all the saints throughout time and space.

On the other hand, Johnson emphasizes the benefits that flow to Roman Catholics and to all Christians from the wise use of the Nicene Creed in particular. His three main points are that the creed allows the community of faith to define itself properly, that it empowers the more effective communication of a prophetic witness needed desperately in our dying world, and that the creed-as-rule-of-faith serves to guide the appropriate behaviors—individual and collective—that help us conform more closely to the will of God. Johnson also concludes with the suggestion of a reflective process that can assist each local church in reclaiming its connection to the creed in different areas of its life.

Both of these authors make a case that is relevant to the current situation of The United Church. Despite the significant contextual differences, they address faith-communities that, like The United Church, either do not use the classical creeds frequently or do not use them well. We can find in their compelling presentations ample reason to justify a reevaluation of the classical creeds in the life of The United Church. With Johnson, we can say that the creed allows for a proper and healthy definition of the church, that the theological vision of the creed is badly needed in our fallen world, and that this simple confession provides the framework for a soundly Christian rule of faith and practice. With Harmon, we can concur that the church needs the classical creeds, if it wishes to understand better the biblical story of salvation and to find itself in a closer spiritual proximity to the universal church. Though Harmon's briefer presentation does not emphasize the political-prophetic implications of the creeds, that may be only because his discussion is set specifically within a presentation on ecumenism and the broader tradition of the church universal. For his part, Johnson offers a very detailed treatment of the Nicene Creed but rather neglects the tremendous value and opportunity that accompanies the use of the Apostles' Creed also. Together, these two scholars demonstrate mutually reenforcing perspectives that harmonize nicely to create an attractive picture of credal Christianity. The people of The United Church would do well to hear what they say on the subject of creeds and consider beginning to reintroduce the Apostles' and Nicene Creeds into the worship of the assembly, the instruction of the faithful, and the theological reflection of the church in all aspects of its life.

Conclusion

Before thinking concretely about a particular creed or its use, we need to consider what it means to label a confessional text as a creed. More broadly, we need to ponder the significance of credal confession as an activity, regardless of the title assigned to a given text that is used in such a manner. By no means will the fruit of this reflection be easy answers. It is evident that a great diversity of perspectives exists across the Christian church—and, in this day and age, even within an individual denomination such as The United Church of Canada—as to what a creed properly is, what it means, and to what extent it is appealing or not. Though it is not easy or simple to do so, we must try to make some sense out of these challenging issues.

I have argued in this chapter that the best way of understanding credal confession is offered by Mary John Mananzan when she suggests that the act of faith-confession should be conceived as a speech-act or language game. Collective, confessional speech gives both rise and shape to a community of faith and makes sense within the context of that community. Moreover, such speaking serves to enable a faith-connection with God. This set of helpful ideas allows us to understand our situation more clearly and to interpret our creeds more insightfully, while also indicating some preferred ways forward. We have seen also in the work of Steven R. Harmon and Luke Timothy Johnson the wisdom, benefit, and beauty of confessing our faith using the Apostles' and Nicene Creeds. The so-called classical creeds offer consensus summaries of the biblical story within the broader Christian tradition, and therefore their study and recitation help to shape our Christian mind, individually and collectively. The use of these texts, whether in worship or other settings, can help us to experience joy, to articulate a powerful witness, and to strengthen the bonds of fellowship we have with God's people throughout time and space—the communion of the saints.

Conclusion

Finding Our Center

Centered or Bounded?

In recent decades, it has become increasingly popular to draw upon the mathematical metaphor of bounded and centered sets in seeking to understand how communities of the Christian church are defined. First proposed as a model for ecclesial thinking by Paul G. Hiebert in 1978, bounded sets are defined by the line between inside and out, while centered sets are clustered to varying degree around fixed points.[1] Peter Wyatt proposed the same sort of idea but in a more pastoral imagery: a pasture could be marked with a fence or, if the context allowed it, merely centered by wells from which the flocks would not want to travel too far.[2] Depending on the situation, either orientation could be more or less helpful. As with any analogy, these ones can be pushed too far. However, they may have some utility in helping us to think about the theological definition of The United Church. Is The United Church bounded theologically or confessionally? It would seem difficult to assert that there is a clear boundary or to say where it would be. Instead, most of its participants would likely see the idea of a centered set as more descriptively helpful for The United Church, and more appealing. One of the more popular hymns in The United Church has become

1. Hiebert, "Conversion, Culture," 24–29.

2. Wyatt, "Doctrine Matters," 5.

Gordon Light's "Draw the Circle Wide," and it expresses this well. Its phrases include: "Draw the circle wide, draw it wider still"; "God the still-point of the circle, 'round whom all creation turns"; and "Let our hearts touch far horizons . . . let our loving know no borders."[3]

If The United Church is a centered set, or seeks to be, what is its center? As we have seen, many have pointed to "A New Creed," implicitly or explicitly, as articulating the denomination's theological center. Yet, as we have learned, despite the poetic and other merits of this text, it does not really articulate a shared theology, and certainly not clearly. It has been variously described as open-ended, suggestive, and allusive, but evidently it is often interpreted in ways that are not just diverse but sometimes incompatible. Therefore, although it uses some theological words and phrases, it does not actually appear to be the center of a common theological vision. Originally intended both to accommodate and to take advantage of an existentialist theological trend in the 1960s, it has since come to be seen as a politically useful tool in holding together the fragile coalition which makes up The United Church of Canada. *A Song of Faith* says not just that "A New Creed" is open-ended but that it is "*usefully* open-ended."[4] What is this utility if not political? Theologically at least, the denomination seems to me neither bound nor centered.[5]

Of course, this is not a new critique of The United Church. Thanks to the fierce conflict it aroused among Canada's Presbyterians in the first quarter of the twentieth century, we know the movement for church union was subject to the same appraisal from its beginnings. Indeed, one of the criticisms levelled at The United Church even before its incorporation was the insufficiency of the theological statement in its proposed Basis of Union (now known as the "Twenty Articles of Doctrine"). E. Lloyd Morrow, a Toronto-based Presbyterian anti-unionist of the era, catalogued a series of statements made by various church leaders about the doctrinal section of the Basis of Union. Given that disparagement of the document, such as it was, generally came from those who opposed the idea of

3. *More Voices*, #145.

4. *Song of Faith*, 17 (emphasis added).

5. In arguing that The United Church is "awash in theology," Bourgeois and others seem to be in agreement that the denomination often discusses theology but without an ability to define either a common center or a boundary, albeit with a different evaluation of this reality. See Michael Bourgeois, "Awash in Theology: Issues in Theology in The United Church of Canada," in Schweitzer, *United Church of Canada*, 259–77; and Bourgeois, "Awash in Theology," a lecture given at West Hill United Church.

church union on a variety of grounds—particularly from a strong desire to maintain their distinctly Presbyterian identity—these analyses must be taken with a grain of salt. However, a careful reading of their critiques remains instructive. A few unionists, Morrow acknowledges, were enthusiastic about the theology of the proposed Basis of Union. Naturally, many of his fellow anti-unionists were vehemently opposed to church union on purely theological grounds; their beliefs did not align with what it claimed. Among the anti-unionists were also a number who viewed the "Twenty Articles of Doctrine" not as a statement of constructive theology but rather as a political document designed to accommodate the creation of an unsustainable coalition—that of Arminian, free-will Methodism with Calvinist, predestinarian Presbyterianism and non-confessional Congregationalism. Morrow notes in addition the presence of a cynical, political realism among the many unionists from all three denominations who had little interest in or love for the Basis of Union's doctrine. "This basis of union which I support is a platform not to stand on but to get into union on," he quotes one Methodist leader as saying.[6] Even those who disagree with this assessment of The United Church's theology acknowledge that it is still sometimes offered today.[7]

Some years ago, in a short essay, I made a similar point about the political utility of the pervasive use of "A New Creed" in The United Church.[8] One of the denomination's leading thinkers kindly told me that he liked the narrative aspect of my paper but that he would want to "push back" against my conclusion. However, whether out of politeness or other considerations, he did not suggest an alternative interpretation. That essay seems to have been read somewhat widely in The United Church and has been cited on occasion by other scholars. Yet, in the intervening time period, I have not seen any attempted refutations of its thesis or other explanations proposed in its place. Of course, it could be that my argument has found acceptance or that it is considered unworthy of response. Either would be fine, but I would be curious to know what others think of a question that lingers in my mind: why was "A New Creed" not subject to remit when it was proposed in 1968, or when it was revised in 1980, or again in 1995, to test the will of the church?[9] If not seen as necessary

6. Morrow, *Church Union in Canada*, 146–56.

7. Young, "Introduction," 1.

8. Haughton, "A New Creed."

9. Under The United Church's original governance structure, proposed changes to the Basis of Union would be sent from the General Council by remit to the presbyteries

on those earlier occasions, why then was its status as a fully adequate baptismal and liturgical symbol subject to remit in the period 2009–2012 after it had already been used and promoted as such extensively for decades? A pent-up impatience to publish the *Service Book* may provide some explanation for the approval process used in 1968 but not in later years. That the theological and liturgical significance of "A New Creed" did not have implications for The United Church's constitution in its first forty years of use seems to stretch the imagination. The best explanation I can see that fits in all the evidence presented in this book is a politically oriented one. It is not that this was some kind of conspiracy hatched in smoke-filled rooms. It is that so permitting and even promoting "A New Creed," without the level of open discussion and reflection one might have expected, has been seen as the path of least resistance for a church struggling to live with its irreducible theological diversity.

Some years ago, *The United Church Observer* magazine published the transcript of a discussion between famed atheist-minister Gretta Vosper and the noted evangelical minister Connie den Bok. Seaton helpfully highlights some telling portions of their conversation in his book, *Who's Minding the Story?*[10] "We are," suggested den Bok, "a kind of anarchistic loose alliance of individuals and congregations held together by a common property owner, by a common love of nobody telling us exactly what we should do." "One of the things The United Church failed to do," replied Vosper, "was to name why we come together. We got close to having those important conversations in the 1960s, but we veered away because we were afraid it was going to tear the fabric apart . . . . We should have kept with this work in the 1960s." "Or," said den Bok, "honourably split, way back when." "Honourably split," agreed Vosper, "way back when. Exactly." I am *not* prescribing such a split but am seeking to describe one of The United Church's key problems: it does not have a theological center.[11] Instead, it relies on institutional centers such as a pension plan, a governance structure, *The Manual*, myriad extra-manual policies, and perhaps others as well—including statements of faith, which, in saying little concretely or unambiguously, clearly function politically more than theologically or confessionally. In order to be acceptable to the

---

and congregations for approval, and then, if sufficient votes in favor were returned, the subsequent General Council would formalize the change.

10. Seaton, *Who's Minding the Story*, 108–9.

11. This claim does not rely only on reference to the denomination's theological extremes but to evidence and experiences everywhere present.

denomination's various constituencies, it has been simply assumed that any theological statement needs to have the capacity to accommodate vastly different interpretations, belief sets, and worldviews. The philosophy of language that enables "A New Creed" in particular to do this promotes private reflection rather than the building of community around the Christian gospel.

Ecumenism

As we have seen in this study, certain viewpoints have predominated within The United Church over the last four to five decades that see the faith of the classical creeds as irrelevant or even damaging and therefore impossible to affirm. Those holding such perspectives have often asserted that the particular confession called "A New Creed" is the only one needed, beneficial, or acceptable in The United Church. Seen from the wider angle of the whole church throughout time and space, however, the exclusive use of "A New Creed" within The United Church is surprising. Christians in other churches have noticed. The late United Methodist theologian Thomas C. Oden used harsh words like "basket case" and "dysfunction" to describe The United Church's theological situation.[12] Arnold L. Cook, former president of the Christian and Missionary Alliance in Canada, once commented that The United Church had "departed radically" from its own founding vision of a church, "[built] upon the foundation of the Apostles and the Prophets, Jesus Christ Himself being the chief cornerstone."[13] More recently, Stanley Hauerwas—once labeled by *Time* magazine, much to his chagrin, as America's best theologian—told a United Church minister-student of his in characteristically salty language that the student's denomination was "in deep shit."[14]

If theological critiques of an emergent sectarianism coming from outside The United Church present a challenge, even more so do those of a similar nature that have originated within. Searcy, cited earlier, declared that he was no longer satisfied with The United Church's wholesale replacement of the classical creeds with "A New Creed." Whereas the exclusive use of the latter has effected "our alienation from those foundational affirmations that have long belonged to the world-wide church," he

12. Oden, *Rebirth of Orthodoxy*, 144.

13. Cook singles out The United Church in his book *Historical Drift*, 208, 301–5.

14. Personal conversation with Jeff Seaton, 17 Feb. 2021.

expressed a longing for more catholic expressions of the faith, of which he acquired a greater appreciation through his "growing engagement with the historic and contemporary ecumenical church beyond our own denomination." He writes:

> I owe my rebirth in the faith to writers, teachers and colleagues who have shared with me the riches of the historic ecumenical tradition, and to parishioners who have responded eagerly to my attempts to give voice to this peculiar language and world. In learning the rhythms and cadences of the early creeds I have been given back a memory, and with it a transformed trust in a Triune God so much more peculiar and mysterious and wonderful than the One I met "in-house" in the beloved denomination of my upbringing. I am so profoundly grateful to have been met by the wonderfully relevant gospel of new life in the most surprising places—in the language and texts and traditions that I had learned to label as irrelevant.[15]

We can all acknowledge that the global church is the body of Christ, consisting of and needing different parts and a diversity of gifts. Seeking to balance the uniqueness of The United Church with the almost two-thousand-year heritage of Christianity, Seaton advocates "a progressive orthodox United Church . . . that would seek to push beyond the limitations of reliance upon only one creedal statement, the 1968 New Creed, to recover the challenges and adventure of a broader engagement of the universal church."[16] "A New Creed," he suggests, is "beautiful, but partial."[17] "A New Creed" was originally designed to hold together a fracturing religious consensus in The United Church in the turmoil of the 1960s. Its continued use, however, has crystallized the orientation of The United Church at a unique point in the past when its cultural context was at its most tumultuous and, at the same time, when its confidence to cope with that situation was most insufficient.[18]

Some readers might wish to respond that my hermeneutic here has been too simplistic, that I have drawn too heavily on the stated aims of the text's authors in reaching conclusions. After all, the meaning of authorial intent is controversial in literary criticism. In anticipation of this possible reply, I would make two points. First, "A New Creed" would not have been

15. Searcy, "Story of My Conversion," 38.

16. Seaton, *Who's Minding the Story*, 118.

17. Seaton, *Who's Minding the Story*, 99.

18. Seaton, *Who's Minding the Story*, xvii.

created apart from the institutional aims of its authors. Further to these aims, The United Church published an accompanying final report of the Committee on Christian Faith, *Creeds*, in order to communicate its reason for being and to guide its interpretation. "A New Creed" did not arise organically and therefore it does not lend itself as well as other kinds of texts might to such a recontextualizing of meaning as would be suggested by a different hermeneutic. Indeed, ample evidence has been presented in these pages to show that "A New Creed" continues to function within The United Church largely as initially envisioned. In this case, authorial intent still matters. Second, there are obviously alternate interpretive lenses—whether raised by advocates of the new criticism, reader response, or other schools of thought—that give primacy to a meaning located elsewhere: objectively in the text itself or subjectively as created by the reader or interpreter. While I remain interested in authorial intent, I acknowledge that these other kinds of approaches are often required or beneficial. I also agree that the creation of meaning above the text, with the interpreter, is precisely what is happening whenever the words and phrases of "A New Creed" are read or recited. The nature of the text requires it. What I contend is that this dynamic does not work well as a method of theological confession or as the sustaining basis for a faith-community. Such concerns are only amplified in an ecumenical context in which "A New Creed" has been used by only a small group within the universal church.

There are of course those who take a different view than I and claim that "A New Creed" has gained, or is gaining, greater acceptance in the wider church—that it is, so to speak, a wave of the future. I have yet to see good evidence that this is the case or is likely to become so.[19] Conversely, as Airhart points out, the initial approval of "A New Creed" by the General Council Executive was one of the developments that eventually scuttled plans for a potential union between the United and Anglican

19. Anecdotal support for this claim tends to rely on rather weak indicators, in my opinion, suggesting that perhaps stronger argumentation is unavailable. See Young, "Introduction,"15, 20n23. As of 2009, The United Church had given permission to use "A New Creed" in approximately two dozen publications, several of which were actually from within The United Church tradition, such as for Sunday school curricula and *The United Church Observer*. The primary ecumenical borrower at that time was the United Methodist Church which, in addition to its hymn book, had used the text in some small group study resources. Other permissions of note were given to the PCUSA for use in a Bible study leaflet and the Church of Scotland for its *The Church of Scotland Ordinal and Service Book* (interim edition) in 2001 (email correspondence from Zara D. Garcia-Alvarez, 25 Mar. 2009).

churches in the 1970s.[20] This notable consequence was felt even before "A New Creed" developed such a pride of place as it has in more recent times. "Doctrine is important," write MacLean and Young helpfully, "[because] in a world where we function so frequently as individuals, we need community." They add,

> We need it not to have a sense that others share our convictions, important as that can be. Rather, we need it to check our own reading of scripture, our own understanding of where and how God is active in the world. Former United Church Moderator Lois Wilson spent the fall of 2009 at the Queen's School of Religion as a scholar-in-residence. In one presentation during her time there, she offered several criticisms of the contemporary United Church. She perceived a decline of the denomination's ecumenical spirit and therefore its increasing isolation. Worse still, she said, as a denomination we have become quite contented with that, quite contented to hear only our own voice.[21]

Though not specifically about "A New Creed," these remarks speak insightfully to the reality of The United Church in the twenty-first century—one in which the almost exclusive use of one confessional text is both symptom and cause.

Conflict and Decline

In their impressively researched book, *Leaving Christianity: Changing Allegiances in Canada Since 1945*, Clarke and Macdonald trace what has been a precipitous numerical decline, measured in any level of participation, in The United Church of Canada (and many other denominations as well) since the early 1960s. Flatt argues that the denomination's theological drift from Evangelicalism to liberalism is a key reason for this decline. While there is some helpful analysis in Flatt's work, the broader statistical evidence suggests that the Canadian population has been sliding away from Christianity altogether rather than abandoning so-called liberal churches for more so-called conservative ones. While the latter move would doubtless describe the experience of some individuals, such a hypothesis provides an insufficient explanation for the larger trends. Considering the situation of The United Church during this period of decline, Airhart

20. Airhart, *Church with Soul*, 279.

21. MacLean and Young, *Preaching the Big Questions*, 157.

offers a helpful and succinct summary: "In many respects the church that was born in 1925 did not survive the tumultuous 1960s."[22] As Beardsall notes, it is remarkable in retrospect how quickly United Church leaders realized what was happening around them in that era, and how dire might be their denomination's future if radical changes were not made.[23] In that context, it is understandable that the denomination would seek to chart something of a new course, including the attempt to craft a new confessional text that would help it ride the incoming wave. Even if, in hindsight, some might disagree with certain of the decisions made, we can continue to honor the attempt of our forebears to wrestle with the difficult "adaptive challenges" they faced.[24] Given the politically oriented approach to doctrinal confession that was embedded into the DNA of The United Church at its founding, such a move would almost be expected.

In a brilliant but little known study, *Conflict and Decline: Ministers and Laymen in an Australian Country Town*, Kenneth Dempsey shows how the onset of institutional decline after 1950 rattled the once happy Methodist congregations of the Barool Circuit in New South Wales. Where once ministers and congregations had gotten along consistently well, the subsequent thirty years saw a succession of pastorates that for the most part went badly and ended badly. Dempsey convincingly identifies the nature of the problem. As the churches declined, the congregations blamed their ministers, and the ministers in turn blamed their congregations. Though not a Methodist himself, Dempsey sees this is as somewhat tragic, for the decline of the churches in the circuit was obviously related to inexorable changes going on in the society around them. Neither better ministers nor more faithful, committed lay persons were likely to have materially altered the overarching trend that was becoming demonstrable across their country and in a variety of Protestant denominations. Writ large, this study of the Barool Circuit could have been done on the decline of The United Church of Canada and even of mainstream Christianity in the West, the precise causes of which are so complex as to not yet be fully understood. Seen in that light, "A New Creed" has clearly not caused the decline of The United Church. Its writing and adoption were simply some of the responses taken by United Church leaders in the midst of what was evidently a tumultuous and unsettling

22. Airhart, *Church with Soul*, 256.

23. Beardsall, "Sin and Redemption," 113–14.

24. Airhart, *Church with Soul*, 255–61.

time. Moreover, as the social context of the denomination's ministry has become increasingly inhospitable in the intervening years, the nature of "A New Creed" has allowed it to remain relevant as a confessional text. The continued promotion of this particular statement of faith is therefore correlated with the ongoing challenge and decline being faced by The United Church. Having been written to help manage the reality of a breakdown in theological consensus, which emerged forcefully in the 1960s, this text has continued to be used for that reason and is celebrated within the denomination for admittedly doing so somewhat effectively.

A Call for Conversation

The aim of this book is not to be negative or critical. I acknowledge: in a challenging cultural context, most people in The United Church have been trying their best to be faithful to their God. Among the many good and faithful servants who belong to The United Church will be those who disagree with my conclusions. My intention has been to offer a classically Christian perspective on "A New Creed" and its place in the life and liturgy of The United Church, while making positive and constructive suggestions that can help and strengthen the denomination going forward. Though I propose that the use of "A New Creed" ought to be revised and curtailed, that is not to say that I think it can never be used profitably or that it is not a treasured piece of our common heritage. Rather, I contend that "A New Creed" should be regarded more as the classical creeds came to be by the Committee on Christian Faith in the 1960s—as an option, but not the primary one. I further hope that the people of The United Church will be open to conversation about reconsidering their disregard of the Apostles' and Nicene Creeds.

Gretta Vosper describes "A New Creed" as a reflection of The United Church's desire in the 1960s "to have a softer gentler version of the denomination's Statement of Faith," which, she concludes, "allowed those in the church who were questioning some of the traditional beliefs of the Christian Church to remain within the embrace of the United Church." Yet, Vosper also argues at length that a satisfactory vision for religious life cannot be found through intentionally vague language and the replacement of confession with mere obfuscation.[25] In other words, it is no longer enough for Vosper or others to recite empty words, which are

25. Vosper, *With or Without God*, 94. On this rare point, I agree with her.

capable of being "filled with personal content by those who say the creed." Moreover, it is no longer enough to assume that such an approach to confessional language will be able to sustain the illusion of a nonexistent theological center. We in The United Church need to have a real conversation about theology, even if it is, at times, a difficult one. As with other areas of life, honest tension would be more productive and healthier than an ongoing denial of the issue.

Since the constitution of The United Church, the Basis of Union, continues to acknowledge the teaching of the Apostles' and Nicene Creeds and the bulk of the global church remains committed to the theological vision they narrate, I believe it would be greatly enriching if these texts were studied, recited, and even debated within our fellowship. The love generated by "A New Creed" in The United Church goes to show the amazing potential for good that practices of credal confession can have within a community of faith. I believe that this potential could be harnessed with even greater benefit if we made regular and joyful use of the classical creeds and allowed ourselves to be shaped by the gospel story they tell. Mary John Mananzan confirms this when she writes that distinctly Christian belief is "anchored in human experiences and therefore can be the basis for a way of life that is engaged in by human beings. Consequently, the Christian religious discourse, which is the linguistic expression of this way of life, finds its significance in its attempt to articulate these experiences."[26] I realize there are those whose personal, ideological commitments will not allow them to consider this. However, as Stanley Hauerwas added in speaking to his United-Church-student, at this point we should, "try everything—[we] have nothing to lose."[27] As we were reminded by the writings of Steven R. Harmon and Luke Timothy Johnson, the classical creeds are among the jewels of the Christian tradition. Used wisely, they can help to nurture understandings of the biblical story of salvation and enable Christians reciting them to participate worshipfully in the divine-human relationship. Further, these ancient ecumenical confessions can unite God's people in fellowship throughout time and space, and center the church on beliefs that are essential to its core good-news message, thereby freeing us from the burden of the harmful barriers that are typically erected when nonessentials are brought to the fore.

26. Mananzan, *"Language Game" of Confessing*, 149.

27. Personal conversation with Jeff Seaton, 17 Feb. 2021.

Bibliography

"Affirmations of Faith." *Expository Times* 83, no. 11 (Aug. 1972), 345.

Airhart, Phyllis D. *A Church with the Soul of a Nation: Making and Remaking the United Church of Canada*. Montreal: McGill-Queen's University Press, 2014.

"The Approved Guideline of Covenanting Service for Use in Waterloo Presbytery." Unpublished document, from Waterloo Presbytery, Waterloo, ON, n.d. Copy in author's possession.

Bauer, Walter. *Orthodoxy and Heresy in Earliest Christianity*. Edited by Robert A. Kraft and Gerhard Krodel. London: SCM, 1972.

———, et al., eds. *A Greek-English Lexicon of the New Testament and Other Early Christian Literature*. 3rd ed. Chicago: University of Chicago Press, 2000.

Baum, Gregory. Review of "A New Creed." *Ecumenist* (July–Aug. 1968) n.p.

Beardsall, Sandra. "'And Whether Pigs Have Wings': The United Church in the 1960s." In *The United Church of Canada: A History*, edited by Don Schweitzer, 97–117. Waterloo, ON: Wilfrid Laurier University Press, 2011.

———. "Sin and Redemption in The United Church of Canada." In *The Theology of The United Church of Canada*, edited by Don Schweitzer et al., 101–125. Waterloo, ON: Wilfrid Laurier University Press, 2019.

Bennett, John C. "Some Objections to Coexistence." *Christian Century* 77, no. 14 (6 Apr. 1960) 408–9.

Berger, Peter L. "A Market Model for the Analysis of Ecumenicity." *Social Research* 30, no. 1 (1963) 77–93.

———, and Thomas Luckmann. "Secularization and Pluralism." *International Yearbook for the Sociology of Religion* 2 (1966) 73–84.

Berton, Pierre. *The Comfortable Pew: A Critical Look at Christianity and the Religious Establishment in the New Age*. Toronto: McClelland and Stewart, 1965.

Best, Marion. *Will Our Church Disappear? Strategies for the Renewal of The United Church of Canada*. Winfield, BC: Wood Lake Books, 1994.

The Book of Common Order of The United Church of Canada. 2nd ed. Toronto: United Church, 1950.

Bourgeois, Michael. "Awash in Theology." Lecture given at West Hill United Church, Toronto, 25 Feb. 2007.

Bradley-St.-Cyr, Ruth. "The Downfall of the Ryerson Press." PhD diss., University of Ottawa, 2014.

Bromiley, G. W. *Theological Dictionary of the New Testament: Abridged in One Volume.* Grand Rapids: Eerdmans, 1985.

Bruce, David. *Jesus 24/7: A Short Course in Faith for the Questing Christian.* Toronto: United Church, 2008.

———. "Swimming the Tiber." *Touchstone* 30, no. 2 (May 2012) 52–55.

Bryson, Bill. *Made in America: An Informal History of the English Language in the United States.* New York: William Morrow, 1994.

Bultmann, Rudolf. "The Primitive Christian Kerygma and the Historical Jesus." In *The Historical Jesus and the Kerygmatic Christ,* edited by C. E. Braaten and R. A. Harrisville, 15–42. New York: Abingdon, 1964.

———. *Translating Theology into the Modern Age.* Edited by Robert W. Funk. New York: Harper and Row, 1965.

Campbell, Douglas F. "The Anglican and United Churches in Church Union Dialogue, 1943–75." *Studies in Religion* 17, no. 3 (Summer 1988) 303–14.

Catechism: The United Church of Canada. Toronto: Board of Evangelism and Social Service, 1944.

Cavanaugh, William T. *The Myth of Religious Violence.* New York: Oxford University Press, 2009.

Cawley, Janet. "The United Church of Canada and the Trinitarian Formula." *Ecumenical Trends* 17, no. 5 (May 1988) 72–74.

Celebrate God's Presence: A Book of Services for The United Church of Canada. Toronto: United Church, 2000.

Chalmers, Randolph Carleton. *The Happy Science.* Toronto: United Church Observer, 1975.

———. "The New Creed." Unpublished manuscript. The United Church of Canada Archives, Standing Committee on Christian Faith fonds, 82.204c, box 3, file 41.

———. *See the Christ Stand! A Study in Doctrine in The United Church of Canada.* Toronto: Ryerson, 1945.

Chambers, Steven. *This Is Your Church: A Guide to the Beliefs, Policies and Positions of The United Church of Canada,* 2nd ed. Toronto: CANEC, 1986.

Clarke, Brian, and Stuart Macdonald. *Leaving Christianity: Changing Allegiances in Canada Since 1945.* Montreal: McGill-Queen's University Press, 2017.

Clifford, N. Keith. "The United Church of Canada and Doctrinal Confession." *Touchstone* 2, no. 2 (May 1984) 6–21.

Cook, Arnold L. *Historical Drift.* Camp Hill, PA: Christian, 2000.

"Covenanting Service." Shining Waters Regional Council, Sept. 2019. https://shiningwatersregionalcouncil.ca/wp-content/uploads/2019/09/Covenanting-Service-Template-SWRC-Sept-2019.docx .

Cox, Harvey. *The Secular City: Secularization and Urbanization in Theological Perspective.* New York: Macmillan, 1965.

"A Creed." *United Church Observer* (1 Feb. 1969) 18–19, 30, 40.

Cross, F. L., and E. A. Livingstone, eds. *The Oxford Dictionary of the Christian Church.* 3rd ed. Oxford, UK: Oxford University Press, 1997.

Crossley, Russel. *This You Can Believe: A Commentary on a Contemporary Creed of The United Church of Canada.* Guelph, ON: Dublin Street United Church, 1976.

Dare to Be: Remembering Our History. Toronto: United Church, 2010.

DeLorme, Richard. "A Revised Creed Based on the Original by M. Freeman, November, 1967." Unpublished manuscript. The United Church of Canada Archives, Standing Committee on Christian Faith fonds, 82.204c, box 3, file 41.

Dempsey, Kenneth. *Conflict and Decline: Ministers and Laymen in an Australian Country Town*. Sydney: Methuen, 1983.

DeVries, Frederic. "Musical Setting for 'A New Creed' in Honour of the 70th Anniversary of the Sanctuary, St. Paul's United Church, Dundas." Privately published in Dundas, ON, 2003.

Dolan, Rex. *The Big Change: The Challenge to Radical Change in the Church*. Toronto: United Church, 1967.

"Don't Make Us Recite the Apostles' Creed." *United Church Observer* (1 Feb. 1965) 10.

Dow, John. *This Is Our Faith*. Toronto: Board of Evangelism and Social Service of The United Church of Canada, 1943.

Evans, Donald. "A Possible Revision of the Creed." Unpublished manuscript. The United Church of Canada Archives, Standing Committee on Christian Faith fonds, 82.204c, box 3, file 41.

Flatt, Kevin N. *After Evangelicalism: The Sixties and the United Church of Canada*. Montreal: McGill-Queen's University Press, 2013.

Forms of Service for the Offices of the Church. Toronto: United Church, 1926.

Frye, Northrop. *The Double Vision: Language and Meaning in Religion*. Toronto: United Church, 1991.

———. *The Great Code: The Bible and Literature*. Toronto: Academic Press Canada, 1983.

———. *Words with Power: Being a Second Study of "The Bible and Literature."* New York: Harcourt, Brace and Jovanovich, 1990.

Gandier, Alfred. *The Doctrinal Basis of Union and Its Relation to the Historic Creeds*. Ryerson Essay 34. Toronto: Ryerson, 1926.

Gorman, William J. *Elements of Biblical Exegesis*. Peabody, MA: Hendrickson, 2001.

Grant, John Webster. *The Church in the Canadian Era*. 2nd ed. Burlington, ON: Welch, 1988.

———. "Leading a Horse to Water: Reflections on Church Union Conversations in Canada." In *Studies of the Church in History: Essays Honouring Robert S. Paul on His Sixty-Fifth Birthday*, edited by Horton Davies, 165–81. Pittsburgh Theological Monographs. Allison Park, PA: Pickwick, 1983.

———. "Only Yesterday." *United Church Observer* 40, no. 3 (Nov. 1979) 37–38.

Harding, Thomas, and Bruce Harding. *Patterns of Worship in The United Church of Canada: 1925–1987*. Toronto: Evensong, 1996.

Harmon, Steven R. *Towards Baptist Catholicity: Essays on Tradition and the Baptist Vision*. Milton Keynes, UK: Paternoster, 2006.

Harmon, William, and C. H. Holman. *A Handbook to Literature*. 8th ed. Upper Saddle River, NJ: Prentice Hall, 2000.

Haughton, William. "Almost Forgotten: R. C. Chalmers and the Liberal Evangelical Heritage of the United Church of Canada." *Touchstone* 29, no. 2 (May 2011) 51–58.

———. "The Genesis and Evolution of A New Creed in the United Church of Canada." *Historical Papers*, Canadian Society of Church History (2011) 5–20.

———. "'A New Creed': Its Origin and Significance." *Touchstone* 29, no. 3 (Sept. 2011) 20–29.

Hays, Richard B. *Echoes of Scripture in the Letters of Paul*. New Haven, CT: Yale University Press, 1989.

Heschel, Abraham J. *Man Is Not Alone: A Philosophy of Religion*. New York: Octagon, 1951.

Hiebert, Paul G. "Conversion, Culture, and Cognitive Categories." *Gospel in Context* 1 (Oct. 1978) 24–29.

Hobsbawm, Eric. *Age of Extremes: The Short Twentieth Century 1914–1991*. London: Joseph, 1994.

Holmes, Michael W., ed. *The Apostolic Fathers: Greek Texts and English Translations*. Grand Rapids: Baker, 1999.

Homewood, E. L., ed. *Faith of the Church*. Toronto: United Church Observer, 1983.

Howse, Ernest Marshall. *Roses in December: The Autobiography of Ernest Marshall Howse*. Winfield, BC: Wood Lake Books, 1982.

Huntly, Alyson C., and Yvonne Cathcart. *The Painted Trunk and Other Stories: A Children's History of The United Church of Canada*. Toronto: United Church, 1999.

Hymn and Worship Resources Committee. *Voices United: Services for Trial Use 1996–1997*. Toronto: United Church, n.d.

The Hymn Book of the Anglican Church of Canada and the United Church of Canada. Toronto: Cooper & Beatty, 1971.

The Hymnary of The United Church of Canada. Toronto: United Church, 1930.

InterChurch and InterFaith Committee. *Mending the World: An Ecumenical Vision for Healing and Reconciliation*. Toronto: United Church, 1997. https://ecumenism.net/archive/docu/1997_ucc_mending_the_world.pdf.

Johnson, Luke Timothy. *The Creed: What Christians Believe and Why it Matters*. New York: Doubleday, 2003.

Johnston, George. "A Proposed New Creed." Unpublished manuscript. The United Church of Canada Archives, Standing Committee on Christian Faith fonds, 82.204c, box 3, file 43.

Joint Committee of the Presbyterian Church in Canada, the Methodist Church, and the Congregational Churches of Canada. "Twenty Articles of Doctrine." The United Church of Canada, 1925. https://united-church.ca/community-faith/welcome-united-church-canada/faith-statements/twenty-articles-doctrine-1925.

Jung, Hae-Bin. "A Wanderer with an Open Mind: From Russia to Canada—A Reflection on the Journey of Sang Chul Lee." *Touchstone* 39, no. 3 (Oct. 2021) 61–67.

Kelly, J. N. D. *Early Christian Creeds*. 3rd ed. New York: Continuum, 1972.

———. *Early Christian Doctrines*. 5th ed. Peabody, MA: Prince, 1976.

Kervin, William S. *The Language of Baptism: A Study of the Authorized Baptismal Liturgies of The United Church of Canada*. Langham, MD: Scarecrow Press, 2003.

———. "Sacraments and Sacramentality in The United Church of Canada." In *The Theology of The United Church of Canada*, edited by Don Schweitzer et al., 223–50. Waterloo, ON: Wilfrid Laurier University Press, 2019.

Kung, Hans, and Jürgen Moltmann, eds. *An Ecumenical Confession of Faith?* New York: Seabury, 1979.

Lee, Sang Chul. "United in Faith." In *Voices and Visions: Sixty-Five Years of The United Church of Canada*, edited by Peter Gordon White, 153–60. Toronto: United Church, 1990.

Liddell, H. G. *An Intermediate Greek-English Lexicon*. Oxford, UK: Clarendon, 1889.

MacLean, Catherine Faith, and John H. Young. *Preaching the Big Questions: Doctrine Isn't Dusty*. Toronto: United Church, 2015.

MacQueen, Angus J. "Revision of Freeman-DeLorme Creed." Unpublished manuscript. The United Church of Canada Archives, Standing Committee on Christian Faith fonds, 82.204c, box 3, file 41.

Mananzan, Mary John. *The "Language Game" of Confessing One's Belief: A Wittgensteinian-Austinian Approach to the Linguistic Analysis of Creedal Statements.* Tübingen, Germ.: Niemeyer, 1974.

The Manual. Toronto: United Church, 2022.

Marshall, I. Howard. *I Believe in the Historical Jesus.* Grand Rapids: Eerdmans, 1977.

Marwick, Arthur. *The Sixties: Cultural Revolution in Britain, France, Italy, and the United States.* Oxford, UK: Oxford University Press, 1998.

McGrath, Alister. *Christianity's Dangerous Idea: The Protestant Revolution—A History from the Sixteenth Century to the Twenty-First.* New York: HarperCollins, 2007.

Miedema, Gary. *For Canada's Sake: Public Religion, Centennial Celebrations, and the Re-Making of Canada in the 1960s.* Montreal: McGill-Queen's University Press, 2005.

Milton, Ralph. *This United Church of Ours.* 3rd ed. Kelowna, BC: Wood Lake, 2000.

More Voices. Toronto: United Church, 2007.

Morrow, E. Lloyd. *Church Union in Canada: Its History, Motives, Doctrine, and Government.* Toronto: Allen, 1923.

"A New Creed." The United Church of Canada, 1968, rev. 1980, 1995. https://united-church.ca/community-faith/welcome-united-church-canada/faith-statements/new-creed-1968.

Nicol, Eric, et al. *Why the Sea Is Boiling Hot: A Symposium on the Church and the World.* Toronto: United Church, 1965.

Nodwell, R. G. "Some Modern Creeds Discussed: A Preliminary Draft." Unpublished manuscript. The United Church of Canada Archives, Standing Committee on Christian Faith fonds, 82.204c, box 3, file 41.

Noll, Mark A. "What Happened to Christian Canada?" *Church History* 75, no. 2 (June 2006) 245–73.

Oden, Thomas C. *The Rebirth of Orthodoxy: Signs of New Life in Christianity.* New York: HarperCollins, 2003.

"Pastoral Relations Liasons." Shining Waters Regional Council, 2019. https://shiningwatersregionalcouncil.ca/pastoral-relations/liaisons/.

Pelikan, Jaroslav. *Credo: Historical and Theological Guide to Creeds and Confessions of Faith in the Christian Tradition.* New Haven, CT: Yale University Press, 2003.

Pentland, John. *Fishing Tips: How Curiosity Transformed a Community of Faith.* Toronto: United Church, 2015.

Putnam, Robert D. *Bowling Alone: The Collapse and Revival of American Community.* New York: Simon and Schuster, 2000.

Ramsey, Michael. *Image Old and New.* London: SPCK, 1963.

Riordan, Michael. *The First Stone: Homosexuality and the United Church.* Toronto: McClelland and Stewart, 1990.

Robinson, John A. T. *Honest to God.* London: SCM, 1963.

Rose, Hugh A. A. "Letter to Richard H. N. Davidson, 19 March 1968." The United Church of Canada Archives, Standing Committee on Christian Faith fonds, 82.204c, box 1, file 3.

Routley, Erik. *Creeds and Confessions: The Reformation and Its Modern Ecumenical Implications.* London: Duckworth and Co., 1962.

Schweitzer, Don. "The Christology of The United Church of Canada." In *The Theology of The United Church of Canada*, edited by Don Schweitzer et al., 127–52. Waterloo, ON: Wilfrid Laurier University Press, 2019.

———, et al., eds. *The Theology of The United Church of Canada.* Waterloo, ON: Wilfrid Laurier University Press, 2019.

———, ed. *The United Church of Canada: A History.* Waterloo, ON: Wilfrid Laurier University Press, 2011.

Searcy, Edwin. "The Story of My Conversion." *Touchstone* 27, no. 1 (Jan. 2009) 36–38.

Seaton, Jeff. *Who's Minding the Story? The United Church of Canada Meets "A Secular Age."* Eugene, OR: Pickwick, 2018.

Service Book for the Use of Ministers Conducting Public Worship. Toronto: United Church, 1969.

Service Book for the Use of the People. Toronto: United Church, 1969.

Service Book for Use in Church Courts. Toronto: United Church, 1993.

"A Service of Covenanting." Unpublished document, from Middlesex Presbytery, London, ON, n.d. Copy in author's possession.

Shephard, Muriel. "Letter to the Editor." In *United Church Observer*, 4 Mar. 2009. http://www.ucobserver.org/letters/index1.php. Site discontinued.

Silcox, C. E. *Church Union in Canada: Its Causes and Consequences.* New York: Institute for Social and Religious Research, 1933.

Simpson, J. A., and E. S. C. Weiner, eds. *The Oxford English Dictionary.* 2nd ed. vol. 2. Oxford, UK: Clarendon, 1989.

"A Song of Faith." The United Church of Canada, 2006. https://united-church.ca/community-faith/welcome-united-church-canada/faith-statements/song-faith-2006.

A Song of Faith: A Statement of Faith of The United Church of Canada. Toronto: United Church, 2006.

Soskice, Janet Martin. *Metaphor and Religious Language.* Oxford, UK: Clarendon, 1985.

Spong, John Shelby. *Why Christianity Must Change or Die: A Bishop Speaks to Believers in Exile.* New York: HarperCollins, 1999.

Standing Committee on Christian Faith. *Creeds: A Report of the Committee on Christian Faith.* Toronto: United Church, 1969.

———. "Meeting Minutes." The United Church of Canada Archives, 82.204c, boxes 3–6.

———. "Report on Creeds." The United Church of Canada Archives, 82.204c, box 3, file 41.

"A Statement of Faith." The United Church of Canada, 1940. https://united-church.ca/community-faith/welcome-united-church-canada/faith-statements/statement-faith-1940.

Strain, Christopher B. *The Long Sixties: America, 1955–1973.* Hoboken, NJ: Wiley and Sons, 2016.

Styles, Frederick A. *A Faith to Live By: A Resource for Adult Study.* Toronto: United Church, 1991.

Task Group on Christian Initiation, Working Unit on Worship and Liturgy, Division of Mission in Canada. *Baptism and Renewal of Baptismal Faith for Optional Use in The United Church of Canada.* Toronto: United Church, 1986.

Taylor, Charles. *A Secular Age.* Cambridge, MA: Harvard University Press, 2007.

Taylor, Jim, ed. *Fire and Grace: Stories of History and Vision*. Toronto: United Church, 1999.

Thielicke, Helmut. *I Believe: The Christian's Creed*. Translated by John W. Doberstein. Philadelphia: Fortress, 1968.

The United Church of Canada. *Record of Proceedings*. Eighteenth General Council. Toronto: United Church, 1958.

———. *Record of Proceedings*. Forty-First General Council. Toronto: United Church, 2012.

———. *Record of Proceedings*. Thirty-Fifth General Council. Toronto: United Church, 1994.

———. *Record of Proceedings*. Twenty-Seventh General Council. Toronto: United Church, 1977.

———. *Record of Proceedings*. Twenty-Third General Council. Toronto: United Church, 1968.

The United Church of Canada General Council. "Executive Meeting Minutes." Correspondence of the Executive and Sub-Executive, The United Church of Canada Archives, 82.001c, boxes 32–34.

The United Methodist Hymnal. Nashville: United Methodist, 2002.

"Vague New Creed for Canadians." *Christianity Today* 12, no. 23 (30 Aug. 1968) 43. https://www.christianitytoday.com/ct/1968/august-30/vague-new-creed-for-canadians.html.

Vischer, Lukas, ed. *Reformed Witness Today: A Collection of Confessions and Statements of Faith Issued by Reformed Churches*: Bern: Evangelische Arbeitsstelle Oekumene Schweiz, 1982.

Voices United: The Hymn and Worship Book of The United Church of Canada. Toronto: United Church, 1996.

Vosper, Gretta. "A Letter to Gary Paterson Regarding Paris." Gretta Vosper, Jan. 9, 2015. https://www.grettavosper.ca/letter-gary-paterson-regarding-paris/.

———. *With or Without God: Why the Way We Live Is More Important Than What We Believe*. Toronto: HarperCollins, 2008.

Waters, Moir. "Sermon on 'A New Creed.'" N.d. The United Church of Canada Archives, Standing Committee on Christian Faith fonds, 82.204c, box 3, file 41.

We Are Not Alone, We Live in God's World. Toronto: United Church, 1996.

Welcome to The United Church: Celebrating the New Creed. Toronto: United Church, 2010.

Wells, Harold. "The Good Creation: From Classical Theism to Ecotheology." In *The Theology of The United Church of Canada*, edited by Don Schweitzer et al., 77–100. Waterloo, ON: Wilfrid Laurier University Press, 2019.

Wells, Patricia. *Welcome to The United Church of Canada: A Newcomer's Introduction to A New Creed*. Toronto: United Church, 1986.

White, Peter Gordon, ed. *Voices and Visions: Sixty-Five Years of The United Church of Canada*. Toronto: United Church, 1990.

Wilson, Paul Scott. "Let Go and Let God." Sermon given at Eglinton-St. George's United Church, Toronto, ON, 22 Nov. 2009.

———, et al. *A Guide to Sunday Worship*. Toronto: United Church, 1988.

Wishart, Vernon R. "Beyond the Gospel of Liberalism." *Touchstone* 11, no. 3 (Sept. 1993) 24–31.

Working Unit on Worship and Liturgy, Division of Mission in Canada. *A Sunday Liturgy for Optional Use in The United Church of Canada*. Toronto: United Church, 1984.

Wright, Lance. *Confirmation That Works: Based on the New Creed of The United Church of Canada*. 3rd ed. Privately published in Hamilton, ON, 2000.

Wright, N. T. *The New Testament and the People of God*. Minneapolis: Fortress, 1992.

———. *The Resurrection of the Son of God*. Minneapolis: Fortress, 2003.

Wyatt, Peter. "Doctrine Matters." *Touchstone* 29, no. 3 (Sept. 2011) 2–6.

———. "Ministering with a High Doctrine of the Trinity in a Liberal Church." *Toronto Journal of Theology* 30, no. 1 (2014) 71–80.

Young, John H. "Introduction." In *The Theology of The United Church of Canada*, edited by Don Schweitzer et al., 1–20. Waterloo, ON: Wilfrid Laurier University Press, 2019.

Zachar, Laurie Ann. "The Renewal/Reform Groups of The United Church of Canada: The Spirit of Methodism." Unpublished manuscript, Dec. 11, 1997. http://web.ncf.ca/dq579/ucrenewal.html.

Zung, Paul. "Bermuda Trial." Sermons & Writings of Victor Shepherd, Mar. 9, 2014. http://victorshepherd.ca/bermuda-trial/.

Manufactured by Amazon.ca
Bolton, ON

25302264R00129